The Presumption

The Presumption

Race and Injustice in the United States

D. Marvin Jones

BLOOMSBURY ACADEMIC

NEW YORK • LONDON • OXFORD • NEW DELHI • SYDNEY

BLOOMSBURY ACADEMIC
Bloomsbury Publishing Inc
1385 Broadway, New York, NY 10018, USA
50 Bedford Square, London, WC1B 3DP, UK
29 Earlsfort Terrace, Dublin 2, Ireland

First published in the United States of America 2024
Paperback edition published 2026

Cover image: Lightfieldstudiosprod/Dreamstime.com

Bloomsbury Publishing Inc does not have any control over, or responsibility for, any
third-party websites referred to or in this book. All internet addresses given in this
book were correct at the time of going to press. The author and publisher regret
any inconvenience caused if addresses have changed or sites have ceased
to exist, but can accept no responsibility for any such changes.

Library of Congress Cataloging-in-Publication Data
Names: Jones, D. Marvin, author.
Title: The presumption : race and injustice in the United States / D. Marvin Jones.
Description: New York : Bloomsbury Academic, 2024. | Includes
bibliographical references and index.
Identifiers: LCCN 2023048293 (print) | LCCN 2023048294 (ebook) | ISBN 9781440867712
(hardback) | ISBN 9781440867729 (ebook) | ISBN 9798216172215 (epub)
Subjects: LCSH: African Americans–Social conditions. | Racism
against Black people–United States. | Racial profiling in law enforcement–
United States. | Discrimination in criminal justice administration–United States. |
Presumption of innocence–United States. | United States–Race relations.
Classification: LCC E185.86 .J6514 2024 (print) | LCC E185.86 (ebook) |
DDC 305.800973–dc23/eng/20231106
LC record available at https://lccn.loc.gov/2023048293
LC ebook record available at https://lccn.loc.gov/2023048294

ISBN: HB: 978-1-4408-6771-2
         PB: 979-8-7651-1562-6
       ePDF: 978-1-4408-6772-9
      eBook: 979-8-2161-7221-5

Typeset by Integra Software Services Pvt. Ltd.

To find out more about our authors and books visit www.bloomsbury.com
and sign up for our newsletters.

Contents

Preface

I grew up in East Baltimore. I lived on a tree-lined street of beautiful brownstone row houses. My mother worked as a freelance hairdresser. I still remember her "doing hair" in our basement, curlers rattling, charging $2.25 per head. She was very industrious. My father worked at Bethlehem Steel. I can still see him, bag lunch in hand, on his way to the Sparrow's Point plant, where he worked nights, on the trains that carried the iron ore.

Every family who lived in my neighborhood, with the exception of the Rosado family which lived a block away, was Black. On the other hand, the police which patrolled our neighborhood were white, the owner of the corner store was white, the man who collected for our insurance was white, the mayor was white.

The schools in my neighborhood were "failing" schools. At my junior high, which was overwhelmingly Black and poor, the average reading level in the ninth grade was second grade. I would later learn that the beautiful neighborhood I grew up in was an urban "ghetto." Very few people made it out.

But I had one big advantage. My mother told me I was "smart" and that if I worked hard, I would be "somebody." So, I did. Every day, sick or well, I went to school. I *never* missed a day. After school, every day, I went to the library to read for a couple of hours. And every day the kids in my neighborhood laughed at me for doing so.

I would go on to graduate from a highly selective private college and later to the prestigious New York University School of Law.

By the time I was hired at the University of Miami in 1988, I had a sense of having lived in two worlds. I had been able to cross over into greater America where there were the elite universities, gleaming condominiums, beautiful suburbs with rolling lawns. But in the inner city it was clear both from my research and from my visits to my mother's house nothing had changed. At the same time, despite the fact that the law is officially color-blind, I experienced, then and now, the fact that all Black bodies remain vulnerable to suspicion, stereotyping, and profiling by police. What explains this racial dualism?

I had help in my journey to answer this question. In 1990 I received an invitation to the Critical Race Theory Conference taking place in Boulder Colorado in June of 1991. This was one of the early meetings that laid the foundation for the Critical Race Theory movement. Even then mainstream scholars and judges had labeled this group radical and dangerous. I went anyway. And they were dangerous: dangerously visionary, and dangerously smart.

At the conference were Professors Derrick Bell (the person I see as the founder and who would later write one of my letters for tenure), Kimberlé Crenshaw, the late Lani Guinier, Gerald Torres, Linda Greene, Charles Lawrence, Mari Matsuda, Kevin Brown, Richard Delgado and many other brilliant scholars. Critical Race Theory was and is less a body of knowledge than it was and is a movement to develop an understanding of legal and political institutions through the lens of the lived experience of Black people. The inspiration I gained from attending that conference is still with me, and the insights I gained there continue to shape my work.

Another formative experience I have had, which contributes to this book, is that, at the University of Miami, I have had the opportunity to work with some incredible people including renowned legal scholars, historians, and social theorists. They taught me to see law, history, philosophy as different rooms of the same house. The cadences of all those disciplines find harmony in my work.

Armed with these critical tools I have spent years of thinking and writing about the question of race: What is it? And why does it remain a central contradiction of our society?

Imagine a criminal finds a cloak which allows them to become invisible. Subsequently, a series of homicides occur. But we never see the perpetrator, only their footprints in the snow. This is a metaphor for the problem of race in the twenty-first century. We recognize racism when it takes the form of hate. But sometimes it takes a more subtle form. Then, too often it is "invisible" to the media and the courts. The purpose of this book is to expose this subtle form of racial bias. I call it "The Presumption."

Introduction

It was December 20, 1970, Christmas time in Tucson, Arizona. Sixteen-year-old Luis Cuen Taylor decided he would join holiday revelers at the Pioneer Hotel for happy hour. But, around midnight, a fire started on the fourth floor of the hotel. Taylor heroically helped to rescue many of the guests. "At a subsequent court proceeding, the custodian of the hotel testified that the teenager [Luis Taylor] helped him try to extinguish the fire, according to a story from the *Arizona Daily Star*. The hotel's beverage manager testified that Taylor helped him carry injured guests to safety, another story said.[1]"

But, the presumption of guilt had followed Taylor to the happy hour. After his heroic efforts, Taylor was arrested and charged with arson.[2] There was no witness who would testify that he or she saw Taylor start the fire.[3] But officers said Taylor could not explain why he was at the hotel.[4] An all-white jury found Taylor guilty of murder in the deaths of twenty-eight people who died immediately in the fire.[5] Taylor would spend forty-two years in jail.[6] However, Taylor's case was reinvestigated decades later by the Arizona Innocence Project. This prompted an investigation by the Tucson Fire Department, which found that "there was no conclusive evidence that the Pioneer fire was intentionally set."[7] Nonetheless, despite the absence of evidence that arson was the cause of the fire, Pima County prosecutors still insisted they believed Taylor was guilty. He was released on April 2, 2013.[8] But, at the prosecution's insistence, in order to be released Taylor was forced to plead no contest to twenty-eight counts of murder.[9] Taylor was released after getting credit for time served.[10]

The presumption of guilt also follows some Black children to school. According to Max Rameau, who operated an organization he called "cop-watch," on February 28, 2008, a teacher at Miami Edison High "put a student in a choke-hold during school."[11] The police later entered the classroom to arrest the student, not the teacher.[12] Subsequently, the students staged a protest.[13] The protest began peacefully. Ultimately, over 70 police cars were called to the scene. Miami Edison students protested by sitting in their school cafeteria. According to one account, "students were told to get up and when they didn't police stormed in using full force."[14] Police were armed with Tasers, nightsticks, and other weapons. Students participating in the sit-in were clubbed, tasered, and arrested by police. At least one pregnant student was struck in her stomach. The police arrested 27 people. All of the 27 students arrested were children of color, and most of them Black. With one exception, the police were unable to identify what, specifically, any particular student did.

> Officers responding to the Feb. 29 brawl changed the names and contact information on each student's form, but the charges and descriptions of what happened are almost identical on 23 of the 26 forms. ... Though each student is charged with resisting arrest with violence, starting a brawl and disrupting a school assembly, none of the 23 reports specifies what an individual student did to merit the charges.[15]

They used form affidavits—general warrants, in essence—in which the offense was stated in conclusory terms. The wording was identical; the names on each form were changed. Many parents felt their children were arrested merely for being present in the vicinity of the demonstration. One parent, Edwin Alvarez, commented that his 18-year-old daughter, who is part of a non-violent student group, "was arrested and treated like a criminal for just being in the area."[16]

The presumption walks with urban youth in the streets of Baltimore. Evan Howard was a freshman engineering student at Morgan State University in Maryland. At 8:30 on a Friday evening, Howard was leaving a corner store a block away from his West Baltimore home when he stopped outside to talk to a friend. The police approached Howard and his friend. According to the police, the two young men were "loitering" and had repeatedly refused orders to move along. The officers took Howard to Baltimore's Central Booking facility, where he spent the next fifty-six hours in a crowded cell with other offending (or perhaps unlucky) individuals from the Baltimore streets. He was released at about four o' clock Monday morning.[17]

The presumption also appears in court. As Luis Cuen discovered, for Blacks and especially Black men, it appears too often as a presumption of guilt. It may also appear as a presumption of dangerousness. In Texas, "future dangerousness" must be established before a death sentence is imposed. In the case of Dwayne Buck, Dr. Walter Quijano testified in a Texas courtroom that the fact that Buck was Black "increased the probability" that he would commit future acts of criminal violence.[18] In the Buck case, the presumption was fully explicit, conscious, and overt.

This presumption of dangerousness is often at the root of moral panic about urban crime. Nixon weaponized widely shared fears about the criminal tendencies of Blacks in forging his "law and order" narrative. As Nixon told the story, "racial discord"—which race-coded the problems of violence and drugs—constituted American society's greatest threat.

> We live in a deeply troubled and profoundly unsettling time. Drugs and crime ... racial discord ... on every hand, we find standards violated, old values discarded, old precepts ignored. ... As a result, all of our institutions in America are undergoing what may be the severest challenge in our history.[19]

This was dog whistle racism. Law and order of course meant racial order. Building on these themes, John Diluio, former aid to George H. W. Bush, developed the myth of the super-predator.

> We're talking about elementary school youngsters who pack guns instead of lunches. We're talking about kids who have absolutely no respect for human life and no sense of the future. In short, we're talking big trouble that hasn't yet begun to crest ...

> They fear neither the stigma of arrest nor the pain of imprisonment. They live by the meanest code of the meanest streets, a code that reinforces rather than restrains their violent, hair-trigger mentality. In prison or out, the things that super-predators get by their criminal behavior—sex, drugs, money—are their own immediate rewards. Nothing else matters to them. So for as long as their youthful energies hold out, they will do what comes "naturally": murder, rape, rob, assault, burglarize, deal deadly drugs, and get high.[20]

These frightening images become part of a cautionary story weaving together statistics, speculation, and hyperbole into an apocalyptic vision.

Since around 6 percent of young males turn out to be career criminals, according to the historical data, this increase will put an estimated 270,000 more young predators on the streets than in 1990, coming at us in waves over the next two decades. Numerous studies show that each succeeding generation of young male criminals commits about three times as much serious crime as the one before it: the occasional fatal knife fight of 1950s street gangs has given way to the frequent drive-by shootings of 1990s gangs.[21]

To prevent the rise of a generation of Black super-predators, Congress enacted laws making penalties for crack cocaine 100 times that of powdered cocaine. Thus, possession of five grams of crack cocaine, worth about $125.00—the drug of choice of inner-city Blacks—resulted in a mandatory sentence of five years. On the other hand, possession of 500 grams of powdered cocaine, worth $500,000.00—the drug of choice of most whites—resulted in the same sentence. While the Fair Sentencing Act of 2010 reduced the crack/cocaine sentencing quantity disparity to 18:1, thousands continue to languish in prison serving sentences applied under the old laws because the act has not been applied retroactively. This disparity persists despite the fact that whites use cocaine at levels statistically identical to Blacks, but simply use it in a different form.

Whether as a presumption of guilt or a presumption of dangerousness, the presumption has been smuggled into urban policing much like the drugs that are smuggled into the United States.

Between 1980 and 2000, the U.S. black drug arrest rate rose from 6.5 to 29.1 per 1,000 persons; during the same period, the white drug arrest rate increased from 3.5 to 4.6 per 1,000 persons. Yet the disparity between the increase in black and white drug arrests does not correspond to any significant disparity in black drug activity. In 2012, for instance, the National Institute on Drug Abuse published a study surveying drug usage among secondary school students in the United States from 1975–2011. The study found that white students were slightly more likely to have abused an illegal substance within the past month than black students. Yet from 1980–2010, black youth were arrested for drug crimes at rates more than double those of white youth.[22]

The disparities are equally apparent between Black and white adults.

Disparity between black drug activity and black arrest rates is also present in adult populations: in Seattle in 2002, for instance, African Americans constituted 16% of observed drug dealers for the five most dangerous drugs but 64% of drug dealing arrests for those drugs. While these arrests were for trafficking rather than possession, the modest evidence available suggests that most drug users purchase drugs from a dealer of their own race.[23]

Similarly, Maryland commissioned a study by Vincent Shiraldi and Jason Zeidenberg in which they found, first of all that, Blacks and whites abused cocaine at statistically identical rates. But while Blacks make up 28 percent of the Maryland population, they made up 68 percent of those arrested and 90 percent of those incarcerated in Maryland prisons as well.[24]

One in six Black men have been incarcerated as of 2001.[25] If current trends continue, one of every three Black American males born today can expect to go to prison in his lifetime, compared to one of every seventeen white males.[26]

The presumption is deadly. In confrontations with police, Blacks are three and a half times more likely than whites to experience the use of force. Black people account for 31 percent of police-killing victims in 2012, while they make up just 13 percent of the population.[27] Of the people killed by police who were not attacking when killed, the percentage increases to 39 percent.[28] And Blacks make up 62.7 percent of the unarmed people killed by police.[29]

Finally, the same presumption that lurks within our criminal justice system also appears on our screens.

A Community of Criminals

In 1990, Robert Entman did a famous study that quantified statistically the way the urban ghetto was caricatured in the evening news. He looked at three ten-day periods covered by ABC, CBS, and NBC news.

1. "77% of the stories in which blacks were accused concerned a violent or a drug crime ... In other words the overwhelming majority of black crime stories concerned violence or drugs."[30]
2. "Blacks were twice as likely as whites to be shown in the grasp of a police officer."

3. "An image of police breaking into a house was shown 7 times during the period. In 6 of the cases the occupants were black."

4. "10 stories during the period focused on people selling drugs. In 6 of those cases such images were of blacks."[31]

Stereotypes found in news are harder to resist because the news is "real." While the images are entirely stereotypical, they are presented as neutral. Entman notes that "the benign guise" of these stereotypical images encourages the racial coding of criminal behavior.[32]

Thus, institutional racism and racism within the meaning-making processes of society are two sides of one coin.

This portrayal both relied upon and perpetuated the presumption that Blacks were prone to crime. In addition to the news, a host of films and television shows are premised on a notion that the inner city is a war zone populated by gangbangers, hoodlums, and thugs. The overwhelming majority of the people in the inner city are law-abiding. But shows like *The Wire*, *Cops*, and *Power* and films from *New Jack City*, *Boyz n the Hood*, and *Training Day* to more recent films like *Waist Deep* and *Snow on Da Bluff* limn out an image of the inner city that embodies a presumption that those who live there are sociopaths.

> If they Gun Me Down, Which Picture will they Use?
> If I walk out of here
> And they gun me down
> ...
> Tell em my skin was a threat
> And my rights were improper conduct.
> Trey G[33]

The presumption is deeply embedded in the reporting about unarmed Black men shot by police. Blacks here, more specifically Black men, who are shot by police, are true victims. A victim is someone who suffers an injustice but has an avenue of redress within our legal system. A true victim is one who suffers an injustice but lacks any means of redress. Unarmed Blacks are victimized first by being shot by police and again as the media unceasingly portrays them as perpetrators. Here the freewheeling criminalization of Black victims of police shooting is premised on a vagrant, unanchored, brooding suspicion that they are thugs, gangbangers, or criminals.

In the Trayvon Martin case, George Zimmerman shot Trayvon as he was walking home from the 7-Eleven armed only with Skittles and iced tea. Trayvon might have been shown as an honor student, as a deceased teen victim of gun violence, or many other ways. But in the racialized portrayals which follow Trayvon's achievements, his innocence was erased. Trayvon was shown on television stereotypically, in a hoodie staring into a camera at the 7-Eleven, or smiling broadly with a mouth full of gold teeth. Other photographs circulated as well.

> Also circulating the web are unauthenticated photographs of a young black teenager said to be Trayvon, shirtless, pants sagging, and throwing up gang signs. This photo is coupled with another picture of George Zimmerman where he is smiling and in a suit. By posting these questionably sourced pictures of Martin, which depict him as stereotypical black male thug, it makes it much easier to believe that the kid with the Skittles might actually be suspicious somehow, validating Zimmerman's racial bias.[34]

Breitbart openly called Trayvon a thug who got what he deserved.

Something similar happened to Michael Brown. Michael Brown was a Ferguson teenager who was shot six times by Officer Darren Wilson. Brown was shot despite the fact that, according to witnesses, he was unarmed and famously holding his hands up when he was shot. Wilson set the stage for Brown's subsequent media portrayal by describing Brown in his statements to news sources as a beast.

> When he stopped, he turned, looked at me, made like a grunting noise and had the most intense, aggressive face I've ever seen on a person. When he looked at me, he then did like the hop ... you know, like people do to start running. And, he started running at me. During his first stride, he took his right hand put it under his shirt into his waistband. And I ordered him to stop and get on the ground again. He didn't. I fired multiple shots. After I fired the multiple shots, I paused a second, yelled at him to get on the ground again, he was still in the same state. Still charging, hand still in his waistband, hadn't slowed down.[35]

Social media went into high gear, producing a spate of images to demonize the unarmed teen who was shot. On December 9, 2014, a Facebook user named Shawn Spall posted a video purporting to be footage of Mike Brown (the teenager shot and killed by Officer Darren Wilson in Ferguson, Missouri) brutally assaulting a much older man over the theft of a backpack.[36] The video was totally false.

More famously, the police released a security video supposedly of Michael Brown robbing a cigar store.

> Photos from the video footage released by police show a large man dressed in a T-shirt and red St. Louis Cardinals cap, the same clothing Mike Brown was wearing when he was killed, shoving the liquor store clerk.
>
> ...
>
> "Brown, still holding a box of Swisher Sweets [cigars] in his right hand, grabs [store cashier] by his shirt with his left hand. Brown aggressively pulls [the store clerk] in close to him and then immediately pushes him back into a display rack ... Brown then abruptly turns back around and advances on [the store clerk] appearing to intimidate him," says the Ferguson police report, describing the video footage.[37]

But the video left out scenes that would have shown a much friendlier Michael Brown; it mischievously cuts to an altercation to suggest Brown robbed the store. Filmmaker Jason Pollock released a film showing the whole transaction which shows a friendlier Michael Brown and shows clearly there was no robbery. "Let America and the world see that Mike didn't rob the store—that that was all a lie."[38] The videos were catalysts. They set off the psychological equivalent of a chain reaction by activating the already pervasively present narrative/presumption that Black men are urban thugs, savages, or beasts.

So what is the presumption of guilt? It is in the first instance a legacy of our racial past. It is the crystallization of racial ideology that upheld slavery and the Jim Crow regime.

In the *Prison Notebooks* the philosopher Gramsci remarked that while they had overthrown fascism and dismantled the bureaucratic infrastructure through which it operated, the belief system on which the bureaucracy had rested remained intact. "[W]hen the state trembled, a sturdy structure of civil society was at once revealed. The state was only an outer ditch behind which there stood a powerful system of fortresses and earthworks."

By earthworks, Gramsci referred to beliefs and attitudes, which functioned as "ideological institutions" that consolidate political arrangements. While we have torn down the wall of law and policy which relegated Blacks to inferior schools and housing, this wall of formal policy was only the equivalent of an outer ditch. What remains is the deeply embedded earthwork of racial ideology, which upheld it. It was axiomatic of the Jim Crow regime that Blacks were held to be both innately inferior, and innately prone to crime. Thus, Fredrick L. Hoffman, a German-born insurance statistician, wrote in his popular book of 1896, *Race Traits and the Tendencies of the American Negro*, that an "immense amount of immorality … is a race trait." He went on to write, "as for Negro poverty it was not the result of white discrimination or lack of opportunity but stemmed directly from an innate tendency toward crime and immorality."[39] The presumption of guilt or dangerousness is a crystallization of this racial ideology into a lens of suspicion. It inheres in a notion that blacks are innately prone to crime or innately dangerous or innately deviant or a combination of the three. It is this lens through which Luis Cuen and Michael Brown were viewed.

The question becomes: how does this presumption survive in an era in which we are formally committed to equal opportunity? The simple answer is that it hides in plain sight. More shocking than the existence of this form of racism is the fact that it is generally invisible. What invisibilizes it are a set of blinding assumptions, which mask its operation. These blinding assumptions repose in our concept of prejudice or discrimination itself.

Claims of Knowledge

Our ideas about race and racism are rooted in sets of images and stories, which date back to the civil rights era. In the film *Selma*,[40] for example, we watched as policeman beat demonstrators trying to cross the Edmund Pettus Bridge. And many of us have seen newsreels of police dogs biting "negro demonstrators," or Sheriff Bull Connor water-hosing them. These images shout hatred and aversive racism. This civil rights imagery is at the core of our current understanding of prejudice as something irrational,[41] based on hate. (A corollary is that it is deviant, something done by ignorant people.)

To understand racism in the post-civil rights era, we need a paradigm shift of sorts. While I certainly agree that racism is irrational, *racism in the post-civil rights era nonetheless masquerades as rationality*—in the form of "a claim of knowledge."

George Zimmerman's comments on Trayvon moments before he shot him exemplify this claim of knowledge. Zimmerman stated:

> "This guy looks like he's up to no good, or he's on drugs or something," Zimmerman tells the 911 operators. "He's just staring, looking at all the houses. Now he's coming toward me. He's got his hand in his waistband. Something's wrong with him."
>
> Zimmerman described Martin as wearing a hoodie and sweatpants or jeans. He continues: "He's coming to check me out. He's got something in his hands. I don't know what his deal is. Can we get an officer over here?"
>
> "These assholes. They always get away," he says to the operator.[42]

How did Zimmerman know all this about Trayvon—a person he had never met—just by watching him walk down the street in Sanford, Florida? By stating, "These assholes always get away," he was implying that we all know that this kind of person, like Trayvon, was dangerous, and that he, Zimmerman, did not need to see Trayvon commit a crime because it was "obvious" that Trayvon was a criminal. But the only distinguishing features about Trayvon were that he was Black and wearing a hoodie.

Trayvon was, in the words of Derrida, an "already read text." He was the cover of a storybook. We all know his type so well, we can judge the book by its cover; we do not have to read the book.

Interviewed about this, Zimmerman's friend Frank Taffe stated,

> We had eight burglaries in our neighborhood all perpetrated by young black males in the 15 months prior to Trayvon being shot. It would have been nine—there would have been nine, but George Zimmerman through his efforts of being a neighborhood watch captain helped stop one in progress, documented in the 911 calls February 2 ... Taffe continues, "All of the perpetrators of the burglaries, the prior burglaries, were young black males."[43]

When O'Brien presses on how this comment relates to Trayvon Martin, Taffe responds, "There's an old saying if you plant corn, you get corn."[44]

O'Brien asks for further clarification, and Taffe says, "It is what it is. It is what it is. I would go on record by stating that of the eight prior burglaries in the 15 months prior to the Trayvon Martin shooting, all of the perpetrators were young Black males."

Racial Essence v. Facts

What does link Trayvon to the burglaries? What makes Trayvon's criminality "obvious" is an unstated and unanchored assumption that race and crime are inextricably linked. Said another way, the notion is that the stereotypes about Blacks are true: Blacks are innately prone to crime, whites are innately law abiding. Zimmerman and Taffe both mistake this unanchored assumption for a fact. Their conflation reflects a reliance on a notion of race as "essence."

There are two different ways of determining the character of something. Empiricism represents the method of using observation. In Criminal Law, this process of basing a conclusion that a person is a criminal on empirical observation and on a case-by-case basis is linked to the liberal premise that each individual is both precious and unique. Race essentialism rejects this liberal premise.

Race essentialism represents the notion that once you know the character of something, you need not test further. Snakes are poisonous, wild dogs bite, spiders spin webs, and corn planted in the ground grows into stalks. This is the meaning of Taffe's comment, "You plant corn seeds you get corn."

In the Zimmerman–Taffe racial narrative, it is as if criminality is as much a part of the essence of Blacks as growing into a corn stalk is to a corn seed.

No Evidence Required

The effect of this presumption—grounded as it is in a kind of race essentialism— is that no evidence of Trayvon's conduct, no observation of Trayvon's actions is required.

His mere presence in a place where "he does not belong is sufficient" to justify suspicion. We see the same logic in the case of Louis Taylor. He could not explain why he was there. The burden was not on the police to explain the arrest—as the presumption of innocence requires—the burden is on Taylor to explain his presence. The same logic was used to justify anti-loitering laws in *City of Chicago v. Morales*, the detention of Black men like Fred Gray who run from police, the arrest of Henry Louis Gates Jr—"What was he doing in a house in upscale neighborhood?" The suspicionless stop and frisk of hundreds of thousands of Black men in New York is well documented in the famous case of *Floyd v. New York*.[45]

This reduction of Blacks as a group to a community of suspects appears reasonable to Zimmerman and Taffe. I believe it's because these assumptions are widely shared. These assumptions are seen as "common sense." I say all this to say the presumption certainly is irrational, but it relies on pseudo-logic as a mask.

Conscious or Unconscious

Sometimes the presumption is unconscious—walking the feather line between the imaginary and the real.

> This bias can be tested when participants play a video game that instructs them to shoot perpetrators (who are holding guns) as fast as they can but not to shoot innocent bystanders (who are unarmed but holding a non-gun object, such as a cell phone). The "shooter bias" refers to participants' propensity to shoot Black perpetrators more quickly and more frequently than White perpetrators and to decide not to shoot White bystanders more quickly and frequently than Black bystanders. Studies have also shown that participants more quickly identify handguns as weapons after seeing a Black face, and more quickly identify other objects (such as tools) as non-weapons after seeing a White face.[46]

Justin Levinson argues in a famous article that Jurors in criminal cases have memory illusions: they misremember facts concerning Black defendants, altering the facts in the record to conform to stereotypes of criminality associated with Blacks.

But while racism may be unconscious, the premise of this book is that it is generally both conscious and unconscious—a kind of hybrid. Thus, Zimmerman and Taffe consciously and militantly believe it is reasonable to stop, detain, and interrogate a Black person simply because he is Black. What they are "unconscious of" in making their claims of knowledge about Blacks is the fact that there is no objective anchor to their racial essentialist fantasy. The conflation of assumption with fact occurs unconsciously. The claim that they know the character of Trayvon, however unanchored, is in their minds, and is based on common sense, not hate. I would note with interest that, according to philosopher Waheema Lubiano, the "common sense" idea invisibilizes this as racism as that term is traditionally understood. They apply a presumption of guilt, premised largely by race, but see no wrong.

> Imagine this scenario: officers … are patrolling … [in a rich neighborhood]. They spot a new Mercedes at a stop sign being driven by two African American teens wearing baseball caps backward …
>
> [T]hese guys don't belong here. Those guys are cruising the neighborhood. What if they break in, or hurt someone.
>
> [R]acial profiling exists-not as written policy de facto.

it's subtle, a product of the gut …

> [G]ood street sense and a nose for suspicious activity is the most valuable tool a cop can possess. That's what he is paid to develop. That's what people … want him or her to have. That's what prevents crime …
>
> Label me a racist if you wish, but the cold fact remains that African-Americans comprise 12 percent of the population, but occupy nearly half the state and federal prison cells.[47]

The policeman goes on to argue, incredibly, that being a Black and male (and teenager) in that car in that neighborhood is as obviously suspicious as a "car weaving across lanes of traffic at midnight.[48]"

Both the claim that three Blacks in a car in an expensive neighborhood and a Black man walking in a white neighborhood equals probable cause, is racial paranoia. But, it appears to be reasonable—common knowledge—i.e. common sense to all of these men. In fact, whenever one says something is common sense, one can always say this is ideology. That is, *ideology is internalized common sense.* Under the sway of racial ideology, a racist does not see that he is being paranoid—or racist.

Why Do I Write This Book?

So much of our discourse about race is about racism as hate, conscious or unconscious. I write to explore how it operates paradoxically consciously and unconsciously under a cloak of reasonableness or rationality. This bias crystallizes as a presumption of guilt. I want to show how it operated in the era of Jim Crow, in the civil rights era. I want to explore the role it continues to play—how it is smuggled into the decisions of police about whether to shoot and kill, and too often in urban areas seamlessly integrated into standard operating procedure by police, legislators, and courts. I will show finally that this presumption has been pervasively smuggled into the meaning-making machinery of society, i.e. the news, television, and film. The meaning-making machinery—the social imaginary—and the political and legal machinery—the social real—are intimately intertwined.

We inhabit a paradox. If segregation represents the veil, the premise of our legal system (formal equality) is that the veil has been lifted. Formally it has. But in a real sense, there has been no meaningful change. We have noted that racism hides as common sense. What results is that *the pervasiveness of this presumption is as invisible to educated elites as it is to the Zimmermans, Taffes, and so-called fringe elements.* Ironically, the ubiquitous presence of the presumption of guilt in our criminal justice system occurs even as a new movements targeting its effects have gained steam. In the aftermath of the brutal and senseless killing of George Floyd—I cannot erase from my mind the image of a white police officer, hands in his pockets nonchalantly kneeling on the neck of a Black man as he pleaded pitifully "I can't breathe"—there was a national and international outpouring of concern, i.e. massive demonstrations all over the world. This is the beginning of a new civil rights movement. But over a year after this atrocity, while progress has been made, the basic problem is still there. Statistica reports, "Sadly the trend of fatal police shootings seems only to be increasing." According to the same website, "As of June 15, 112 Black people were killed by the police in the United States in 2023. This compares to 90 Hispanics and 253 white people. The rate of police shootings of Black Americans is … 5.8 per million people … compared to 2.3 per million for whites.[49]"

Our national conversation about these massive disparities is stalling or simply has stalled. In part the stall is due to the focus on police violence. There are two stages on which the discourse is taking place. There is a liberal stage in which those who genuinely are committed to real change are engaging each other. On this stage the main impediment is that there is an assumption that police violence is "THE PROBLEM." On this stage—those focusing on police violence—there is also splintering of groups as some, a minority I believe, advocated "defunding the police." Blacks are rightly angry about the police killing Blacks and systemic discrimination in general. I heard this "defund the police" as a righteous expression of anger and/or call for less police militarism. But some actually sought to literally defund—which would result in affluent whites getting their own police and lower-class whites forming armed neighborhood watch groups—not one but thousands of Zimmermans unleashed—and Blacks in the ghetto without any police protection but suffering *the same or more violence as gangs and organized criminals in the inner city would have no check.*[50]

The starting point of my analysis is that a narrow focus on police violence as "THE PROBLEM" creates a horizon on our thinking. This book is about an ideological institution which is at the root of police violence—and other forms of racism against Blacks. This book discusses what is beyond that horizon of much of today's liberal discourse.

On the larger stage where the majority of Americans engage, there is a deeper problem—most whites (and some black conservatives) see race through a web of stereotypes and false narratives, which mystify or distort the problem. Conservatives like John McWhorter respond that the root cause is that Blacks make bad choices (i.e. they commit more crimes).[51] Conservatives like John Hudgens, Director of Human Services in Baltimore, argues that "some Black people are a much greater threat to other Black people than the Ku Klux Klan."[52]

Accidental Racism

Liberals, at least publicly, reject this narrative but argue generally the statistical disparities result from the fact that Blacks are socially isolated and disadvantaged. Thus, Judge Scheindlin found that New York's stop-and-frisk law targeted neighborhoods that were predominantly Black. The police and the New York mayor argued this was inadvertent—Blacks simply happen to live in high-crime areas.

Implicit Bias

A parallel discourse has developed that the disparities we are seeing are racially motivated, but the bias is unconscious, i.e. "implicit." All of these narratives, particularly the implicit bias discourse, feed the post-racial narrative—which has become hegemonic.

But the presumption of guilt is explicit racism. As long as the discourse stays within the parameters of implicit bias, unconscious racism or institutional policies which inadvertently harm Blacks—accidental racism—the discourse terminates before it reaches the problem at the heart of racism in the criminal justice system today. I feel almost as much boxed in by the liberal discourse as the conservative discourse. The problem is not merely one of unconscious bias or "accidental racism" but a conscious bias—a presumption of dangerousness or guilt veiled as common sense.

How racism can be "veiled" has much to do with the transformation of race. Race is no longer simply a matter of color, but spectrum; it includes class and cultural aspects (was he wearing a hoodie?) and the zip code one lives in. Spatial metaphors of inner-city underclass are often simply code words, metaphors for race. "Inner city" is in turn recoded in police terminology as high-crime areas. Police in New York did not target all Blacks generally; they targeted *inner-city* neighborhoods with dense concentrations of Black and brown people. The mob chasing Bigger Thomas called him n—ger. Trayvon was referred to as an "urban" thug. As a result, based on little more than the notion "Zimmerman shot an urban thug," Trayvon's humanity was erased. Beast, n—ger, and urban thug become a signifying chain reflecting not the lifting of the veil of race, but the veiling or recoding of race itself. The presumption is a conflation of race and criminality. The sheer racism of this is invisibilized by recoding race in spatial terms. Part of telling the story of how the presumption of guilt has evolved—and has become invisibilized—is telling the story of how our notions of race have evolved.

Organization

We begin with the past.

Just as the psychiatrist must take the patient back to the origins of his psychic trauma, in Chapter One I take us back to the origins of the presumption.

Slavery was born out of an act of violence. To maintain the state of master and slave the master must establish his absolute dominance. This oppression constantly bred resistance. Even when there was no resistance, the nature of the relationship produced a constant fear. In Chapter One we explore how the presumption originates as an invention of the master class to rationalize their domination of the slave.

In Chapter Two, "This is a White Man's Country!" we explore the case of Ossian Sweet and his family attacked by a mob. The whites were engaged in riots. Sweet and his family made the mistake of trying to defend themselves. When a white man was killed the police charged Sweet, his family, and friends with murder. This was true, despite the fact there was no evidence that the bullet that killed the man was fired from Sweet's house. We will explore how the presumption obviated any need for evidence.

In Chapter Three we explore the social construction of the second ghetto. As millions of Blacks migrated North during the 1940s and 1950s, they were systemically confined, like carriers of a dangerous disease, to urban ghettos on the ragged edge of industry. We explore how presumption of deviance, immorality, and criminal tendencies more so than any overt hate shaped both private prejudice and government policy that led to the post-war expansion of urban ghettos.

In Chapter Four we explore the social history of the drug war. We explore how the drug war is really two wars. One was a social war in which the media and politicians demonized first crack and ultimately the inner city as the source of both users and dealers. The second was a real war waged not against drugs but the Black community. In this chapter we explore the role of the presumption as the linchpin in each of these racial projects.

In Chapter Five we explore the problem of the perceived incongruence of Blacks in white spaces. We have had a Black president and now a Black woman as vice president. Perhaps because of it we are witnessing a kind of backlash against Blacks moving into or spending time in certain spaces, white spaces, shall we say. From Henry Louis Gates Jr in Cambridge to the young lady who went to sleep momentarily in the common areas of her dorm, we will explore the role of a presumption in these claims of racial trespass.

Too often both scholars and popular culture image racism as something that is rooted in the realm of law, economics, or politics. But the problem is deeply rooted in the meaning-making realm of our society. In Chapters Six and Seven

I explore how films from *Birth of a Nation* to blaxplotiation to the hood films of the later twentieth century created controlling images and narratives—from Sambo to the Magical Negro—which normalized first Jim Crow and later mass incarceration. The presumption of Black inferiority or Black deviance is rooted as much in these films as it is in the policies and practices of the criminal justice system.

Throughout the book we are exploring racism as an evolving structure of thought. In each period, the presumption of guilt has been associated with widely shared racial fears of the dominant society. Initially, these fears were associated with breaches of the color line drawn in black and white. Initially, also, this presumption was associated with notions of hate. Then we see that aversive racism—racism as hate—is increasingly replaced with racism masquerading as something rational—common sense. Still, later we see incredible transformation in society in which universalism of race as a dividing line between black and white is replaced with a spectrum.

Finally, we see that what remains the same is that in each period the presumption of guilt operates as a distorting prism in which no objective evidence is necessary to condemn a Black person.

It is a mistake to think that in any era this presumption is a problem of individual decision making. It is, directly. But the presumption is always a crystallization of the social meaning of race in any particular period. Race is like a lake in which all of these narratives have, over time, deposited their streams. The police officer, the mob, the judge who sentences, the reporters who lynch, unjustly arrest, unjustly convict, or unjustly disparage Blacks, all indulge in this toxic presumption. But they are like mosquitos who are drunk from the polluted lake. The lake is our culture; the pollution is the social meaning of racial identity (Black=dangerous or guilty) embedded in and polluting our social culture. We cannot bring about change by swatting the mosquitos that come off the polluted lake. But the meaning of race—which has polluted our culture and our discourse—is always a function of the stories we tell. My goal is to tell stories which can help transform what we, as a society, perceive the meaning of race to be.

Notes

1   Richard Ruelas, "Man Convicted in Deadly Arizona Fire Released after 41 Years," *The Arizona Republic* (April 2, 2013).

2   Ruelas, "Man Convicted in Deadly Arizona Fire."

3   Tucson Fire Foundation, "Louis Taylor Served 42 Years," *Tucson Fire Department*, www.tucsonfirefoundation.com/…/uploads/2015/10/Louis-Taylor. pdf.

4   David Cieslak, "Police May Test Pioneer Hotel Fire Evidence—If Any Exists," *Tucson Citizen*, April 11, 2002.

5   Ruelas, "Man Convicted in Deadly Arizona Fire."

6   Jody Woodruff, "After 42 Years in Jail, Conviction Overturned in Case of Deadly Fire," PBS News hour April 3, 2013, www.tucsonfirefoundation.com/…/uploads/2015/10/Louis-Taylor.pdf

7   Pima County Liberator, "The Case of Louis Taylor," https://pimaliberator.com/louis-taylor/; Brian Skolaff, "Man Convicted in 1970 Arizona Fire Set, Free", *The San Diego Tribune*, April 3, 2013.

8   Skolaff, "Man Convicted in 1970."

9   Ibid.

10 Louis Taylor, Freed after More than 40 Years in Prison: "It Was Shameful What They Did," *CBS This Morning* April 4, 2013, https://www.cbsnews.com/news/louis-taylor-freed-after-more-than-40-years-in-prison-it-was-shameful-what-they-did/.

11 "Students Arrested, Police Injured after Miami School Protest," *WSVN, Channel & News*, February 29, 2008, http://www.wsvn.com/news/articles/local/MI78504/.

12 Ibid.

13 Ibid.

14 Michael Martinez, "Students Stand up to Racist Police Terror," *Worker's World*, March 7, 2008, http://www.workers.org/2008/us/miami_0313MichaelMartinez.

15 Max Rameau, "Miami Edison Senior High: Students Protest and Police Riot," *Miami Indymedia.org*, March 3, 2008, http://miami.indymedia.org/news/2008/03/10567_comment.php.

16 Nathalie Hrizi, "Police Arrests Miami Students for Peaceful Protest," *PSLweb.org*, last modified March 7, 2008, http://www2.pslweb.org/site/News2/796392023?page=NewsArticle&id=8614&news_iv_ctrl=1261.

17 R. Collins, "Strolling While Poor: How Broken-Windows Policing Created a
    New Crime in Baltimore," *Georgetown Journal on Poverty Law & Policy* 14, no. 3
    (2007) 419.

18 The Sentencing Project, "Shadow Report of the United Nations on Racial
    Disparities in the United States Criminal Justice System," August 31, 2013, p. 4,
        https://www.sentencingproject.org/publications/shadow-report-to-the-
    united-nations-human-rights-committee-regarding-racial-disparities-in-the-
    united-states-criminal-justice-system/.

19 President Richard Nixon, "Address at the Dedication of the Karle E. Mundt
    Library Beadle State College," Madison, South Dakota, June 3, 1969. Quoted in
    D. Marvin Jones, *Dangerous Spaces: Beyond the Racial Profile* (Santa Barbara,
    CA: Praeger, 2016), 28.

20 John J. Dilulio, "Super-Predator," *The Weekly Standard*, November 27, 1995.

21 John J. Dilulio, "My Black Crime Problem and Ours, Public Safety," *Social Order*,
    Spring, 1996.

22 The Sentencing Project, "Shadow Report of the United Nations."

23 Ibid.

24 Vincent Schiraldi and Jason Ziedenberg. *Race and Incarceration in Maryland.*
    Policy Report Commissioned by the Maryland Legislative Black Caucus.
    Washington DC: Justice Policy Institute, 2003.

25 M. Mauer and Ryan S. King, "Uneven Justice: State Rates of Incarceration by
    Race and Ethnicity," The Sentencing Project, page 2, August 2013.

26 Marc Mauer, *Addressing Racial Disparities in Incarceration*, 91 Supp. 3 *The Prison
    Journal* 87S, 88S (Sept. 2011) (hereinafter Mauer).

27 German Lopez, "Police Shootings and Brutality: 9 Things You Should Know,"
    Vox, https://www.vox.com/cards/police-brutality-shootings-us/us-police-racism.

28 Lopez, "Police Shootings and Brutality."

29 Ibid.

30 Robert Entman, "Representation and Reality in the Portrayal of Blacks on
    Network and Television News," *Journalism Quarterly* 71, no. 3 (1994) 511–12.

31 Entman, "Representation and Reality."

32 Ibid.

33 Trey G. "If they Gun Me Down," All Def Poetry, https://www.youtube.com/
    watch?v=LFaymN257KY, last visited October 10, 2023.

34 Zerlina Maxwell, "The Thug-ification of Trayvon Martin: Smear campaign
    distracts from the case," *The Grio*, March 28, 2012, https://www.google.com/

search?ei=UsGPWpjiKp-jjwSlp5nwDA&q=%22This+photo+is+coupled+wi
th+another+picture+of+George+Zimmerman%22&oq=%22This+photo+is
+coupled+with+another+picture+of+George+Zimmerman%22&gs_l=psy-
ab.3…6160.9153.0.9365.2.2.0.0.0.0.82.160.2.2.0….0…1.1.64.psy-ab..0.0.0…
.0.gdPWOS3ULCM.

35   Ezra Klein, "Officer Darren Wilson's Story Is Unbelievable, Literally," *Vox*,
     November 25, 2014, https://www.vox.com/2014/11/25/7281165/darren-wilsons-
     story-side.

36   David Mikkelson, "Mike Brown Beating Video," *Snopes*, December 8, 2014,
     https://www.snopes.com/fact-check/mike-brown-beating-video/.

37   David Clark Scott, "Ferguson Shooting: What's Known Now about Michael
     Brown" (video), *The Christian Science Monitor*, August 17, 2014.

38   Susannah Cullinane, "Breaking Down the Michael Brown video and What It
     Reveals." *CNN*, March 14, 2017, https://www.cnn.com/2017/03/14/us/michael-
     brown-ferguson-video-claims/index.html.

39   Vincent Schiraldi and Jason Ziedenberg. *Race and Incarceration in
     Maryland*. Policy Report Commissioned by the Maryland Legislative Black
     Caucus. (Washington DC: Justice Policy Institute, 2003), 251, quoting
     Frederick L. Hoffman's book *Race Traits and the American Negro* published
     in 1896.

40   *Selma*, directed by Ava Duvernay, 2014 Hollywood: Paramount Pictures.
     2014, film.

41   Gordon Allport, *The Nature of Race Prejudice* (New York: Basic Books, 1979), 22.

42   Trymaine Lee, "Black Voices," "Trayvon Martin Case: 911 Audio Released of
     Teen Shot by Neighborhood Watch Captain (Audio)," *Huffington Post*, March 16,
     2012.

43   CNN Press Room, "Zimmerman Neighbor, fmr. Neighborhood Watch Captain:
     Prior burglaries were by 'young black males'; 'if you plant corn, you get
     corn,'" *CNN* (April 3, 2012), http://cnnpressroom.blogs.cnn.com/2012/04/03/
     zimmerman-neighbor-fmr-neighborhood-watch-captain-prior-burglaries-were-
     by-young-black-males-if-you-plant-corn-you-get-corn.

44   CNN Press Room, "Zimmerman Neighbor."

45   959 F. Supp. 2d 540 (2013).

46   Statista Research Department, number of people killed by police in the United
     States from 2013 to 2023, August 1, 2023:

https://www.statista.com/statistics/1124036/number-people-killed-police-ethnicity-us/.

47   Marshall Frank, "Better Safe Than Sorry," *The Miami Herald*, October 19, 1999.

48   Ibid.

49   Justin D. Levinson and Robert J. Smith, *Implicit Racial Bias Across the Law* (Chapel Hill, NC, University of North Carolina, 2012).

50   In poor neighborhoods in Haiti and Jamaica and in some neighborhoods in Rio (see the film *City of God*) we have glimpses of what life is like in areas where the police have withdrawn from providing protective services—garrison communities arise in which local gangs divide territories.

51   It is certainly true that FBI statistics attribute more violent crimes to Blacks. However, the racial status of this perpetrator has nothing to do with the disproportionate pattern. This mistakes cause for effect. The problem is that Blacks tend to live in inner-city areas where poverty is concentrated and in these areas there is chronic epidemic joblessness, failing schools. The increased violence is due to environmental factors related to this social isolation not to race.

52   I agree with John McWhorter that Blacks do make bad choices. I agree with Dr. Hudgins that of course it is true that Blacks kill each other disproportionately. But these are superficial truths. There is a context to why Blacks make bad choices. Their choices are constrained by structural inequality and systemic racism. Dr. Hudgins could be paraphrased to say much of the violence Blacks experience is due to cultural pathology—which on its face may appear to be distinct from white racism. It is not. Dr. Elijah Anderson frames this cultural pathology in his analysis of street culture as part of "the code of the street." Under this code violence performed toward others is in fact seen as a source of respect or something necessary for survival. But this cultural pathology is itself deeply rooted in an "alienation" which results from systemic inequality as well. See Elijah Anderson, *Code of the Street: Decency, Violence, and the Moral Life of the Inner City* (New York: W. W. Norton, 1999).

1

Crimes of Identity: The Slave Ship, the Plantation, and the Presumption

Slavery originates from captivity in war.[1] For American slaves it generally began as a result of armed conflict between other African tribes, in which the slave became a prisoner under threat of death.

While the slave's physical life was spared, he suffered what Orlando Patterson aptly calls "social death": the slave had no rights, no honor, no power to make any decisions for him/herself.[2] Thus slavery constitutes "absolute dominion."

Figure 1.1 Fitting shackles onboard slave ship.

The slave was a dominated thing, an animated instrument, a body with natural movements, but without its own reason, an existence entirely absorbed in another. The proprietor of this thing, the mover of this instrument, the soul and reason of this body, the source of this life was the master. The master was everything for him: his father, his God, which is to say his authority and his duty ... Thus God, fatherland, family, existence.[3]

This condition of absolute dominion was unnatural and could only be maintained through violence. More specifically, to maintain the institution of slavery it was necessary to continually repeat the original violent act of transforming free people into slaves. Slaves were kidnapped from their native lands, yoked together, and marched, sometimes for days, to waiting slave ships, and later packed spoon-fashion for a trans-Atlantic voyage—which could take months—in conditions of "indescribable horror." Once on the plantation they were branded, forced to work from just before sun-up until it was too dark to see, from "can to can't," and punished horrifically for the most minute infractions: a slave could have his ears cut off for stealing a pig.[4] Black women were often raped by the master or overseer, sometimes as punishment. Every slave faced the prospect of being sometimes sold away from their mother, fathers, or children. This is the meaning of absolute domination. This, for slave society, was order.

Thus, in the folklore of plantation life we see the master, dressed in finery, rocking on a porch behind soaring Doric columns, drinking mint julep tea, his wife with a hooped skirt presiding over happy docile slaves tending to their every whim. This picture of life on the plantation in popular culture is often portrayed as one of "idyllic repose."[5] But this was a romantic illusion. Behind the façade of supremacy, control, and order there was perpetual fear.

The never-ending rituals of buying, whipping, and owning "slaves" was knotted together in the mind of the master with a never-ending nightmare that these same "slaves" would rise up and slit his throat. Said one southern gentlewoman, "If they want to kill us, they can do it when they please, they are noiseless as panthers .... We ought to be grateful that anyone of us is alive."[6]

Reflecting the same sense of perpetual fear, a Louisiana planter exclaimed, "I have known times here, when there was not a single planter who had a calm night's rest; they then never lay down to sleep without a brace of loaded pistols at their sides."[7] Similarly, Jefferson says in *Notes of a State of Virginia*, "Indeed I tremble for my country when I reflect that God is just and that his justice cannot sleep forever."[8]

The master class channeled their anxiety into building interlocking institutions of control. First, they designed a system of punishment "rituals" intended to intimidate and control whole communities of slaves.

Slaves did steal, run away, and damage property, etc. Punishment did serve reflexively as a means of policing infractions, of getting control over a particular slave. But at a deeper level, the so-called punishment on the plantation was fundamentally designed to intimidate and control the slave population as a whole. It was "a means of transforming force into right, obedience into duty."[9] This transformation is a matter of controlling private and public symbols and "ritual processes" that "induce and seduce people to obey."[10] In the simplest terms they were "rituals to inscribe into the flesh of the slave the meaning of being a slave" (a slave had no honor and no power). Concomitantly the punishment was a way of expressing that the master had both great honor and power, absolute power.[11] The master could never be punished, regardless of how cruel or arbitrary the punishment. There is an echo of this symbolic linkage between ritual use of violence and honor in the slave regime and the shooting of Black men with impunity.

The Origin of the Presumption Itself

The idea of "Blacks" as both ethnically distinct and inferior precedes slavery. Africa is called Ifrichia in Arabic, from the word *faraca* which has the meaning of the Latin word *separavit* ("it has separated"). The Greeks spoke of Africa as the land of "the sunburnt races." Similarly, racism in an abstract sense precedes slavery as well. Thus, David Brion Davis writes,

> Recent scholarship has immensely enriched our knowledge of mediaeval European stereotypes of supposedly Black skinned serfs and peasants (who were darkened by dirt and by labor in the sun); of early Arab stereotypes of Black African slaves (millions of whom were transported from East Africa to the Near East).[12]

But Davis himself speaks of the special harshness of new-world slavery: "there can be no doubt that racial slavery in the United States widened the gap between slaves and the descendants of slaves [versus] non-slave populations that, despite their internal hierarchies, now appeared to be forever free, gave new meaning to both race and slave."[13]

To say that someone is Black is to engage in a thick description of a unique, shared history and experience. Within this welter of experience, one particular experience is the most formative and paradigmatic of the power relations between Blacks and whites: the experience of slavery.[14] The meaning of Blackness, in America, is largely constituted of the treatment Blacks received on the slave ship, on the plantation and the social, political, and legal status that flows from that treatment. What is implicit in this is a history of violence arising from a dialectic of oppression and resistance.

More specifically, the violent practices used by the master class to capture and later control slave populations defined more than any other feature what American slavery truly was. While slavery was upended, the ideology of slavery, by which the violence was rationalized, crystallized into a logic that reduced Blacks to a lower order of human life. During slavery this "logic" was inscribed on the bodies of Blacks. Today the same logic is implicit in the perpetuation of racial hierarchies, in racial projects like the drug war, and in state-sponsored violence against Blacks in the inner city.

The discussion in this chapter will unfold as follows. First, we will detail what I refer to as the spectrum of resistance: there was individual resistance on the plantation; there was both individual and collective resistance manifested in attempts to escape. And finally, there was open revolt.

After detailing this spectrum of resistance and exploring the threat it posed to the slave regime, we explore the plantation as prison, more specifically the mechanisms of control masters used to prevent rebellion—from whipping and slave patrols to quarantine.

Finally, we will suggest that these brutal mechanisms of control and the need to legitimate them is the root of the presumption we confront today.

The Spectrum of Resistance

Rebellion at Sea

The rebellion began as early as the middle passage. Thus, C. L. R. James writes, "[C]ontrary to the lies that have been spread so perniciously about Negro docility, the revolts at the port of embarkation and on board were incessant, so that the slaves had to be chained, right leg, left hand to left leg, and attached in rows to long iron bars."[15] He goes on to write, "They undertook vast hunger strikes; undid their chains anded themselves at the crew in futile attempts at insurrection."[16]

The most famous rebellion took place on the *Amistad* in 1839. The *Amistad* was a Spanish ship—*amistad* means friendship in Spanish—which left the port of Havana in August of 1839 bound for Gunaja, the port of entry of Puerto Principe in Cuba.[17] On board were fifty-three Africans the Spanish slavers had purchased at a slave market in Cuba.[18]

> [L]ed by Joseph Cinque, the natives had armed themselves with cane knives and risen in revolt, seizing control of the vessel after killing its Captain and owner Ramon Ferrar, and the cook, Celestino ... The two crew members disappeared, the two Spaniards declared, presumably murdered and thrown overboard with the other victims.[19]

Although they wrested power over the ship, they lacked the navigational skills to find their way home. Sparing and later trusting a Spanish navigator named Montes,[20] they were promptly tricked when he sailed East by day and North or West by night, zigzagging up the American coast.

Eventually the slave rebels landed on Montauk Point, Long Island.[21] Cinque and thirty-eight surviving Africans were promptly captured and indicted for murder.[22] This was true despite the fact that the Africans aboard ship had fought for the same values espoused by Patrick Henry and Jefferson a few decades earlier. Although the indictments were later dismissed, the Africans were still held to determine whether or not they were properly denominated as cargo or people.[23]

On the Plantation: "Individual Acts of Resistance"

As soon as they landed in the colonies, Africans resisted in a wide variety of ways. Sometimes they tried to assault or cause harm to their owners. "Slaves frequently spat, urinated in and polluted the master's food; they also, in moments of desperation struck back, responding to blows with blows."[24]

But most of what historians have termed "day to day" resistance involved crimes against property. Slaves "pulled down fences, sabotaged farm equipment, broke implements, damaged boats, vandalized wagons, ruined clothing, and committed various other destructive acts. They set fire to outbuildings, barns and stables, mistreated horses, mules, cattle."[25]

Slaves also struck back at the master by stealing his property: "They stole with impunity: sheep, hogs, cattle, poultry, money, watches produce liquor, tobacco flour, cotton, indigo, corn, nearly anything that was not under lock and key—and they occasionally found the key."[26]

They also stole the master's time. "[S]ome blacks worked slowly, or indifferently, took unscheduled respites, performed careless or sloppy labor when planting, hoeing and harvesting crops. Some chopped cotton so nonchalantly they cut the young plants nearly into fodder ... Slaves feigned illness, hid in outbuildings, did not complete their tasks."[27]

This "theft of time" "could not be obvious—absence from the gang or late return from meal breaks ... Theft had to be subtle theft through energy conservation and the deliberate reduction of performance level."[28]

Figure 1.2 A late nineteenth-century illustration of picking cotton on a plantation, in Louisiana, USA.

Source: De Luan/Alamy Stock Photo.

In all these instances slaves were engaged in a struggle for power. Slaves saw the master's property as an extension of the master himself. Whether through sabotage, theft, slow-downs, spitting in the soup, or physical assault, these were expressions of defiance and rebellion, an effort "to survive psychologically,"[29] to make their lives their own.

Running Away as Resistance

In the dialectic of oppression and resistance many slaves tried to escape, though only a small percentage did. According to Franklin, the ratio of slaves who escaped permanently to those held in bondage was 1 to 5,000.[30] Nonetheless, even at these extreme ratios, in any given year hundreds of slaves would make good their escape. In addition, thousands more would attempt to flee, some surviving for months. This means that there was at any given time a lurking population of fugitive slaves, threatening livestock, property, and the slave-owners themselves if they got in their way. Frequently they would band together in fugitive gangs.

> In virtually every state there were gangs of ten to twenty outlying slaves. The largest bodies of maroons, as they were sometimes called, reached only a few hundred members (with the exception of those in the great dismal Swamp between North Carolina and Virginia, which numbered several thousand). "… [R]unaway gangs were a constant source of fear and anxiety for whites."[31]

Resistance by Revolt

The most feared form of resistance was slave insurrection.

According to Apthecker, there were 250 slave revolts in America.[32] The small number of revolts is due to the fact that, in order for a slave revolt to succeed, slaves needed two things: numerical superiority and a great leader. Those two conditions came together in Haiti with cataclysmic force.

The Haitian Revolution

> A courageous chief only is wanted. Where is he, that great man whom Nature owes to her vexed, oppressed and tormented children? Where is he? He will

appear, doubt it not; he will come forth and raise the sacred standard of liberty. This venerable signal will gather around him the companions of his misfortune. More impetuous than the torrents, they will everywhere leave the indelible traces of their just resentment. Everywhere people will bless the name of the hero who shall have reestablished the rights of the human race; everywhere will they raise trophies in his honor.[33]

The Haitian revolution was the most successful slave insurrection in world history. Haitian slaves defeated, one after another, French, Spanish, and British armies. It shocked and horrified planters in North America and Europe that supposedly inferior Black slaves could rise up and defeat a European army and establish their own state.

The insurrection had its roots in a particularly brutal slave regime: the same "egalitarian" society which brought forth the French Revolution converted its half of the island of Santo Domingo into "a vast killing field" "sacrificing life for profit." The French, awash with egalitarian notions about the "rights of man," did enact a "Code Noir" which admonished slave owners to feed, clothe, and refrain from raping slaves.[34] Nonetheless, despite this "Code Noir," many slaves were worked to death because "it was usually cheaper to buy than raise a slave."[35] As Erica Hepburn writes, the labor conditions were so brutal that half the slaves died within ten years of arrival.[36]

But [t]he very conditions of their labor brought them together in a fashion that made "class struggle" more possible. "[W]orking together in gangs of hundreds on huge sugar factories which covered the northern plain,"[37] C. L. R. James compares the slaves[38] to a "proletariat" ready to rise, already "a thoroughly prepared and organized mass movement."[39]

In a sense the Haitian revolution began in France in 1789. "[T]hey had heard of the revolution and construed it in their own image: the white slaves of France had risen, and killed their masters and were now enjoying the fruits of the Earth." The spark of the French example ignited the explosive mix of desperation and hope among the slaves in Saint Dominique. The Haitian revolt began in August of 1791, led by Bookman.

Each slave gang murdered its masters and burnt the plantation [the Gallaudet plantation] to the ground … and in a few days one half of the famous Northern plain was a flaming ruin.

…

From their masters they had known rape, torture, degradation, and at the slightest provocation, death. They returned in kind. For two centuries the higher civilisation had shown them that power was used for wreaking your will on those whom you controlled. Now they held the power they did as they had been taught. In the frenzy of the first encounters they killed all. Vengeance! Vengeance was their war cry.[40]

One month after the revolt began, Francois-Dominique Toussaint L'Ouverture, a free man and born leader, joined the rebels (see Figure 1.3). He had studied the words of Abbé Raynal and answered his call: he was the "the great man" that Raynal had prophetically described. L'Ouverture transformed these "gangs of slaves" into a professional army loyal to him. Inspired morally by the ideals of the French Revolution, he led his army of slaves first against the Spanish and defeated them. In 1793, concerned that L'Ouverture's revolt would spread to the British Colonies, King George III sent 27,000 troops against him. Incredibly, L'Ouverture defeated them as well. In May 1798 Toussaint L'Ouverture accepted the surrender of the British at Port-Au-Prince.[41] In part the victories stemmed from L'Ouverture's strategic brilliance; in part it was tropical disease which killed thousands of redcoats before they surrendered to L'Ouverture. The victory of this army of slaves over the imperial British forces inspired William Blake's 1793 "America: A Prophecy."

> Let the slave grinding at the mill run out into the field;
> Let him look into the Heavens and laugh in the bright air[42]

Through intrigue and betrayal, L'Ouverture was captured and imprisoned by the French in 1802. But Dessalines and others continued the revolution which would create the first Black independent state in the Western Hemisphere.

The Haitian revolution had explosive impact on the American master class. Slavery was a paradox in the American social order. America's moral foundation was built on egalitarian ideals invoked in their rebellion against King George. At the same time, the economic foundation and the driving force of union between the North and the South, originally, was in large part slavery. As such, the Haitian revolution sent shock waves through the corridors of power in the U.S. President George Washington reflected on "a spirit of revolt among Blacks." "Where will it stop," he said.[43] In sum, the Haitian revolution was seen "as a formidable threat to the entire system,"[44] a "flame"[45] that could

Figure 1.3 Toussaint L'Ouverture, Haitian General.
Source: Alamy.

spread throughout slave-holding America. This no doubt had much to do with why the U.S. agreed with Britain to end slavery on the high seas after 1808. But the spirit of revolt would spread. It would spark the Gabriel conspiracy in Virginia.

The Gabriel Conspiracy

Ironically, in the year the declaration proclaimed all men are created equal, Gabriel Prosser was born into slavery on the plantation of Thomas Prosser at Brookfield, a plantation in Henrico County, Virginia.[46] He became a skilled artisan, a blacksmith who had gained a measure of freedom by virtue of his skills. His master hired him out to work in Richmond foundries. This practice of hiring out slaves was in part the result of war between England

and France, which "wrought havoc on the ability of Virginians to market their tobacco profitably in Europe." At the same time, the Haitian revolution had begun in what was then San Dominique in 1791. By 1795 "as many as twelve thousand Dominican slaves had entered the United States,"[47] many into Virginia. They brought with them news of Black victories over their colonial masters.

By 1799, Gabriel had met Charles Quersey, a veteran of the American Revolutionary War, in which French troops had helped Americans overthrow British tyranny. Egerton suggests Quersey—whose abolitionism was midwifed by the French revolution—both inspired and conspired with Gabriel to plot his rebellion. The Haitian revolution succeeded in part because of political division within the master class. Gabriel hoped to leverage homegrown division between the artisans, Black and white, who often labored beside each other, and the merchants, who set the prices and were mutually seen to oppress them. When Gabriel began his rebellion with an army of urbanized Black slaves, he thought, erroneously, that white artisans would join him.

He devised a brilliant, complex plan. He recruited artisans to fashion swords from scythes, and he recruited 500–600 bondsmen to serve as his rebel army. He would create a diversion, seize guns at the warehouse, take Richmond, fortify the city, and demand the end of slavery in Virginia. The plan might have succeeded, but for torrential rain that washed out fragile wooden bridges and cut off communications. Then a slave named Pharoah, owned by Phillip Sheppard, used the intervening pause to tell his master about the planned uprising.

Denmark Vesey's Revolt

Even more famous was the Charleston uprising led by Denmark Vesey. Vesey "was born a slave and worked in the sugar fields in Haiti until purchased by Captain Joseph Vesey, who brought him to Charles Town (renamed Charleston in 1783) in the 1780s."[48] In 1799 Vesey won the East Bay lottery and bought his freedom. He was devoutly religious. He established, with others, a Methodist church. Tragically, in June 1818 he and 140 free blacks and slaves were arrested for worshipping there together in violation of city ordinances.

Radicalized, by 1822 Vesey had recruited and organized over 9,000 Blacks to begin a war of insurrection. Christianity, at least under the New Testament, preaches peace: "If anyone slaps you on the right cheek, turn to them the other cheek also."[49] But as Douglas Egerton has written, Vesey "turned his back on Christian passivity commonly taught by white ministers and free Black preachers in favor of an Old Testament Activism forged of wrath and justice." According to one slave witness, Rolla, Vesey exhorted his followers "not to spare one white skin alive,"[50] which Vesey allegedly justified using passages from the Old Testament.[51] Vesey was arrested on June 22 a few weeks before his rebellion was scheduled to begin. Over 100 Blacks were tried and thirty-five hanged, including Denmark Vesey.[52]

But the most important and successful rebellion in the United States was led by Nat Turner, or General Nat.

The Nat Turner Rebellion

> Nat Turner reminds us that oppression is a kind of violence which pays in coin of its own minting. He reminds us that the first and greatest of the gospels is this: individuals and systems always reap what they sow.[53]

The Nat Turner revolt which erupted in Southampton County, Virginia, during the early morning hours on August 22, 1831, was the bloodiest slave revolt in Southern history. As Herbert Aptheker explains,

> At its height, the revolt involved approximately forty active rebels and ultimately led to the death of approximately fifty-five white victims. While we can be reasonably certain of the number and identities of the black rebels who were executed after trials, and we can clearly identify the white victims, there were scores of additional anonymous deaths: unrecorded summary executions of "suspected" insurrectionists by infuriated local residents and militiamen.[54]

Like Gabriel Prosser and Denmark Vesey, Nat Turner, the slave revolutionary who led the rebellion, was reputed to be a man of unusual gifts. Nat could read at an early age, which was unusual because most slaves were illiterate. Who taught him? It was a crime to even teach slaves to read and write. Nat states in his confession it just came to him miraculously,

> The manner in which I learned to read and write, not only had a great influence astonishment on my mind, as I acquired it with the most perfect ease, so much so, that I have no recollection whatever of learning the alphabet—but to the astonishment of my family, one day, when a book was shewn to keep me from crying, I began spelling the names of different objects—this was a source of wonder to all in the neighborhood, particularly the blacks.[55]

While Gabriel Prosser and Denmark Vesey were inspired by Lockean ideals of freedom and liberty, Nat found inspiration in the gospels of Christianity. Slave masters, in their religious instruction of their slaves, carefully picking passages in which the Bible urged obedience of servants to their masters, deployed the scriptures as yet another device to control them.

> If they did not obey their masters and perform their allotted tasks God would burn them in flames of an eternal hell. The bible said that God wanted negroes to be the white man's slaves, that this was their proper station in life. One must not question the wisdom of the almighty ... To be good children of the lord the slaves must accept their lot, be meek and faithful, patient and submissive, even if their masters were cruel.[56]

But the slaves had their own Church, in a forest clearing or a tumble-down shack, where "black exhorters preached a different version of Christianity from what the white man offered, an alternative version that condemned slavery and fueled resistance to it." [57]

"One day while Nat was praying at his plow, Nat thought he heard a voice in the wind—the spirit called out to him—'Seek ye the kingdom of Heaven and all things shall be added unto you—as to the prophets of old.'"[58] By 1825 Nat had styled himself as both itinerant preacher and "cotton patch prophet."[59] In his praise meetings he told his parishioners about prophetic visions of "warring angels in the sky." By 1829 he had his most "epochal" vision in which he stated that the lord had told him he "should fight against the serpent" and the time had come for the last to be first. In February 1831 there was an eclipse, which Nat took as the sign that it was time to begin. Nat gathered four slaves who functioned as his lieutenants—Hark, Nelson, Henry, and Sam. They in turn gathered others. On Sunday, August 21, the revolt began. Unlike Vesey, Nat's goal was to make a "march of extermination": to "kill all the white people" on the 10-mile route to Jerusalem, ironically the name of the county seat. Oates suggests that once the insurrection began he (Nat Turner) expected God to lead him.[60] In Ezekiel God says, "Go ye after him through the city and smite, let not your eye spare, neither have ye pity." Armed with a dull sword and his conviction to spare neither women nor children, Nat led his followers on a deadly rampage. After two days the rebellious slaves met organized resistance and were dispersed by the militia. Nat was beheaded and over fifty other Blacks were executed.[61]

Slavery as a Disciplinary Regime

Slave revolts were an existential threat. Any act of defiance was an inchoate threat to the slave regime as a whole. Any infraction was an act of defiance. To preempt violence by slaves, the master class created a regime of constant violence and intimidation.

> The slaves were punished for stealing … not doing what their master told them, and for talking back to their master. If any of these rules were disobeyed their feet and hands were chained together and they were put across a log or barrel and whipped until the blood came from them. There were no jails; the white man was the slaves' jail.[62]

There was no limit to the master's discretion. Thus the punishment could be quite severe. The *La Grange True Issue* in July, 1860, described how a master in Coryell whipped a girl from sunrise until noon. The editor wrote, "One observer said the slave, who was accused of stealing, was the most inhumanely whipped creature he had ever seen, including horses and oxen."[63]

Slaves were often whipped on the most arbitrary grounds.

> It would astonish one unaccustomed to a slaveholding life, to see with what wonderful ease a slaveholder can find things, of which to make occasion to

whip a slave. A mere look, word, or motion—a mistake, accident, or want of power—are all matters for which a slave may be whipped at any time. Does a slave look dissatisfied? It is said, he has the devil in him, it must be whipped out.[64]

At prayer:

[T]he white folks would come in when the colored people would have a prayer meeting, and whip every one of them. Most of them thought that when the colored people were praying it was against them. For they would catch them praying for God to lift things out of their way.[65]

And

Henry Bibb was threatened with five hundred lashes on the naked back for attending a prayer meeting conducted by slaves on the neighboring plantation because he had no permission to do so ... Charlotte Martin was whipped to death for taking part in one of the religious ceremonies.[66]

For whites, the whipping served deep psychological needs. Southern whites defined slaves as persons without honor. Therefore, whites being persons with honor or gentlemen meant being wholly unlike a slave. The ritual of white master inflicting injury on the body of the Black slave the mark of their dishonor. Thus as Professor Andrew Taslitz writes,

For white southerners, the whip on the back of the slave was a sign of the slave's bad character. ... Southerners saw the scars of whipping as permanently marking the slaves as flawed and outside of the community of equals. The scar spoke for itself—or rather about the man whose body carried it regardless of the process or the larger set of relations that brought it into existence.[67]

For the white master class it was about honor. But it was also equally about power. The power to dominate the slave totally to make the slave an empty vessel, devoid of any will of his own, was necessary to the slave relationship.

With slavery it is far otherwise. The end is the profit of the master, his security and the public safety; the subject, one doomed in his own person, and his posterity, to live without knowledge, and without the capacity to make anything his own, and to toil that another may reap the fruits. What moral considerations shall be addressed to such a being, to convince him what, it is impossible but that the most stupid must feel and know can never be true—that he is thus to labour upon a principle of natural duty, or for the sake of his own personal happiness, such services can only be expected from one who has no will of his own; who surrenders his will in implicit obedience to that of another. Such obedience is the consequence only of uncontrolled authority over the body. There is nothing else which can operate to produce the effect. The power of the master must be absolute, to render the submission of the slave perfect.[68]

Whipping was equally a way of inscribing onto the Black slave the mark not only of bad character but the mark of powerlessness, rightlessness.

As Southerners well understood, the purpose of the violence was not solely to discipline the slaves, but also to venerate the owner. The honor of the white man depended upon his lordship over the black man. That lordship required violence so that slaves understood that they could have no world of their own. They could not work, sleep, or protect their families; they could not rest, or pray, or gossip. They were allowed no existence except for that dictated by the master. Only violence, most often in the form of whipping, but including rape, branding, and murder, among other methods, demonstrated the absolute command of the white master over the black slave.[69]

At absolute bottom the act of whipping repeated the act of enslavement in which Africans were herded and stowed onto ships like cattle to be sold as chattel. The mark of the whip signified that they were the slave and the whipper was the slave owner. The meaning of being a slave was that a slave was no better than an animal. Most simply put, they were treated as beasts.

This, beast/sub-human characterization anchors the notion that it is natural and normal for Blacks to be treated in this manner. The more they were treated as animals the more they came to be seen as animals.[70] This sub-humanization is the essence of the presumption—which traces back to slavery. Whether it is a presumption of dangerousness or guilt, or a notion that Blacks belong in certain places and are dangerous in others, the presumption originates implicitly in the notion of Blacks as being not merely non-citizens but being in "essence" animals—and that they were dangerous and inferior as such. These notions of inferiority or dangerousness were implicit in the brutality, the constant surveillance, which were typical features of plantation life. These same notions of inferiority and dangerousness justified whites in taking freedom away from Blacks, and hunting them if they dared to escape. These practices themselves were not merely part of a race-making process; they were the race-making process. Through the specific ideas of a presumption of dangerousness, or guilt, or a "presumption" of "you don't belong here," the dominant society legitimates the treatment of those who were treated as beasts.

The fact that this private violence was authorized and sometimes required by law intensified the message. The fact that the master could do this with impunity illustrates that Blacks were outside of the law's protection. They were objects of the law's control, not subjects. Since Blacks and only Blacks experienced chattel slavery, the inside/outside dichotomy this created between slave and master was also racialized. Racial violence, racial caste, and honor are all knotted together in this ritual of violence.

This linkage is mirrored in the way Southern violence was used during the era of segregation. Recall the fact that Emmet Till was tortured and murdered for nothing more than, allegedly,[71] "wolf-whistling at a white woman" (Carolyn Dunham), an offense to Southern honor. Blacks were also often lynched for failing to walk on the opposite side of the street or for having an "uppity attitude." These were "honor crimes" as well. Lynching Blacks during the Jim Crow era, sometimes for the pettiest infractions, was reminiscent of slavery, policing the boundaries of racial caste.

Similarly, consider the case of Michael Brown. He was shot after resisting arrest for allegedly jaywalking. Jaywalking is quintessentially a petty offense. After Brown resisted what he felt was an unjustified arrest, Officer Darren Wilson shot him, according to three witnesses, in the back with his hands up. If the three witnesses' account is true, the true motive for the shooting was that, in the officer's mind, he had been disrespected. There is a mirroring among the shooting of Michael Brown, for disrespect of a police officer, the violence during the era of Jim Crow, and the violence of whipping Blacks on the plantation for talking back.

Slave Patrols

Beginning in the Caribbean, slave society developed slave patrols, which originally were associated with the "militia." Slave patrols borrowed from the concept of *posse comitus*. Sometimes the states paid a group of armed men to patrol. But the perceived danger was such that every citizen could be called upon to support the cause.

> With us every citizen in the maintenance of order and in promoting honesty and industry among those of the lowest class who are our slaves and our habitual vigilance renders standing armies, whether soldiers or policeman entirely unnecessary. Small guards in our cities and occasional patrols in the country insure us in repose and security known nowhere else.[72]

Often depicted as men on horseback with bloodhounds chasing runaways, slave patrols did much more:

> Then the paddy rollers they keep close watch on pore niggers so they have no chance to do anything or go anywhere. They jes like policemen, only worser. Cause they never let the niggers go anywhere without a pass from his masters. If you wasn't in your proper place when the paddy-rollers come they lash you til' you was black and blue. The woman got 15 lashes and the men 30. That was for jes bein out without a pass. If the nigger done anything worse he was taken to jail and put in the whipping post.[73]

They looked for weapons and stolen goods in slave cabins, questioned slaves they met on the road and broke up slave meetings. Patrollers could detain and question whites and search their homes without warrants.[74]

Sometimes they pursued slaves far into the North. The constitution itself contains a Fugitive Slave clause. When first adopted, this clause applied to fugitive slaves and required that they be extradited upon the claims of their masters, but it provided no means for doing so. The Fugitive Slave Act of 1793 created the mechanism for recovering a fugitive slave, overruled any state laws giving sanctuary, made it a federal crime to assist an escaped slave, and allowed slave-catchers into every US state and territory.[75] As free states sought to undermine the federal law, the even more severe Fugitive Slave Act of 1850 was enacted. It required that all escaped slaves, upon capture, be returned to their masters and that officials and citizens of free states had to cooperate.[76] Abolitionists called this the bloodhound law. Under this law slaves could not ask for a jury trial or testify on their own behalf.

The slave patrols, fugitive slave laws, and a particular presumption worked in tandem. The presumption, at least in the South was that Black people generally were slaves. Thus in *Hudgins v. Wright* the judge Roane Tucker stated, "Nature has stampt upon the African and his descendants two characteristic marks besides the difference of complexion."[77] The two characteristics were a flat nose and wooly hair.

Similarly, Frederick Nash wrote, "let the presumption rest upon the African color, that is a decided mark, … and against the rule that presumptions are always in favor of liberty".[78] While in the North the presumption was otherwise, the mischief of denying the alleged fugitive slave a trial effectively prejudged him. All the judge could do was to determine whether the identity of the suspect corresponded to the description in the affidavit.

The presumption of guilt and dangerousness that is implicated in the systemic disparities of Blacks arrested and incarcerated in the drug war is linked historically to the presumption in the ante-bellum era that a Black person was a slave.

Quarantine

Slave revolts were the sum of all fears for the master class. At a deep level the master class knew, of course, that the revolts were repayment, in the coin of blood, for their oppression. But in a feat of denial, the public discourse of the master class focused not on the slaves themselves as the problem but agitators from outside.

Thus, in response to the near successful revolt of Denmark Vesey, the white population of Charleston constructed a narrative of Vesey as a Trans-Atlantic sailor who brought in his ideas of rebellion from his travels over the seas.[79]

The city's white population constructed a narrative of causation for the botched revolt, and within it Denmark Vesey assumed Herculean characteristics. He was the mastermind, and because of his central role, white Charlestonians sought to explain the impetus behind his murderous designs. Mayor James Hamilton wrote that Vesey was once an Atlantic-savvy sailor who had traveled for years around the revolutionary Atlantic and even resided in St. Domingo immediately before the Haitian Revolution. The official trial "transcripts," which were actually authored after the executions by two of the sitting magistrates, confidently proclaimed that Vesey kept close contact with transnational black sailors.[80]

Immersed in this narrative of outside influences a key feature of the slave regime became quarantine. Following the Denmark Vesey rebellion South Carolina adopted legislation criminalizing the very presence of "free negroes."[81] It commanded local authorities to arrest all free Black sailors found on board ships that docked in South Carolina ports and to imprison them until their ships were ready to depart. The statute also required the Captain of the ship to pay for the incarceration of the imprisoned sailor. If the captain did not pay, the captain himself would be imprisoned and fined while the sailor would be "taken as [an] absolute slave."[82] Under the statutory scheme the Black sailor was jailed and sometimes sold into slavery without the benefit of a trial.

The Negro Seamen's law treated free Black sailors as carriers of a deadly disease. In fact, when challenged in the federal court the state of South Carolina argued that it was operating no differently than the state of New York when it quarantined vessels carrying contagion.[83] The "contagion" here was not disease, however, but free Black sailors, outsiders "who might undermine slave society." South Carolina argued they had a basic right to protect themselves from this outsider-borne contagion. "The civilized man can secure his family against the contagion of the dissolute or the depraved, by closing its doors or selecting its visitors a state must be the sole judge to decide what strangers may remain or enter."[84]

The source of the contagion was knowledge. Free Blacks from other states and foreign lands had access to abolitionist ideas. These free Blacks were prone to spread these ideas among the plantation slaves: "[F]reed negroes and persons of color, coming from the North … [had] attempted to corrupt our colored population by instilling into their minds false ideas … till by their insidious and exaggerated statements, they succeeded in exciting in the midst of this community a formidable insurrection."[85]

Under this scheme the place for Blacks in South Carolina society was clear: either in jail or on the plantation.

Similarly, after the bloody Nat Turner revolt, Virginia whites blamed this revolt on "outside agitators."

> Desperately needing to blame somebody for Nat Turner besides themselves [some] Southern whites inevitably linked the revolt to sinister Northern abolitionist plot to destroy their cherished way of life … Southern zealots declared that the antislavery movement, gathering momentum throughout the 1820's had now burst into a full-blown crusade against the South.[86]

The Governor of Virginia also blamed "negro preachers." He "became [convinced] that a heinous Yankee conspiracy, with Garrison and Knapp as its high priests and *Negro Preachers* as its agents lay behind the Southampton uprising and all other slave troubles as well."[87]

In response the Virginia authorities enacted several measures mirroring the quarantine strategy of their South Carolina counterparts. "To prevent any future uprising Floyd enjoined the legislature to outlaw these preachers, enact sever punishments against outside agitators, remove the state's free Black population, rearm and strengthen the militia no matter what the cost."[88]

In addition to these post-insurrection measures there were of course, as standard operating procedure, pass laws to restrict Blacks from being "off the plantation" without permission. Any white citizen could check to see if they had a proper pass.

The significance of these restrictions on the right of free Blacks to enter a slave state and of Blacks on the plantation to leave was a knotting together of the notion of race and place. Slavery was a caste system. A caste system is defined by the notion that the members of the lower caste had to stay in their place. But "place" in both the thinking and the law of the ante bellum South had a double meaning. It refers first to a physical space: Blacks "belong on the plantation or in jail." At the same time it refers to an inferior position within the social hierarchy: Blacks belonged either on a plantation, as slaves, or in jail. The concept of Blacks as beasts is implicit here.

But if slavery, and the violence that was necessary to maintain it, was rationalized in the culture of slavery by the notion that Blacks were beasts, how was this rationalized in the law? Taney says it was because Blacks were regarded in law and morals as inferior, and so far inferior they could justly be "reduced to slavery." He says,

> They had for more than a century before being regarded as beings of an inferior order, and altogether unfit to associate with the white race, either in social or political relations; and so far inferior, that they had no rights which the white man was bound to respect; and that the negro might justly and lawfully be reduced to slavery for his benefit ... This opinion was at that time fixed and universal in the civilized portion of the white race. It was regarded as an axiom in morals as well as in politics, which no one thought of disputing, or supposed to be open to dispute; and men in every grade and position in society daily and habitually acted upon it in their private pursuits, as well as in matters of public concern.[89]

An "axiom" is no more than an assumption. But this assumption, an untethered and perverse assumption, anchored the ideology of slavery.

The regime of slaves and masters has disappeared. We now have formal equality. But what remains—deeper and stronger in Gramsci's terms— is a pernicious logic, or narrative or mentality. The logic is a distillation of the ideology of slavery. The "logic" of Justice Taney. This "logic" and the presumption we are talking about is the same.

During the era of slavery this logic attached to Black bodies by force of law. Now it continues to attach not by force of law but as a set of widely shared narratives and myths. Since slavery we have erased the color-line as a formal barrier between Blacks and equal opportunity. The fault lines are between two Americas, one suburban with beautiful late model cars in the driveway—here there are jobs, good schools, opportunities, and one can purchase soybean milk at the grocery store. In another America there is joblessness, squalor, a landscape of urban despair with acres of ruined abandoned houses that stare back at you with plywood sheets for eyes. Here when one asks a child what they will be when they grow up they say, "I want to be 18." Here, mirroring the rules of the plantation, the right of locomotion has disappeared, as police systemically target these areas for military style stop and frisk campaigns. The color line has disappeared, but here are two distinct Americas with Blacks on both sides.

But despite this dualism, America still has a racial caste system. It is simply that race has become a spectrum with Blacks who live in greater America at one end and poor Blacks in the urban core at the other. The source of the fault line between the two Americas, a fault line that reaches into our criminal justice system as well—so much so that one could say we do not have one criminal justice system; we have two—is a presumption. Sometimes it is a presumption of dangerousness. Sometimes it is a presumption of guilt; sometimes, if you're Black, it is a presumption that in certain spaces you don't belong. That presumption is the legacy of slavery, it is the legacy of mark: the mark of criminality inscribed by the master class on a collective Black body with whips and branding irons as a "sign" of dishonor. The mark is still there.

Notes

1   Gunnar Landtman, *The Origin of the Inequality of the Social Classes* (New York: Routledge, 2015), 248.

2   Orlando Patterson, *Slavery and Social Death* (Cambridge, MA: Harvard University Press, 1985).

3   Patterson, *Slavery and Social Death*.

4   Oliver Perry Chitwood, *Justice in Colonial Virginia* (Baltimore, MD: Johns Hopkins Press, 1905), 83.

5   Paula T. Connolly, *Slavery in American Children's Literature, 1790–2010* (Iowa City, IA: University of Iowa Press, 2013).

6   Mary Boykin Chesnut, *A Diary from Dixie* (Boston, MA: Houghton Mifflin, 1949), 147–8.

7   Fredrika Brewer, *The Homes of the New World: Impressions of America* (2 vols.) (New York: Harper, 1853), 190.

8   Thomas Jefferson, *Notes of the State of Virginia* (New York: W.W. Norton, 1972), 162–3.

9   Patterson, *Slavery and Social Death*.

10   Ibid.

11   Of course it is precisely at the point that power becomes absolute that it becomes a form of dependency. Orlando Patterson writes,

> As Georg Hegel realized, total personal power taken to its extreme contradicts itself by its very existence, for total domination can

become a form of dependence on the object of one's power and total
powerlessness can become the secret path to control the subject that
attempts to exercise such power.

Patterson, *Slavery and Social Death*, 2.

12 David Brion Davis, *Inhuman Bondage: The Rise and Fall of Slavery in the New World* (Oxford, UK: Oxford University Press, 2008).

13 David Brion Davis, *Inhuman Bondage*, 3.

14 D. Marvin Jones, "Darkness Made Visible: Law, Metaphor, and the Racial Self," *Georgetown Law Journal* 82 (1993) 437.

15 C. L. R. James, *The Black Jacobins* (New York: Random House, 1963).

16 James, *The Black Jacobins*.

17 Christopher Martin, *The Amistad Affair* (New York: Abelard-Schuman, 1970), 35–6.

18 Martin, *The Amistad Affair*.

19 Ibid.

20 William Owens, *Slave Mutiny* (New York: John Day, 1953) 71–110.

21 Martin, *The Amistad Affair*, fn. 183, 52–3.

22 Ibid., 60.

23 Ibid.

24 Anthony Tibbles, *Trans-Atlantic Slavery: Against Human Dignity* (Liverpool, UK: Liverpool University Press, 2005).

25 John Hope Franklin and Loren Schweninger, *Runaway Slaves: Rebels on the Plantation* (Oxford, UK: Oxford University Press, 1999).

26 Ibid.

27 Ibid.

28 Gad J. Heuman and James Walvin, eds., *The Slavery Reader* (NewYork: Routledge, 2003), 481.

29 Junious P. Rodriguez, *Encyclopedia of Slave Resistance and Rebellion*. Volume 2 (Westport, CT: Greenwood Publishing Group 2007), 446.

30 Franklin and Schweninger, *Runaway Slaves*. Franklin notes "although the underground railroad was a reality much of the material relating to it belongs to the realm of folklore rather than history," xiv.

31 Franklin and Schweninger, *Runaway Slaves*.

32 Herbert Apthecker, *American Negro Slave Revolts*, 50th Anniversary Edition (New York: International Publishers, 1993).

33 Toussaint L'Ouverture: *A Bibliography and Autobiography* (Boston, MA : James Redpath, 1863).

34 Phillip Girard, Haiti, *The Tumultuous History: From Pearl of The Caribbean to Broken Nation* (New York: MacMillan, 2010), 25.

35 Dady Chery, *Toussaint L'Ouverture, The Genius Who Embodied the Enlightenment*, November 1, 2011, https://www.dadychery.org/2011/11/01/toussaint-louverture-the-genius-who-embodied-the-enlightenment-2/; See also Daniel P. Mannix, *Black Cargoes: The Atlantic Slave Trade 1518–1865* (New York: Penguin Books, 2002).

36 Erica Hepburn, *The Haitian Revolution: Misconceptions and the Dangers of Teaching It in Western Society* (June 6, 2014). https://www.academia.edu/7277007/The_Haitian_Revolution_Misconceptions_and_the_Dangers_of_Teaching_it_in_Western_Society.

37 Cyril Lionel Robert James and Robin D. G. Kelly, *A History of Pan African Revolt* (Oakland, CA: PM Press, 2012), 5.

38 James and Kelly, *A History of Pan African Revolt*.

39 Ibid., 15.

40 Ibid., 40.

41 Ibid.

42 W. H. Stevenson, *Blake: The Complete Poems* (New York: Routledge, 2014).

43 Gerald Horne, *Confronting Black Jacobins, The U.S., The Haitian Revolution, and the Origins of the Dominican Republic* (New York: Monthly Review Press, 2015).

44 Horne, *Confronting Black Jacobins*.

45 Ibid.

46 Douglas R. Egerton, *Gabriel's Rebellion: The Virginia Slave Conspiracies of 1800 and 1802* (Chapel Hill, NC: University of North Carolina Press, 2000), 19–20.

47 Egerton, *Gabriel's Rebellion*.

48 Douglas R. Egerton, *He Shall Go Out Free: The Lives of Denmark Vesey* (Lanham, MD: Rowman & Littlefield, 2004), 13–14.

49 Matthew 5:39.

50 David Brion Davis, *Inhuman Bondage: The Rise and Fall of Slavery in the New World* (Oxford: Oxford University Press, 2008), 224.

51 Ibid.

52 Douglas R. Egerton and Robert L. Paguette, *The Denmark Vesey Affair: A Documentary History* (Gainesville, Florida: University Press of Florida, 2017).

53 Stephen B. Oates, *The Fires of Jubilee: Nat Turner's Fierce Rebellion* (New York: Harper Collins, 2016).

54 Herbert Aptheker, *Nat Turner's Slave Rebellion: Including the 1831 Confessions* (N. Chelmsford, MA: Courier Corporation, 2012).

55 Oates, *The Fires of Jubilee*.

56   Aptheker, *Nat Turner's Slave Rebellion.*

57   Ibid.

58   James Thomas Baker, *Nat Turner: Cry Freedom in America* (San Diego, CA: Harcourt Brace, 1998).

59   Oates, *The Fires of Jubilee.*

60   Ibid., 198.

61   For all of the information in this paragraph I rely upon Oates.

62   T. Lindsay Baker and Julie Phillips, eds. *The WPA Oklahoma Slave Narratives* (Norman, OK: University of Oklahoma Press, 1996).

63   Randolph B. Campbell, *An Empire of Slavery: The Peculiar Institution in Texas, 1821–1865* (Baton Rouge, LA, Louisiana State University Press, 1991).

64   *Breaking the Chains—The Essential Powerful Narratives that Shook the Roots of Slavery, Memoirs of Frederick Douglass, Underground Railroad, 12 Years A Slave, Incidents in the Life of a Slave Girl, Narrative of Sojourner Truth, Running a Thousand Miles for Freedom*, and many more (Slovakia: e-artnow.org 2017).

65   Albert J. Robateau, *Slave Religion: The Invisible Institution in the Ante-Bellum South* (Oxford, UK: Oxford University Press, 2004), xcii.

66   Robateau, *Slave Religion.*

67   Andrew E. Taslitz, *Reconstructing the Fourth Amendment: A History of Search and Seizure, 1789–1868* (New York: New York University Press, 2009).

68   *State v. Mann*, 13 N.C. 263 (1829), 266

69   Andrew E. Taslitz, "Hate Crimes, Free Speech, and the Contract of Mutual Indifference," *Boston University Law Review* 80 (2000) 1283.

70   D. Marvin Jones, "Darkness Made Visible: Law, Metaphor, and the Racial Self," *Georgetown Law Journal* 82 (1993) 437.

71   We now know that Carolyn Dunham lied. Emmett Till accuser admits to giving false testimony at murder trial. https://www.chicagotribune.com/nation-world/ct-emmett-till-accuser-false-testimony-20170128-story.html.

72   James Henry Hammond, Thomas Clarkson, *Governor Henry Hammonds Letters on Southern Slavery*, https://books.google.com/books?id=4xFiCQAAQBAJ&dq=%22with+us+every+citizen%22&source=gbs_navlinks_s; see also Kenneth Morgan, *Slavery in America: A Reader and Guide* (Athens, NY: University of Georgia Press 2005).

73   Salley E. Hadden, *Slave Patrols: Law and Violence in Virginia and the Carolinas* (Cambridge, MA: Harvard University Press 2001).

74   It is popular today to argue for an analogy between the "paddyrollers" and modern police. I would argue that the better analogy is between the plantation

as a police regime whose goal was not to control and to intimidate the Black population and the ghetto as a police regime. The police functioning today in the same fashion for the same purpose. Of course in slavery times the "paddyrollers" were only the most obvious body of police. In reality all whites in the slave regime functioned as "police" and had the right to inspect the papers of Blacks whom they encountered in the street.

75   See Robert Cover, *Justice Accused: Antislavery and the Judicial Process* (New Haven, CT: Yale University Press, 1975), 162.

76   Eric Arnessen, *Encyclopedia of U.S. Labor and Working class History*, Volume 1 (Abingdon-on-Thames, UK: Taylor & Francis, 2007).

77   *Hudgins v. Wrights*, 11 Va. 134 (1806), p. 138.

78   Thomas D. Morris, *Southern Slavery and the Law, 1619—1860* (Durham, NC: University of North Carolina Press, 2004).

79   Michael Scheppner, "Peculiar Quarantines: The Seamen's Acts and Revolutionary Authority in the Ante-Bellum South," *Law and History Review* 31, no. 3 (2013) 559.

80   Scheppner, "Peculiar Quarantines".

81   Paul Finkelman, "The Crime of Color," *Tulane Law Review* 67 (1993) 2063.

82   D. Marvin Jones, *Dangerous Spaces: Beyond the Racial Profile* (Santa Barbara, CA: Praeger, 2016), 38.

83   Eddie l. Wong, *Neither Fugitive Nor Free: Atlantic Slavery, Freedom Suits and the Legal Culture of Travel* (New York: New York University Press 2009), 197.

84   Wong, *Neither Fugitive Nor Free*.

85   Ibid. The statute provided,

    [W]hen said vessel is ready to sail the captain of said vessel shall be bound to carry away the said free negro, or free person of color, and to pay the expenses of his detention; and, in case of his neglect or refusal so to do, he shall be liable to be indicted, and on conviction thereof shall be fined in a sum not less than one thousand dollars, and imprisoned not less than two months; and such free negroes, or persons of color, shall be deemed and taken as absolute slaves, and sold in conformity to the provisions of the act passed on the 20th December, 1820, aforesaid. Id.

86   Stephen B. Oates, *The Fires of Jubilee*.

87   Ibid.

88   Ibid.

89   *Scott v. Sandford*, 60 U.S. 393, 407.

2

"This Is a White Man's Country!": The Eviction of Ossian Sweet

In the silent black and white films depicting the 1920s, this era appears as a time of "Flappers," Charleston dances, ragtime music, and sports cars with rumble seats. Trying to capture the cultural exuberance of the time, F. Scott

Figure 2.1 Dr. Ossian Sweet.

Source: Detroit Public Library.

Fitzgerald called the decade following World War I "the jazz age."[1] But what is missing from this picture are images of racial violence and death. From November of 1918 to February of 1920, there were nine major race riots across the United States as well as ninety-seven lynchings.[2]

Yet, in spite of the racial horrors they confronted, this era was for American Negroes a time of rising hope.

> Having fought for their country abroad they were resolved to end discrimination at home. as participants in the war in uniform and on the home front they had gained self-confidence and a sense of solidarity with other black Americans.
>
> ...
>
> The world war had produced a "new negro." They were proud, not easily intimidated, and determined to win their rights.[3]

In a word, they were ready to fight.

> [T]his new negro, this new man, ... shed the costume of the shuffling darky, the uncle, the aunty, and the subservient and docile retainer, the clown. He was, rather, a man and citizen in his own right ... intelligent, articulate, self-assured. The new negro was telling all Americans that it was a new ballgame, and that he was revived as an inspired competitor. No longer could he be dismissed by contempt, pity, or terror. He would insist upon his rights, and, if necessary, return violence, blow for blow.[4]

But this new mood of determination and optimism could not take root in the South. A rigid caste system remained in place. And the economy of the South was failing. At the same time, Northern cities like Detroit were booming in the aftermath of World War I, and there was a shortage of labor.

Water flows because of gravity; people flow because of hope. "Between 1917 and 1920 an estimated 700,000 to 1 million Blacks left. Another 800,000 to 1 million left during the 1920s."[5] By the 1920s, seven cities—Philadelphia, New York, Chicago, Detroit, Pittsburgh, Indianapolis, and Cleveland—contained 40 percent of the North's Black population (see Figure 2.2).[6]

Detroit's Black population shot up at an extraordinary rate. Between 1910 and 1920, it had increased by 600 percent. No other colored community

A NEGRO FAMILY JUST ARRIVED IN CHICAGO FROM THE RURAL SOUTH

Figure 2.2 African American extended family arriving in Chicago from the rural South, *ca.*1920. From *The Negro in Chicago: a Study of Race Relations and a Race Riot,* 1922 (BSLOC_2015_16_134).

Source: Alamy.

above the Mason-Dixon Line, not even Harlem, had grown so fast.[7] But Black aspiration collided with white racial fears: whites in the North saw the mass migration of Blacks into their neighborhoods as an invasion. Between July 1, 1917, and March 1921, there had been fifty-eight bombings of Negro houses.[8]

It was in the midst of this social and moral drama that Dr. Ossian Sweet stepped onto the stage of history.

Dr. Ossian Sweet was born in Bartow, Florida in 1895. When he was five years old, he was out alone at night about a mile from his house. He then witnessed a powerless Black man at the mercy of a mob.

Dr. Ossian Sweet, then a boy, saw a crowd of some five thousand white people driving along a Negro youth. Fred Rochelle was his name. He saw them pour kerosene over him and set fire to the living flesh. With his own ears he heard the poor wretch's shrieks and groans. Hidden and terrified, he watched the crowd turn the whole occasion into a Roman holiday, and their victim, dead.[9]

Lynchings, while typically justified as a punishment for alleged sexual assault committed by Blacks, were driven by the economic insecurities of whites at the time.

[T]he economic strains that began during 1879 and 1910 resulted in a generation of white men failing to achieve the financial success of their fathers. As the economic decline continued into the twentieth century white men used lynching usually a black male victim to overcome their economic anxiety by expressing their power as white men.[10]

Ossian would always remember Fred Rochelle's death as "the most terrifying moment of his young life."[11] It terrified Ossian's parents as well. In the shadow of this racial terror, in the form of the lynching of and other atrocities, Ossian's parents made the decision to send Ossian North to Wilberforce University when he was 13.

While the Sweets could not afford the $118.00 tuition, Wilberforce was owned and operated by the African Methodist Episcopal (AME) church and Ossian received a full scholarship from the AME's Florida Conference to attend. But when he arrived at Wilberforce, Ohio, 986 miles away, he learned there was no money for the scholarship.[12]

Ossian was undaunted. Like a Black Horatio Alger, Ossian "made a courageous decision for a thirteen-year-old many hundreds of miles from his home." His courage was forged in the fire of his witness to racial powerlessness. Seeing race hatred in its ugliest forms instilled in Sweet a deep race consciousness and determination not to let bigotry prevent him from achieving his own personal goals. He exemplified the character of the New Negro, which Alain Locke and others would extol. "He decided to stay at Wilberforce and worked many hard jobs on campus to cover his expenses, such as shoveling snow and stoking the campus furnaces."[13]

Years later, the arc of his determination would take him to Howard Medical School, where he graduated in 1921. In the same year, Ossian moved to Detroit and set up a practice in pharmacy in Detroit's Black Bottom area where he served the poor Blacks there. Kevin Boyle describes the Black Bottom as "a magical place."

As the trains rumbled away without them, the migrants turned toward the dazzling lights. The main thoroughfares were magical places. Newcomers were amazed by the sweep of black-owned businesses: "restaurants, barbershops, pool halls, cabarets, blind pigs, gamblin' joints camouflaged as 'Recreation Clubs,'" a migrant to Detroit remembered. They were awed by the street life, by the pushcart vendors hawking fresh fruits and vegetables; by the street-corner orators selling socialism, separatism, or salvation; by the jazz and blues clubs pitching their performers to the locals and the slummers.[14]

But, however romanticized, the Black Bottom was both slum and ghetto. "In the later nineteenth and early twentieth century it was the first destination for most southern and eastern European immigrants, many of whom moved out." Here Blacks lived cheek by jowl alongside immigrants from Greece, Italy, and other countries of Southern Europe.

In the center of Black Bottom, along Hastings and St. Antoine streets, Negroes lived alongside recently arrived Russian Jews, refugees from the czar's pogroms. On the neighborhood's fringes, blacks shared streets with Italians, Greeks, and Syrians, refugees from grinding poverty.[15]

All the residents of Black Bottom shared overcrowding and squalor.

Knowing that the migrants had nowhere else to go, landlords had carved Harlem's brownstones and the workmen's cottages of Black Bottom and the Black Belt into tiny apartments, which they rented at exorbitant rates. The profits rarely found their way back into the buildings. Paint peeled from the clapboards. Broken windows remained unmended, leaky roofs unrepaired.[16]

For Blacks, conditions were worse. The huge influx of Black migrants combined with rigid *de facto* residential segregation resulted, for the Black Bottom's new Black immigrants, in conditions of overcrowding far worse than any previous immigrant had seen.[17]

Black Bottom represented the ceiling beyond which few Blacks could aspire in segregated 1920s Detroit. These conditions represented a ceiling of impoverished and decrepit conditions beyond which Blacks were not allowed to rise. The powerlessness of Blacks to escape these conditions mirrored the powerlessness of Rochelle to escape the lynch mob, mirrored the brutality that Ossian had witnessed as a child. Ossian wanted to make a statement with his life that he would rise above the wall of powerlessness that Jim Crow represented, that he would surmount the wall to take his place in society. This meant moving into a white neighborhood. Sweet's aspiration to "move on up" coincided with a resurgence of white hostility to maintain the regime of de facto segregation in Detroit.

> It is significant, I think, that it was shortly after that Klan-Anti-Klan campaign for Mayor in the winter of 1924–1925 that this violent attack of anti-Negro hysteria struck Detroit. From early in March of that year (1925) one outraged Negroe followed swiftly upon the heels of another ... It was in March that the house of a woman with a three-weeks-old baby was stoned and when she attempted to defend herself she was taken down to the police station. Less than a month later, a vicious crowd routed out a colored family from a block that bordered on a Negro neighborhood.[18]

Even closer to home was the case of Dr. Turner, a colored physician and surgeon, a peer of Dr. Sweet.

> He had bought a house in a neighborhood, almost twenty miles from the one in which Dr. Sweet's home is. When he moved in, a crowd gathered, broke every one of his windows, tore many of the tiles of his roof, and ripped the lamps down from his ceiling. More, they backed a van up to his door, pitched his furniture into it, and at the point of a gun made him sign away his interest in the property. His wife, more spirited, refused to sign. The angry crowd took to stones, literally tore up his Lincoln car and the Turners barely escaped with their lives.[19]

Earlier immigrants to Detroit faced what might be called "new-world prejudice"—fear and loathing associated with people who were foreign. Blacks faced "old-world prejudice" driven by narratives used to rationalize racial violence in the south.

> Some of the men must have feared for the safety of their wives and children, knowing that the black beast was moving into their midst ... Surely it crossed the parents' minds that their daughters soon would be sharing the street with brooding Negro men and sitting in classrooms next to colored boys whose passions knew no restraint.[20]

The narrative of Blacks as a beast was combined with a narrative of Blacks as carriers of a kind of cultural or moral degradation; if they move in they will have a toxic effect on neighborhood "standards." "Having Negroes in the neighborhood would ruin standards, Harry Monet insisted, dragging whites down to the coloreds' level, degrading everything people up and down the block had worked so hard to achieve."[21] At the Tiremens's Association meeting, convened on July 14, to which 700 people came, the speaker outright referred to the Blacks trying to move in as a disease.

Ossian Sweet knew clearly that to achieve his dream he would have to face racist threats, and even the prospect of violent mobs outside his door. But Ossian Sweet was like a person cast by a storm into a river, the river of history, and he was being carried along by its currents.

In response to the pattern of white racial violence against Blacks, A. Philip Randolph and Chandler Owen preached the power of armed resistance: "We are … urging Negroes and other oppressed groups confronted with lynching and mob violence to act upon the recognized and accepted law of self-defense, the pair wrote during the bloody summer of 1919."[22] Poets of the Harlem Renaissance, like Claude McKay, captured the new post-war spirit of militancy in his timeless poem:

> If we must die, let it not be like hogs /
> Hunted and penned in an inglorious spot. …
> If we must die, O let us nobly die,
>
> …
>
> Like men well face the murderous, cowardly pack /
> Pressed to the wall, dying, but fighting back![23]

Concomitantly, the Black press trumpeted the same notion that it was time to meet force with force.

> For three centuries we have suffered and cowered. No race ever gave Passive Resistance and submission to Evil longer, more piteous trial. Today we raise the terrible weapon of self-defense. When the murderer comes, he shall no longer strike us in the back. When the armed lynchers gather, we too must gather armed. When the mob moves, we propose to meet it with bricks and clubs and guns … If the United States is to be a land of law, we would live humbly and peaceably in it; if it is to be a land of mobs and lynchers, we might as well die today as tomorrow.[24]

But probably the most powerful current was Garveyism. Garvey, ascendant as Bookerism was in decline (Booker T. Washington died in late 1915), espoused an awakening of Blacks to a shared national (and Pan-African) identity, a race consciousness in which Blacks were not powerless, but unified captains of their own destiny. "Up you mighty race you may accomplish what you will!"[25] He founded the Universal negro improvement Association, the UNIA,[26] which ultimately boasted hundreds of thousands of members in the U.S. and abroad.

Detroit in this period was a major center for the UNIA, which preached African American self-help and self-defense. Garvey famously stated, "For every Negro lynched by whites in the south, Negroes ought to lynch a white in the north."[27] During the Knoxville riots, in 1919, when Blacks were attacked by whites, the Blacks shot back. Garvey, through his paper, *The Negro World*, cheered their courage in meeting force with force,

> They saw new things that day and they met a new people. They saw fire-deadly, well directed fire, and volley after volley of it, belch from the mouths of rifles and revolvers haled by the hands of black men who now have stiff backs and straight shoulders ... they saw what others had seen in Chicago, at Washington and at Longview, Tex – that Uncle Tom is dead and that a New Negro rises in his tracks.[28]

It was in this context that Dr. Ossian Sweet made the momentous decision to buy a house in an "all-white" neighborhood in Detroit in 1925. On June 7, 1945, Ossian Sweet handed over the down payment of $3,500 and signed the purchase agreement on a "yellow brick" bungalow at 2905 Garland Avenue.[29]

He knew the risks.[30] In moving into the no-Black man's land of an all-white neighborhood, he would be as much in a theater of war as the Black soldiers who fought in France a few years earlier. They had to cross no man's land in the face of enemy fire. He had to cross a no man's land—what an all-white neighborhood was for a Black man in the 1920s. The army he faced was a mob of angry whites; they wore no uniforms, and they carried bricks instead of guns. But the risk of death for him and his family was just as real. In the face of danger, Dr. Sweet's mind, like the stage of history, was set. "I have to die like a man or live like a coward, he told his brother."[31]

Home Sweet Home!

When I opened the door I saw the mob and I realized I was facing the same mob that had hounded my people throughout its entire history. I was filled with a fear that only one could experience who knows the history and strivings of my race.[32]

The invisible line separating Black and white neighborhoods was efficiently guarded by anxious whites who, in Detroit, used the market rather than formal laws to exclude Blacks. One practice was steering.

> Since the early 1910s, white real estate agents and landlords in Chicago and New York had refused to so much as show Negroes homes in white neighborhoods, saying that the presence of colored people depressed property values. In the course of the Great War, those practices spread to Detroit.[33]

Another was a practice by banks of routinely denying mortgages to Blacks.

> [H]ousing appraisers made it official practice to downgrade the value of any neighborhood that had even a single black resident, a requirement that immediately transformed even the most well-to-do colored homebuyers into credit risks, since the moment a purchase was complete the property wasn't worth as much as it had been. And because blacks drove down property values, there wasn't a bank in Detroit willing to give Negroes a mortgage.[34]

"In addition, white insurance agents would not provide them coverage for their homes if they did get them and developers wrote legal restrictions into … deeds, banning Blacks from new housing tracts."[35]
But Dr. Sweet had a stroke of "luck."

> One day in May, Lucius Riley stopped into Ossian's office with a bit of news. Riley had been a devoted patient of Ossian's ever since the day he'd brought his wife into Palace Drugs fearing she had lockjaw. Now Riley extended his own professional courtesy. He knew of a fine house just about to go on the market, he told Ossian, a nine-year-old bungalow, well-built and well maintained, in a white neighborhood a few miles east of Black Bottom.[36]

The owners were Ed and Marie Smith, both of whom appeared to be white. Mr. Smith was, however, merely a light-skinned Negro passing for white. They sold the house on 2905 Garland Avenue for $18,500. It was highly overpriced, but the Sweets "had nowhere else to go" if they wanted a house in a white neighborhood. The Smiths agreed to hold the mortgage. Ossian and Gladys Sweet would repay the loan over ten years at $150.00 a month. On June 7, 1925, the Sweets paid the down-payment of $3,500 and signed the mortgage.

Sweet knew what he could expect and accordingly made preparations to defend his home.

> He asked several relatives and acquaintances to spend the first day or two at his new home. Making the move with Ossian and Gladys on September 8 were two of Ossian's brothers, Dr. Otis Sweet, a Detroit dentist, and Henry Sweet, a twenty-one-year-old student at Wilberforce University. Other members of the moving party included a friend of Henry, a friend of Otis, and Ossian's chauffeur and his handyman.[37]

In addition, he made sure they were properly armed. "I could never respect myself if I allowed a gang of hoodlums to keep me out."[38] Sweet purchased ten guns—two rifles, a double-barreled shotgun, and seven revolvers—and notified police that he planned to move in on Tuesday morning, September 8.

By the evening, a crowd of hundreds of whites had gathered around his house, but no assault occurred.

> By evening, however, a dense scene developed at the new Sweet home. Though Detroit police tried to keep people moving, a crowd had begun to grow. People stopped, looked into the house, pointed, and talked with neighbors. Inside the Sweet home, the two young interior decorators, afraid to go out through the crowd, asked if they could spend the night. At midnight, some 500 to 800 people still mingled outside the home. From time to time, groups of persons met in a nearby confectionery store to discuss plans for dislodging their new neighbors. Not until near daybreak did the last of the crowd leave.[39]

The next night the violence began.

[A]bout 8:15 in the evening, a taxi managed to pull up, dropping off Otis Sweet and his friend, William Davis. The two fled into the house under a barrage of stones, coal, and other missiles. Shouts came from the crowd: "Niggers!

Niggers! They're niggers—Get 'em! Get the damn niggers!" Ossian opened the door to let them in. "When I opened that door," Ossian would recall later, "the whole situation filled me with an appalling fear—a fear that no one could comprehend but a Negro, and that a Negro who knew the history behind his people." Henry Sweet also reported being filled with dread: "It looked like death if we tried to hide, and it looked like death if we tried to get out. We didn't know what to do.[40]

The mob then bombed the house with rocks and chunks of coal.

The first stones flew as the cab came to a stop, rocks and chunks of coal grabbed from the alleyway arching gracefully over the policemen's heads and thudding onto the bungalow's sloping roof. A dormer window shattered, though in the sudden noise and confusion the sound of breaking glass was hard to hear.

. . .

The stones kept coming maybe a minute more, maybe two. Then the bungalow's upstairs guns blazed, brilliant flashes of light illuminating the blackening sky.[41]

The bombing went on for several minutes. It was in response to this, according to Dr. Sweet, that the defenders fired.

Henry Sweet would later say he and his brother fired warning shots above the heads of the crowd. The shots had the desired effect: screams arose from the crowd. People ran in terror. But two white men had been shot. One white man, Eric Houghberg, was wounded, shot in the thigh, but was expected to survive. Another, Leon Briner, was struck by a single bullet in the back and died. Did the fatal shots come from the volley fired from the house ? Or were the fatal shots fired by police on the scene or others in the crowd?[42]

The police had done nothing to restrain the mob; they had come as spectators. Nonetheless, police arrested all eleven people in the Sweet house. None of the whites, not a single one, was arrested or charged.

The Trial of Ossian Sweet

Arthur Garfield Hayes: State your mind at the time of the shooting.

Dr. Ossian Sweet: When I opened the door and saw the mob, I realized I was facing the same mob that had hounded my people throughout its entire history. In my mind, I was pretty confident of what I was up against, with my back against the wall. I was filled with a peculiar fear, the kind no one could feel unless they know the history of our race. I knew what mobs had done to my people before.[43]

It's useful to understand the legal landscape at the time.

In 1859 David Plant made threats against Augustus Pond, who lived in the same fishing village as himself in Mackinac County, Michigan.[44] On Thursday, Plant was heard by witnesses threatening to "whip Augustus Pond."[45] Later that same day, about six o'clock, Plant struck Augustus Pond with his fist and knocked his hat off without Provocation.[46] Pond left. David Plant threatened August Pond again. "I want to see Augustus Pond; he abused an Irishman, and I want to abuse him just as bad … I must have a fight with Gus Pond, and if I can't whip him, Isaac will whip him."[47]

David Plant spoke of himself, Isaac Blanchard, and Joseph Robillard as an army. He was the Captain, Robillard was Bonaparte, and Blanchard was the soldier.

The "army" attacked after drinking. They begin tearing down Pond's net house located within 12 yards of Pond's makeshift residence.[48] They find David Cull, Pond's servant inside and Pond begins to choke him. Pond comes outside, observes the violence, and commands the trespassers to leave. "Leave or I'll shoot." He repeated the warning. When they failed to obey, he fired, killing Isaac Blanchard.[49] The court, in the case of *Augustus Pond v. The People*, held that: A man's home is his castle; and there was no duty to retreat in one's own house. "A man assaulted in his dwelling is not obliged to retreat, but use such means as are absolutely necessary to repel the assailant from his house, or prevent his forcible entry, even to the taking of his life."[50]

The court went on to say, "The making of an attack upon a dwelling, especially at night, the law regards as equivalent to an assault on a man's person."[51]

Reasonable Mistake

The court held as well that the question is not whether the defendant was or was not in imminent danger; it is whether he reasonably believed he was. The law, the court held, does not require the necessity for taking human life to be one arising out of actual and imminent danger.

"The guilt of the accused must depend upon the circumstances as they appear to him."[52]

Finally, the defendant in these cases is not merely excused for using force where he reasonably believes he is in imminent danger, but he is justified in doing so. That is, it is his duty to defend his home.

> It is held to be the duty of every man who sees a felony to prevent it if possible, and in the performance of this duty, which is an active one, there is a legal right to use all necessary means to make the resistance effectual.

> It has also been laid down by the authorities, that … Private persons who cannot otherwise suppress them, or defend themselves from them may justify homicide in killing them, as it is their right and duty to aid in preserving the peace.[53]

This case was law at the time Ossian Sweet defended his home and at the time of his trial.

Abolitionist William Goodell, lamenting the plight of American slaves, wrote that the slave "can know law only as an enemy, and not as a friend."[54] This was true, according to Goddell, because the slave was always treated as property, as an object instead of a human being, except when he was punished. Something similar happens under segregation. If, like Ossian Sweet, they overcome the seemingly insurmountable barriers to buying a house—steering, relining, banks that would not lend—the police will not protect them from an angry mob. When in response to a mob attack on their home, they defend themselves, the police arrest not the attackers, but the people trying to defend themselves. The authorities winked at and acquiesced in private discrimination, and the police, who came as spectators as the mob attacked, all treated Ossian Sweet as an enemy, not as a friend.

Ironically, the law on paper was on the side of Ossian Sweet when he, his family, and his supporters defended his home. Was not the bombing of his house with bricks and the breaking of his windows an attack on Sweet's family's dwelling? Pound was threatened by three men, which David Plant called his army, tearing down his net house. Sweet was threatened by a mob "which surged toward him like a human sea." In the eyes of the law, Ossian Sweet had as much right as Augustus Pond to use deadly force to protect himself and his family from felonious assault. And an attack on his dwelling was the same as an attack on himself.

The law was clear, but the prosecutor spun the facts. The prosecutor argued that Ossian Sweet had not engaged in self-defense, but rather a conspiracy to kill.

> [T]he theory of the state is that no one of these defendants, at the time of the shooting, was in danger of his life or of serious bodily harm; that he had no right to believe … that his life or safety was in jeopardy, that the property was not being trespassed upon, that it was – that there was no justification for shooting – that no damage to the property or to the persons of any of the defendants was imminent, or was threatened, and if it was, it was not sufficiently serious to justify the taking a life … we contend, that these eleven defendants, banded themselves together, and armed themselves with ten deadly weapons, in pursuance of an agreement and understanding between them that in the event of a threatened trespass on this property, or in the event of threatened damage to the house, or to any one of the people in it, one or more of the defendants would shoot to kill; that they actually did that; they did shoot to kill, not even waiting for a trespass property or damage to their persons or to the house … Now, that is the theory on which we claim that this killing was felonious; that it was premeditated; premeditated because they went there with it in mind.[55]

The claim that there was no danger was buttressed by the self-serving testimony of whites who were part of the mob:

> Prosecution witnesses continually denied that a large crowd had formed in front of the Sweet home and that rocks were being thrown at the house. One of the witnesses only conceded that it sounded like pebbles hitting the house. Darrow had one of the large rocks that had been thrown that night

and at one point in the trial, he "dropped" one of the pebbles as he was about to hand it to the witness. It resounded loudly as it bumped along the floor.[56]

The police commissioner testified that they came to protect Ossian Sweet and preserve law and order.

> On direct examination, Schuknecht claimed that he told the men under his command they "would have to act impartially; that we were there to preserve peace and order so that man, Dr. Sweet could live there, if we had to take every man in the department to protect his home; that we wanted no recurrence of the happening on the west side."[57]

He also denied there was a mob, white or otherwise, or that anything unusual was going on before the shooting.

> Q: There was no one there when you got there? The time of your arrival is about 7:30?
> A: There were people on the street, but they were walking up and down and there was no congregating ….
> Q: Did you see anyone armed with clubs or other weapons?
> A: Not any time.[58]

Schuknecht testified that there was no white mob surrounding the Sweet home; there were just a few people occasionally walking by as in any neighborhood. According to Schuknecht, nothing was out of the ordinary—certainly nothing to justify the occupants of the house shooting at anyone.[59]

Even if true, none of this would have been sufficient to convict any particular defendant. The bullet was never found. The prosecution could not establish if anyone inside the house fired the shot. To convict Ossian Sweet or any other member of his family, they needed to prove they acted in concert, in essence that there was some prior arrangement or understanding. That is, they had to prove conspiracy. That was explicitly their theory. It was a theory in search of the facts. They could show that ten guns were found in the house and little food, but there was no documentation or witness to the existence of a prior agreement: there was no evidence of conspiracy. The evidence the prosecution presented was like a bridge stretching across the water reaching for the other side but falling short.

Without this, there was not a prima facie case against any particular person. Even if they could establish a prima facie case of murder, once the mob began to throw large stones through the windows and surge forward like a sea, that would be enough under *Pond* to show self-defense.

No white person would ever have been charged.

But race in a real sense renders strict proof unnecessary. They saw Blacks mobbing into a "white" neighborhood as "a pestilence" threatening to bring down moral standards. Through the prism of these narratives, Blacks appeared to be dangerous and bad, regardless of what they had done on a particular night. Their racial identity was itself evidence of danger. As such they were already guilty.

> If I thought any of you had any opinion about the guilt of my clients, I wouldn't worry, because that might be changed. What I'm worried about is prejudice. They are harder to change. They come with your mother's milk and stick like the color of the skin. I know that if these defendants had been a white group defending themselves from a colored mob, they never would have been arrested or tried. My clients are charged with murder, but they are really charged with being black.[60]

The National Association for the Advancement of Colored People (NAACP) saw the case of Ossian Sweet as a case in which the meaning of Black citizenship was called into question. A Black man should have as much right to defend his home as a white. If Sweet were convicted, the mob would win, the courtroom would become an extension of the lynching tree, and no Black in a white neighborhood would be safe in their home.

> The importance of the case to the Negro cause was obvious. If the Sweets were not given adequate legal defense, if the ancient Anglo-Saxon principle that "a man's home is his castle" were not made applicable to the Negroes as well as others, we knew that other and even more determined attacks would be made upon the homes of Negroes throughout the country. We were equally convinced that legal affirmation that a Negro had the right to defend his home against mob assault would serve to deter other mobs in Detroit and elsewhere.[61]

With those stakes, Walter White met with Clarence Darrow, the greatest lawyer of his day. Darrow's father was an abolitionist. Darrow said of him:

As a little child, I heard my father tell of Frederick Douglas, Parker Pillsbury, Sojourner Truth, Wendell Phillips, and the rest of that advance army of reformers, black and white, who went up and down the land arousing the dull conscience of the people to a sense of justice to the slave. They used to make my father's home their stopping place, and any sort of vacant room was the forum where they told of the black man's wrongs.[62]

Darrow would later say, "I, like all the rest of the boys, inherited my politics and my religion." What made the case particularly controversial is that here was a group of Blacks who had fought back against whites, killing one white man and wounding another. In *Benito Cereno*, Melville writes about Black slaves taking over a slave ship and fighting the white sailors who board the ship to re-enslave them. Melville writes and portrays the Blacks in their act of heroic resistance as wolves, their red tongues lolling. Blacks who attacked whites were perceived in the white mind as the apotheosis of their fears. Through the window of these fears, these Blacks were not merely sub-human, they were wolves. Similarly, in the popular view of Sweet and his family in 1925 Detroit, they would not merely be controversial, they would be seen similarly as vicious and as animalistic as the rebellious Africans in Creon's story. But Darrow took the case precisely because he suspected that Sweet and his family had fought back.

Darrow asked White many questions, including, "Did the defendants shoot into that mob?" White was very hesitant to answer for fear that Darrow might not take the case if the defendants had actually fired into the crowd. Darrow told White, "Don't try to hedge. I know you were not there. But do you believe the defendants fired?" White replied that he thought they did fire and was going to explain that he thought they were justified in defending themselves when Darrow interrupted him by saying, "Then I'll take the case. If they had not had the courage to shoot back in defense of their own lives, I wouldn't think they were worth defending."[63]

Darrow began his work at trial by exposing the claims of the prosecutions witnesses as a tissue of lies.

Darrow cross-examined many of the prosecution's witnesses. He asked them if they were members of the Waterworks Park Improvement Association and he got many to admit they did not want blacks in their neighborhoods.

But all denied there was any large crowd throwing rocks at the Sweet home. One witness, seventeen-year-old Dwight Hubbard accidentally forgot the prosecution's line during direct examination when he blurted out that there was a great crowd gathered outside the Sweet home. Then he immediately stammered that there was just a large crowd but he quickly changed this to just a few people. Darrow of course took notice of this and on cross-examination got Hubbard to admit that he had been coached by a police detective.[64]

Disrupting the false narrative that the whites had only thrown pebbles, Darrow had one of the large rocks that had been thrown that night, and at one point in the trial Darrow "dropped one of the pebbles as he was about to hand it to the witness. It resounded loudly as it bumped along the floor."[65]

But Darrow's problem was not the facts, it was prejudice. "Prejudices do not rest upon facts; they rest upon the ideas that have been taught to us and that began coming to us almost with our mothers' milk, and they stick almost as the color of the skin sticks."[66]

This general prejudice conceals in a criminal context a presumption of guilt—the sense that Ossian Sweet and his family were "already guilty." Racism is an ideology, a system of beliefs, ideas. But it operates even more insidiously as a form of social cognition: as a lens or distorting prism through which the events at issue in the trial were seen. Racism as ideology was the source of the us v. them narratives operating as a distorting prism. Through the prism of these narratives, Ossian Sweet and his family appeared as people who did not belong, as harbingers of moral degradation, etc. Through the prism of these narratives, Ossian Sweet and his family were already guilty. To win the case, Darrow had to take on this underlying ideology: to counter the underlying belief system which produced these stigmatizing images of Blacks. He and Arthur Garfield Hayes had to humanize the defendants.

Dr. Ossian Sweet took the stand. Questioned by Arthur Garfield Hayes on direct, Sweet told the story of his life. Hayes directed him through his journey from poverty in Bartow to working his way through school at Wilberforce.

Under questioning by Arthur Garfield Hays, Sweet told the jury how he, as a black man, grew up in America. He talked of his boyhood in Florida, the oldest of ten children of a poor Methodist preacher. He talked of his struggle to make a life: working as a bellhop, a waiter on steamships, a porter, and a furnace-tender to pay his way through Wilberforce and Howard universities.[67]

Hayes also led Sweet to talk about the racial hostility and the witnesses against Blacks from the time he was a child. The prosecution objected: Prosecutor Toms asked, "Is everything this man saw as a child justification for a crime twenty-five years later?"

"Reasonable Man" or "Reasonable Negro?"

Self-defense is available only to defendants who act reasonably. But reasonable to whom? A reasonable person has no race, no color, no history. This is abstract. This is reasonableness which ignores the particular facts of both why the mob attacked and why Sweet, as a Black man, might have been so afraid. The mob did not attack randomly; it attacked because of race. This, moreover, the perception of Sweet as an individual, was inextricably bound up in this case with Sweet's experience as a Black man, one who throughout his life has experienced racism. In one sense, Darrow argued, in effect due process requires us to consider Sweet not in the abstract, but as a real person, as an individual with relevant personal characteristics and experiences. Reasonableness represents objectivity. Darrow sought to give this objective perspective a subjective dimension: to include the particularity of Sweet's experience.

Darrow, responding to the prosecution's objection, explained it this way.

> This is the question of the psychology of a race, of how everything known to a race affects its actions. What we learn as children we remember—it gets fastened in the mind. I would not claim that the people outside the Sweet home were bad. But they would do to Negroes something they would not do to whites. It's their race psychology. Because the defendant's acts were predicated on the psychology of his past, I ask that this testimony be admitted.[68]

Interrupting the Gaze

To truly humanize Dr. Sweet, Darrow had to interrupt the gaze. The gaze is the perpetrator perspective. Through the perpetrator perspective, Sweet was an interloper seeking to buy a house in a neighborhood he did not belong in. He was seen through a window in which Blacks were essentialized as violent and vicious, like the wolves in the Cereno story. Sweet was the criminal. Breiner was the innocent white victim.

To interrupt this narrative, Hayes and Darrow had to go beyond merely presenting a counter-story; they had to shift the perspective to that of the victim. They sought to have the jury look at the events that unfolded through the eyes of Sweet himself. Ossian Sweet testified.

As Sweet and Davis entered the house or shortly thereafter the violence erupted.

> "We were playing cards about eight o'clock" when "something hit the roof. Somebody went to the window and I heard them remark, "The people! The people!" "And then?" prompted Hays. "I ran out to the kitchen where my wife was. There were several lights burning. I turned them out and opened the door. I heard someone yell, 'Go raise hell in front; I am going back.' Frightened, and after getting a gun, I ran upstairs. Stones were hitting the house intermittently. I threw myself on the bed a short while. Perhaps fifteen when a stone came through a window. Part of the glass hit me." "What happened next?" Hays asked. "Pandemonium—I guess that's the best way to describe it—broke loose. Everyone was running from room to room. There was a general uproar. Somebody yelled, 'There's someone coming!' They said, 'That's your brother.' A car had pulled up to the curb. My brother and Mr. Davis got out. The mob yelled, 'Here's niggers, get them! Get them!' As they rushed in, the mob surged forward fifteen or twenty feet. It looked like a human sea."[69]

Hayes then asked Sweet to "state your mind at the time of the shooting":

> When I opened the door and saw the mob, I realized I was facing the same mob that had hounded my people throughout its entire history. In my mind, I was pretty confident of what I was up against, with my back against the wall. I was filled with a peculiar fear, the kind no one could feel unless they

know the history of our race. I knew what mobs had done to my people before.[70]

Sweet acted in response to imminent danger of an angry mob—reasonable fear: Sweet was innocent. Darrow went on to hold up a mirror to force the whites in the jury, who identified with the whites in the mob, that it was the whites in the mob, whites like Breiner, who were the real criminals that night:

> Ah, let me tell you, gentlemen, Breiner was not an innocent man, but if he had been innocent his blood is on the head of the police department that was around there, that part of it, who should have dispersed Breiner and sent him on his way.
>
> I am sick of this talk about an innocent man being killed. There were no innocent men in that bunch, not one. The evidence in this case shows that he was several doors from his home, that he trice went up and down that street, that he had been lingering around there for some time. Why was he there? Only an inference. He was there just the same as everybody else in this mob was there. He was there to uphold law and order as meted out by the Water Works Improvement Association. That is the evidence in this case. It makes me sick. A man standing there in a mob bent on crime; the court will tell you that, in a mob, which was a criminal organization, waiting to see the sacrifice of some helpless blacks.
>
> And then they say he was innocent. Nobody was innocent. They came there for that purpose with malice in their hearts, with enmity to their fellows, determined to drive them out.[71]

Darrow not only exposed the prosecution witnesses as liars, he exposed the meta narrative that drove the case—that Breiner was an innocent victim was itself a lie.

Mobilizing History

Perhaps more than any other people, Americans have been locked into a deadly struggle with time, with history. We've fled the past and trained ourselves to suppress, if not forget troublesome details of national memory, and a great part of our optimism, like our progress, has been bought at the cost of ignoring the processes through which we have arrived at any given moment of our national existence. We've fought continuously with one another over who and what we are, and with the exception of the Negro, over who and what is American.[72]

Finally, he challenged whites on the jury to confront their own responsibility for what happened that night. He portrayed the violence that happened as a pattern of white violence and white oppression against Blacks which traced back to slavery. He empowered whites in the jury to, through their verdict, take a step toward the right side of history.

[H]e knew the history of his race, he knew that looking back to the terrible year that have marked their history he could see his answer, loaded like sardines in a box in the mid-decks of steamers and brought forcibly from their African homes, half of them dying in the voyage; he knew they were sold like chattels as slaves and were compelled to work without pay; he knew that families were separated when it paid the master to sell them; he knew that even after he had got liberty under the Constitution and the law he knew that the bodies of dead Negroes were hanging from the limbs of trees of every state in the Union where they had been killed by the mob; he knew that in every state of the Union telegraph poles had been decorated by the bodies of Negroes dangling to ropes on account of race hatred and nothing else; he knew they had been tied to stakes in free America and a fire built around living human beings until roasted to death; he knew they had been driven from their home in the north and in great cities and here in Detroit and he was there not only to defend himself and his home and his friends but to stand for the integrity and independence of the abused race to which he belonged, and I say, gentlemen, you may send him to prison if you like, but you will only crown him as a hero who fought a brave fight against fearful odds, a fight for the right, for justice, for freedom.[73]

While it was clear the jury wanted to acquit most of the defendants, the problem was "a white man had been killed." Yet five jurors held out for complete exoneration. The jury hung. Coming into the trial, Sweet and his family were already guilty. Their arrest, indictment, and trial were all machinations of racial hysteria, a racial hysteria over the fact that they as Negroes crossed invisible lines to live in segregated spaces reserved for whites. The hysteria and the presumption of guilt in the case were inextricably intertwined. Darrow and Hayes essentially woke up at least five of the jurors from the hysteria and groupthink which they had been under like a spell.

Notes

1　F. Scott Fitzgerald, *Echoes of the Jazz Age* (New York: C. Scribner, 1931).

2　Heather Bourbeau, "Dr. Ossian Sweet's Black Life Mattered," *JSTOR Daily* (June 17, 2015).

3　Mark Robert Schneider, *African Americans in the Jazz Age: A Decade of Struggle and Promise* (Oxford, UK: Rowman & Littlefield,2006), 1.

4　Nathan Irvin Huggins, *Voices of the Harlem Renaissance* (Oxford, UK: Oxford University Press, 1995).

5　David Goldfield, ed., *Encyclopedia of American Urban History*, Volume 1 (Thousand Oaks, CA: Sage,2006), 11.

6　Harry L. Watson and Jane Dailey *Building the American Republic, Volume 2, A Narrative History from 1877* (Chicago, IL: University of Chicago Press 2018).

7　Kevin Boyle, *Arc of Justice: A Saga of Race, Civil Rights, and Murder in the Jazz Age* (New York: Henry Holt, 2004), Kindle Edition (p. 106).

8　Allan Freeman Davis, Harold D. Woodman, *Conflict and Consensus in American History*, Volume 2 (Boston, MA: Houghton Mifflin 1997), 242.

9　Marcet Haldeman-Julius, *Clarence Darrow's Two Greatest Trials: Reports of the Scopes Anti-Evolution Case and the Dr. Sweet Negro Trial* (Girard, KS: Haldeman-Julius, 1927).

10　Katherine Durocher, *Raising Racists: The Socialization of White Children in the Jim Crow South* (Lexington, KY: University of Kentucky Press, 2011).

11　Michael Hannon, *The People v. Ossian Sweet, Gladys Sweet, et al* (1925). http://moses.law.umn.edu/darrow/trialpdfs/SWEET_TRIALS.pdf, 4.

12　Hannon, *The People v. Ossian Sweet*, 5.

13　Ibid.

14　Boyle, *Arc of Justice*, 105.

15　Ibid.

16　Ibid., 12.

17　Karen R. Miller, *Managing Inequality: Northern Racial Liberalism in inter-War Detroit* (New York: New York University Press, 2016), 107.

18   Haldeman-Julius, *Clarence Darrow's Two Greatest Trials*.

19   Ibid.

20   Boyle, *Arc of Justice*.

21   Ibid., 147.

22   Ibid., 118.

23   James Weldon Johnson, *The American Book of Negro Poetry* (The Floating Press, 2009), 168.

24   W. E. B. Dubois, *The Crisis*, Volume 18 (Baltimore, MD: The Crisis Publishing Company, September, 1919), 231.

25   David Cronon, *Black Moses: The Story of Marcus Garvey and the Universal Negro Improvement Association* (Madison, WI: University of Wisconsin Press, 1960), 39.

26   Garvey founded The Universal Negro Improvement Association (hereinafter the UNIA) in 1914. It has been described as the largest pan-African organization of all time. The UNIA's scope was worldwide ("I know no national boundary where the Negro is concerned," Garvey famously stated) but, according to Cronon, "his [Garvey's] most important work was in the United States." See E. David Cronon, *Black Moses Madison*, (Madison, WI: University of Wisconsin Press, 1969), 3.

27   Marcus Garvey, Robert Hill, *The Marcus Garvey and Universal Negro Improvement Association* (Berkeley, CA: University of California Press, 1984), 401.

28   Investigation Activities of the Department of Justice, 66th Congress, 1st Session, quoting *The Negro World*, September 6, 1919.

29   Boyle, *Arc of Justice*, 146.

30   Douglas O. Linder, *Famous Trials*. "Sweet Trials (1925 & 1926)," http://www.famous-trials.com/sweet.

31   Lloyd Chasson, *Illusive Shadows: Justice, Media, and Socially Significant American Trials* (Westport, CT: Greenwood Publishing Group, 2003), 124.

32   Linder, *Famous Trials*.

33   Boyle, *Arc of Justice*, 108.

34   Ibid., 145.

35   Ibid., 9.

36   Ibid., 145.

37   Douglas O. Linder, *Melting Hearts of Stone, Clarence Darrow and the Sweet Trials*. http://law2.umkc.edu/faculty/projects/ftrials/trialheroes/darrowmelting.html.

38   Linder, *Melting Hearts of Stone*.

39   Ibid.

40 Ibid.

41 Boyle, *Arc of Justice*, 169.

42 Ibid., 38.

43 Linder, *Famous Trials*.

44 *Pond v. People*, 8 Mich. 150 (1860), 151.

45 Ibid., 152.

46 Ibid., 179.

47 Ibid., 158.

48 Ibid., 156.

49 Ibid., 160.

50 Ibid., 176.

51 Ibid., 166.

52 Ibid., 173.

53 Ibid., 176.

54 Paul Finkleman, *Slavery and the Law* (Lanham, MD: Rowman & Littlefield, 2001), 209.

55 Hannon, *The People v. Ossian Sweet*, 28–9.

56 Ibid., 29.

57 Ibid., 30.

58 Clarence Darrow, *The Essential Works and Writings of Clarence Darrow* (New York: Modern Library, 2007), 140.

59 Darrow, *The Essential Works and Writings of Clarence Darrow*.

60 Hannon, *The People v. Ossian Sweet*, 36.

61 Walter Francis White, *A Man Called White: The Autobiography of Walter White* (Athens, NY: University of Georgia Press, 1948), 74.

62 Kevin Tierney, *Darrow, A Biography* (New York: Book Sales, 1981).

63 Hannon, *The People v. Ossian Sweet*.

64 Ibid., 30.

65 Ibid.

66 Ibid., 36.

67 Linder, *Melting Hearts of Stone*.

68 Ibid.

69 Ibid.

70 Ibid.

71 Hannon, *The People v. Ossian Sweet*, 39.

72 Ralph Ellison, "*Blues People*," *Shadow and Act* (New York: New York Vintage International, 1995), 250.

73 Hannon, *The People v. Ossian Sweet*, 38.

3

Makes Me Wanna Holler: The Making of the Second Ghetto

Figure 3.1 View of a young child walking through a path at the Robert Taylor Homes, Chicago, Illinois, 1965.

Source: STM-000383012, *Chicago Sun-Times*.

It is as though one, looking out from a dark cave in a side of an impending mountain, sees the world passing and speaks to it; speaks courteously and persuasively, showing them how these entombed souls are hindered in their natural movement, expression, and development; and how their loosening from prison would be a matter not simply of courtesy, sympathy, and help to them, but aid to all the world. ... It gradually permeates the minds of the prisoners that the people passing do not hear; that some thick sheet of invisible but horribly tangible plate glass is between them and the world. They get excited; they talk louder; they gesticulate. Some of the passing world stop in curiosity; these gesticulations seem so pointless; they laugh and pass on. They still either do not hear at all, or hear but dimly, and even what they hear, they do not understand. Then the people within may become hysterical.

—W.E.B. Du Bois: *Dusk of Dawn*, 1940

The Making of the Second Ghetto

In the great blues song *Going to Chicago* Count Basie sings

Hurry down sunshine, let's just see what tomorrow brings.
Hurry down sunshine, let's see what tomorrow brings.[1]

His deep longing for a new "tomorrow" is a metaphor for the explosive mix of desperation and hope which propelled millions of Blacks to migrate from the rural South to the North between 1940 and 1970. In the song "Goin' to Chicago" Count Basie's character leaves because of a "mucky woman" who was unfaithful to him. But millions of Blacks were propelled to leave the South for reasons that were less romantic. These millions of Blacks left because of wretched conditions they faced as Black sharecroppers in Dixie: they earned often "no more than two dollars a day." The hope of escaping the racial caste system of the South pushed them. They were pulled by Northern newspapers which advertised wages three times that of a sharecropper in the rural south.

This was the second "Great Migration." During the decade of the 1940s alone more than one-third of all Blacks living in the Deep South States of Alabama,

Georgia, Mississippi, and South Carolina left for the North. For the South as a whole 26 percent headed North between 1940 and 1950, and another 25 percent did so in the 1950s.[2] My own parents were among them.

This second Great Migration dwarfed the first. Chicago was its epicenter.

This second Great Migration saw the largest increases to Chicago's black population in history. In fact, Chicago became the epicenter of the greatest demographic shift in American history. During World War II over 60,000 African Americans arrived to work in factories producing airplanes, munitions, and parachutes. In the 1940s, the black population grew from 278,000 to 492,000. In the twenty years after the war, migration continued unabated. The black population of Chicago increased to over 800,000.[3]

In 1965 more African Americans lived in Chicago than in Mississippi.[4] After decades of Black migrants pouring into the North between 1910 and 1930, a rigid color line had developed in housing: by this time "the ghetto," as a place where Blacks were relegated, or quarantined, as if they were the carriers of a deadly disease, had become a familiar feature of urban life north. This was the "first ghetto." The second great migration created the second ghetto. While private prejudice gave birth to the first ghetto, the second ghetto was a child of two fathers, white prejudice and an unvarnished federal policy of residential segregation. Blacks were herded into congested Black belts called Colored Town, Darkytown, Bronzeville, and Niggertown.[5]

This massive wave of humanity moving into the industrial cities of the north faced a housing shortage in the urban areas in which they were forced to live. "Within the main south side Black belt 375,000 Blacks resided in an area equipped to house no more than 110,000. While the Black belt expanded into formerly white areas the population increased faster than the number of dwellings."[6]

The congestion in Chicago mirrored that in other urban areas of the North. Detroit is a case in point.

Detroit blacks were entrapped in the city's worst housing stock, half of it substandard, most of it overcrowded. They lived in overwhelmingly black neighborhoods, a reflection of the almost total segregation in the city's housing market. Detroit's black population had doubled between 1940 and 1950 but the pool of available housing had grown painfully slowly.[7]

Blacks were relegated to areas on the edge of industry, "in a transition area where a sooty conglomeration of factories and mills belch smoke." The desolation of their neighborhoods seemed to express the isolation of the Black community from normal society. "The rickety frame dwellings, sprawled along the railroad tracks bespeak a way of life at an opposite pole from that of the quiet well-groomed orderliness of middle-class neighborhoods."[8]

Greedy unscrupulous whites took advantage of this housing crisis to break up their apartment into smaller Kitchenettes. "Kitchenette apartments, as these units were called, were essentially old houses or larger apartments long since abandoned by Chicago's wealthy whites converted into multiple apartments each installed with a communal restroom, small gas stove, and one small sink."[9] They were also overpriced; "[t]he same apartment for which white people— who can get jobs anywhere and who receive higher wages than we—pay $50.00 a month is rented to us for $42.00 a week."[10] Congestion and squalor were the order of the day. "Poor African American female-headed families were stacked on top of one another ... surrounded by appalling physical neglect, random violence, and social disorder."[11]

In one photo from 1947 a Black woman wearing an overcoat indoors holds a baby in the basement of 3106 Wentworth in 1947.[12] Ten families occupied the basement in cardboard cubicles called apartments. They had no windows or toilets and shared a single broken stairway and stove. Others lived in buildings which had been abandoned or condemned.

Sanitary conditions deteriorated with increasing congestion. "Rat attacks on sleeping children were frequent occurrences and it was not uncommon to hear reports of children being maimed or even killed." Responding to one woman's claim that she had rats big enough to ride on, another woman commented that her rats came in teams; sometimes, she added boastfully, they have enough for a ball game.[13]

> With too many families crammed into airless wood framed dwellings, forced to use alternative heating and cooking methods, with exposed wires ... snaking in every direction from improvised walls ... fires were rampant.[14] ... pneumonia, tuberculosis, all occurred there at many times the rate found in the rest of the city.[15]

"Violent White Resistance"

The hydraulic pressures of constant increasing migration into already overcrowded slums inevitably led the expansion of the Black belt even into what had been white residential preserves.

Blacks moving into these white enclaves were viewed as invaders.

As refugees from the disastrously overcrowded Black Belt sought new homes in previously restricted areas of the city, the number of violent incidents aimed at driving out "black invaders" increased dramatically. The late 1940s became an era analogous to that of 1917–21 when one racially motivated bombing or arson occurred every twenty days. Moreover, large housing riots—the mobbing of black homes by hundreds, if not thousands of whites—broke out, thus revealing a form of resistance rarely seen outside the context of citywide disorder.[16]

In Chicago alone there were 357 incidents of racial violence, most along the southern border of the Black Belt.[17] One of the worst occurs in Fernwood:

Erupting over the placement of black veterans in a temporary CHA project, the community surrounding the project rioted for three successive nights in mid-August 1947. During the first two evenings of disorder crowds ranging from 1,500 to 5,000 persons battled police who frustrated their attempts to enter the project. Unable to penetrate defense lines, mobs broke off their engagement with police and assaulted cars carrying blacks through the area … Police unfortunate enough to get in the way were assaulted with bricks and bottles.[18]

The worst of all takes place in Englewood.

The presence of blacks at an informal Union meeting in a house at 5643 S. Peoria precipitated the rumor that the home was being "sold to niggers." … When a woman spied blacks in Aaron Bindman's living room on November 8, the block organization that had been created to meet the first emergency was mobilized to face a new "crisis." Crowds gathered outside the home … Estimates of the Englewood crowds varied from several hundred at the riot's inception to 10,000 at its peak.[19]

The anti-Black riots were not always about housing. Sometimes they were conflicts that erupted over the use of parks and other public facilities. Consider this riot in Detroit.

> The trouble began when nearly one hundred thousand Detroiters gathered on Belle Isle, Detroit's largest park, on a hot summer Sunday. Brawls between young blacks and whites broke out throughout the afternoon … The following day more than ten thousand angry whites swept through Paradise Valley and rampaged along nearby thoroughfares. Many Detroit police openly sympathized with white rioters, and were especially brutal with blacks; 17 blacks were shot to death by police, no whites were.[20]

White Flight

But despite the violence the Black belt continued to expand. In addition, the Supreme Court had decided *Brown v. Board of Education*.[21] This led to pressure for busing and other racial integration campaigns.

The result was a massive suburbanization of whites. Between 1940 and 1960 in Chicago the white suburban population increased by 1,440,606. In less than a decade in Newark the Black population doubled, from 68,312 to 142,600 while the white population declined by almost 100,000 from 348,856 to 255,800.[22] Between 1940 and 1960, some 250,000 white residents left Detroit.[23] During the 1950s alone, the white population of New York City declined by 7 percent; and Philadelphia's by 13 percent.

According to Ronald Formisano,

> White flight—the gradual evacuation of America's urban cores in the postwar years—[was] the greatest exodus in American history. It drained the white population out of the city limits and engorged the near and far suburbs … The suburbs were almost entirely white, while blacks, Hispanics, and later Asians were ringed into the suburban noose.[24]

This had the effect of concentrating Blacks in the neighborhoods whites had fled from in their migration to the suburbs. In cities receiving large numbers of Black migrants, racial turnover was so regular and so pervasive that most neighborhoods could be classified by their stage in the transition process: all white, invasion, succession, consolidation or all Black.

The Federal Government infamously subsidized the flight of whites to the suburbs. Their primary instrument was Federal Mortgage Assistance, introduced during the new deal. "The practice was conceived as a way to shore up America's tottering banking industry during the great depression."[25] The Federal Housing Administration (FHA) used federal dollars to insure mortgages, which made them safe. In addition, "Congress created a second similar program as part of the G. I. Bill aimed at rewarding America's war-weary military forces." At the same time the federal government refused to fund projects in built-up districts, "interior locations". Prior to the entry of the FHA into the market buyers had to have 50 percent of the home's purchase price and pay off the loan in five years. Under FHA standards the buyer needed only 10 percent and had 30 years.

While the Federal government subsidized white flight, it used the noose of redlining to contain the burgeoning Black population in the ghetto. Thus, "a 1948 Federal Housing Administration manual stated, 'Incompatible racial groups should not be permitted to live in the same communities.' Properties shall continue to be occupied by the same social and racial classes." Concomitantly the federal government "pioneered the practice of redlining" selectively granting loans and insisting that any property it insured be covered by a restrictive covenant—a clause in the deed forbidding the sale of property to anyone other than whites.[26]

But this tacit policy of containment of the Black population in the midst of continuing massive migration of Blacks from the South meant that the Black belt would continue to expand.

This expansion combined with white flight threatened the very life of downtown.

Like individual whites, business owners were frightened by this encroaching blight, but they reacted differently:

> The expansion of the ghetto and the deterioration of the central city alarmed corporate property holders, but their response differed from that of individual homeowners or renters. Downtown businesses and institutions located in slum or transition areas turned not to violence or suburban flight but rather to the use of political and legal power.[27]

The developers wanted to acquire Black belt land—which interestingly enough they could not afford. But there was a symbiotic relationship between the developers and the city: the city wanted to halt central city decline.

> All around us we see the increasing evidence of the decline in the heart of the city—tax delinquencies, slums, absentee ownership. And with them we see the increases in municipal costs—fire, police, juvenile delinquency, health; we see the continual flight away from the city by those who can afford it, the escape to greener pastures.[28]

Harnessing the liberal narrative of slum clearance, they enacted the Redevelopment Act of 1947 and the Urban Community Conservation act of 1953.[29] The city paid for acquisition of land and clearance and turned it over to business interests for development.[30] Ironically, despite good intentions, many slums were not razed. And on the other hand, some well-to-do Negro neighborhoods were destroyed.[31] Only 15 percent of the land was allocated to house the displaced families.[32]

Much of the justification for clearing slums with public funds was to improve the quality of life for the Black families. To do so, liberals argued, the projects needed to be integrated into the city as a whole on scattered sites. But a political hijacking took place. Initially a battle ensued between liberals and Blacks who wanted the public housing on scattered sites, and conservative whites who wanted to maintain the Black belt. But racist leaders won out and the housing projects supposedly designed to improve the quality of life for Black families stayed inside the Black belt.

> When Richard Daley was elected Mayor in 1955, the CHA became his vehicle for urban renewal. Daley authorized urban renewal funds to build massive public housing projects in the existing black ghetto. Under Daley, CHA projects, such as the eight building Stateway Gardens, and the Robert Taylor Homes, the largest public housing complex in the United States, became depressing symbols of the entrapment of African Americans.[33]

The Chicago Housing Authority (CHA) sought a one-to-four ratio of African Americans to whites in the new project.[34] Whites viewed public housing as a step down. Plenty of African Americans applied, but a dearth of white applicants made meeting the quota difficult. By 1960, CHA projects were all African American.[35] These new projects produced, "something of a historical geographical paradox: the new projects were far superior to the horrendous slums they replaced, but inscribed a more severe isolation from the decentralizing urban economy."[36] David Wilson writes,

> The effects on black ghettos were devastating. These projects flagrantly isolated and stigmatized black residents to a degree that embarrassed even some conservative politicians. Chicago's Robert Taylor Homes and Stateway Gardens packed 26,000 and 6,900 people in 28 buildings and 8 buildings respectively. Located in Chicago's sprawling South Side Black Belt, this area became Devira Beverly's (1991) "world unto itself." The Robert Taylor Homes, 4,400 units in 28 identical 16-story buildings, resembled a prison set off from the normal world. Cages of meshed wire, encircling the buildings, guarded a seemingly incarcerated people.[37]

Despite the stigma and obvious racial implications in the practice of "keeping it in the ghetto," public housing projects that densely packed Blacks were built widely but were typically sited within the boundaries of the preexisting Black belt.

> Because public housing so effectively reinforced the concentration of low-waged laborers and walled off dangerous and property-value-threatening people perceived necessities by these growth elites, its use continued. Never had such an unpopular but functionally efficient program gone so far. By 1965, all 50 states had public housing with the program sheltering more than 2 million people.[38]

The Employment Ghetto

"The principal measure of progress toward equality will be that of employment. It is the primary source of individual or group identity. In America what you do is what you are. To do nothing is to be nothing; to do little is to be little. The equations are implacable and blunt and ruthlessly public."[39]

"If they don't stop this discrimination, there is going to be a civil war"— Unemployed Black worker, Detroit, 1950.

In March 1948 Joseph Mays was laid off from a welding job when the Fruehauf Trailer company downsized its Detroit plant. Mays later saw an ad that Chrysler had put in all three Detroit newspapers:

Wanted,
Die Makers, Template Makers,
Machine Operators, Assemblers,
Production workers,
Employment Office
Dodge, Main

Mays was confident he would be hired right away. Production at Dodge main was booming and the plant was hiring hundreds of workers a day. And Mays came with impeccable credentials. He had extensive experience as a welder, both at Fruehauf and in shipyards as a defense worker during World War II. But when he showed up at the Dodge main employment office, Mays's hopes were quickly dashed. When asked about the machine operator openings the personnel representative told him all positions had been filled. The employment representative turned Mays away without a job application.[40]

The state of Michigan passed a Fair Employment Practices Law in 1955. But prior to that, employers regularly specified racial preferences in job listings. Racial classifications were ubiquitous in job orders placed with state agencies. The Michigan State Employment Services (MSES) stated that "in December 1946, 35.1 percent of all job orders placed in its offices contained discriminatory clauses, rising to 44.7 percent in April 1947, and 65 percent in June 1948."[41] The pattern of discriminatory hiring continued through the early 1950s. "[U]nemployment rates for Negroes are double those for whites in every category ... as they have been throughout the postwar period."[42]

During this period the Black unemployment rate was actually more than twice that of whites, "Likewise, just 2.6 percent of white job seekers were unemployed, compared to 6.7 percent of Black job seekers. This disparity in employment was directly related to an equally huge disparity between the poverty rates of whites and Blacks." In 1968, just 10 percent of white people lived below the poverty level, while nearly 34 percent of Blacks did.

Meanest and Dirtiest Jobs

Even if Blacks were able to find work, they were ghettoized within the labor market, relegated to the meanest and dirtiest jobs. According to Sugrue,

> Once hired, blacks found themselves placed in the least desirable jobs, disproportionately in unskilled and semiskilled sectors, usually in the dirtiest and most dangerous parts of the plant. Some employers based hiring decisions on straightforward racial antipathy. One auto company official hired blacks to work in the dangerous paint room. He explained his rationale: "Yes, some jobs white folks will not do: so, they have to take niggers in, particularly in duce work, spraying paint on car bodies. This soon kills a white man." Asked if it killed blacks, he responded, "It shortens their lives, it cuts them down but they're just niggers."[43]

A Nation on Fire

Segregation, determination, demonstration, integration, aggravation, Cities aflame in the summer time, and oh the beat goes on.[44]

—The Temptations

The six million blacks who arrived in the north from the near and deep south had come with empty pockets but with hope filling and kicking in their chest. But hope died. It died in the alleyways of Newark. It died in the fenced-in, cage-like corridors of projects like Cabrini Green, *in the gulf between dream and reality*, between the promise of the white liberals and the squalor and poverty black citizens faced in the ghetto every day. As Du Bois has written,

> It is as though one, looking out from a dark cave in a side of an impending mountain, sees the world passing and speaks to it; speaks courteously and persuasively, showing them how these entombed souls are hindered in their natural movement, expression, and development; and how their loosening from prison would be a matter not simply of courtesy, sympathy, and help to them, but aid to all the world ... It gradually penetrates the mind of the prisoners that the people passing do not hear; that some thick sheet of invisible but horribly tangible plate glass is between them and the world. They get excited; they talk louder; they gesticulate. Some of

the passing world stop in curiosity; these gesticulations seem so pointless; they laugh and pass on. They still either do not hear at all, or hear but dimly, and even what they hear, they do not understand. Then the people within may become hysterical.[45]

Frustrated hope became pent-up anger. It was not simply the "long history of oppression," the entrenched socioeconomic inequality, i.e. the social conditions themselves—which were well-nigh intolerable. It was, even more so, a question of their significance: Blacks perceived the gulf between their conditions and those of whites as a breach of promises of equal treatment that they feel had been made to them, and as well the futility of non-violent protest.

It began with Watts in 1965. The Watts riot, which raged for six days, was the largest and costliest rebellion of the civil rights era.

At least 34 people died ... 1,000 more were injured, and 4,000 arrested. Property damage was estimated at $200 million in the 46.5-square-mile zone (larger than Manhattan or San Francisco) where approximately 35,000 adults "active as rioters" and 72,000 "close spectators" swarmed. ... fewer personnel were used by the United States that same year to subdue the Dominican Republic ... [T]the twenty-square mile district of Watts-Willowbrook was devastated. In its eastern portion lived one-sixth of Los Angeles County's black population of little more than one-half million ... two thirds of the adult residents had less than a high school education and one in eight was illiterate. Income levels were lower than any other section of the county except for the skid row district of downtown LA.[46]

Watts is widely regarded as a pivotal moment in the history of race relations. It certainly marks the rise of Black nationalism—symbolized by the rise of the Black Panther Party for self-defense, and the Nation of Islam—which, though middle class, was fiercely anti-white—as a powerful political force.[47] But there was a double-ness to this historical moment. In 1965, the year major Equal Opportunity laws were passed, liberalism was still alive. America did not choose to make a massive shift of wealth and resources to the Black community. Instead, they provided formal equal opportunity. It was a moment of ambivalence. But it was not the point of rupture between the civil rights era and our own. I argue that rupture takes place in a series of urban rebellions in the Northern United States beginning in 1967 and culminating in Chicago and a number of other U.S. cities in 1968.

More pivotal was the Newark rebellion of July 12, 1967. It started with a story[48] that police illegally arrested and killed a Black taxi driver. This was a half-truth. The driver John Smith was still alive, but hundreds of people gathered the next night in response to flyers calling for a mass rally against police brutality.

> A police officer handed the leader a bullhorn to address the crowd. Bob Curving, a member of CORE, joined by Timothy Still, the president of a poverty program, and Oliver Lofton, who was the administrator of the Newark Legal Services Project. Although the three speakers urged a nonviolent protest march, an unidentified local resident took the bullhorn and urged violence. Young men from the neighborhood began to pick up bricks and bottles and searched for gasoline.
>
> …
>
> Shortly after midnight, two Molotov cocktails were thrown at the precinct. Then a group of 25 people on 17th Avenue began to loot stores.[49]

Hours later protesters roamed the central business district breaking windows and setting fires. On July 14, 1967, Governor Richard J. Hughes declared a state of emergency and called out the New Jersey State Police and the national guard.

The guardsmen, 98 percent of whom were white, arrived in full combat gear carrying loaded rifles. Unprepared for urban violence, nervous guardsman and state police often fired indiscriminately at crowds and at apartment buildings where they believed snipers were hiding. "In most cases they were shooting at shadows and innocent bystanders."[50]

Down in the Springfield area it was so bad police director Dominick Spina recalled the police were firing upon police and police were firing back at them.

> They fell on the city with their mechanical noises and high boots that clacked the streets with thunder. They fired their guns into lifeless buildings as the crowds were dared to move. They brought authority. Their faces were set in white granite and shaded eyes that leapt over the streets like gods, giving laws to the lawless that were all written in books. The riots had ended in an eerie silence as the new sun burned through holes in the sky over

the shameful projects. The passion of rage began to slowly fade and move ubiquitously to a somber pain. Even the dogs took notice.[51]

By the time the guardsman left Newark on Monday, July 17, twenty-three people were dead, including six women and two children, and more than a thousand were injured.

Within a week of the conflagration in Newark, Detroit was in flames. The conflagration started here when police raided five "blind pigs."

> At a quarter to four on the morning of July 23, a black plainclothes officer entered the club. He purchased a beer for fifty cents. Having caught the club selling alcohol illegally, he signaled to a group of fellow officers, who burst through the door … The police herded the customers out onto the street below. Even at four in the morning, however, Twelfth Street was bustling, and a crowd of fifty was standing on the sidewalk.

> After the police left the scene, large crowds continued to mill around the neighborhood. Someone threw a trash can through a store window, and then hundreds of others joined in, tossing rocks and looting stores. The police returned but did nothing to stop the rioting. As word spread that the police were allowing looting, more people poured into the streets. With daybreak thousands of people … joined in. The scene had a carnival atmosphere.[52]

At the time the popular evening news show was the famous Huntley and Brinkley report. They painted a picture which "frightened a nation."

> "Since Sunday morning mobs of angry negroes have paralyzed the city, spreading fire and destruction through large areas … the turmoil has forced businesses to a standstill. Chrysler and General Motors suspended production of new cars." A local correspondent on the scene spoke of smoke that filled the air and fires still burning in a "twelve miles area of the nation's fifth largest city." Michigan Republican governor George Romney spoke about "uncontrollable arson, looting, and the threat to human life by snipers in the city."[53]

By the time the Detroit rebellion was over, forty-three people had been killed and more than 200 buildings burned to the ground.

Enter Dr. Martin Luther King. For Hoover, who had long feared the rise of a "Black messiah," King had long been a threat to the National Security of the United States. Then on August 23, 1968, at the Lincoln Memorial, Dr. King gave his "I Have a Dream" speech,[54] which captured the original American dilemma—America was founded on the premise of Equal Justice under law but yet protected slavery in its constitution.

> When the architects of our republic wrote the magnificent words of the Constitution and the Declaration of Independence, they were signing a promissory note to which every American was to fall heir. This note was a promise that all men, yes, black men as well as white men, would be guaranteed the "unalienable Rights" of "Life, Liberty and the pursuit of Happiness." It is obvious today that America has defaulted on this promissory … Instead of honoring this sacred obligation, America has given the Negro people a bad check, a check which has come back marked "insufficient funds."

But he nonetheless exhorted America to a second founding in which the check—the "promissory note"—would be redeemed. It was the greatest speech of the twentieth century (Figure 3.2).

Outrageously, after King's "I Have a Dream" speech, Hoover wrote:

> Personally, I believe in the light of King's powerful demagogic speech yesterday he stands head and shoulders over all other Negro leaders put together when it comes to influencing great masses of Negroes. We must mark him now, if we have not done so before, as the most dangerous Negro of the future in this Nation from the standpoint of communism, the Negro and national security.[55]

Famously, he initiated a COINTELPRO against Dr. King as early as October 1963.

> From October 24, 1963, to June 21, 1966, the FBI also engaged in an extensive program of electronic surveillance of Dr. King. The committee found it was conducted in a particularly abusive fashion … Private and personal conversations were recorded, as were conversations between Dr. King and Government officials.[5] In fact, the development of personal information that might be derogatory to Dr. King became a major objective of the surveillance effort.[56]

Figure 3.2 Martin Luther King Jr., March on Washington, 1963.

Source: Science History Images/Alamy Stock Photo.

Amidst this increasing new Black militancy, King made a shift from criticizing racism at home to racism in the war in Vietnam. In April 1967 King in his famous riverside speech stated:

> We were taking the black young men who had been crippled by our society and sending them eight thousand miles away to guarantee liberties in Southeast Asia which they had not found in southwest Georgia and East Harlem. So, we have been repeatedly faced with the cruel irony of watching Negro and white boys on TV screens as they kill and die together for a nation that has been unable to seat them together in the same schools.[57]

In May 1967 King told workers in New York city that the movement needed a second phase and effort to change not just unjust laws but the unjust allocation of national resources that upheld poverty.

King was now, if he had not been before, a threat to national security, an enemy of the state.

The investigation of Dr. King and SCLC was handled in the Division by the Internal Security Section. *(9)* In October 1967, the Racial Intelligence Section was formed within the Division, *(10)* and the investigations of Dr. King, the SCLC and the civil rights movement in general became its responsibility. The Racial Intelligence Section also carried out the separate COINTELPRO campaign against so-called Black nationalist hate groups and their leaders, including the SCLC (the campaign was formally initiated in August 1967) ... The Crime Records Division, the Bureau's principal point of contact with Congress and the news media, was the conduit for many of the COINTELPRO initiatives, including derogatory information on Dr. King.[58]

COINTELPRO was a domestic surveillance program that began in 1956. These programs utilize a variety of techniques from surveillance to the spreading of damaging information in the media.

The purpose of this new counterintelligence endeavor is to expose, disrupt, misdirect, discredit, or otherwise neutralize the activities of black nationalist, hate-type organizations ... The activities of all such groups ... must be followed on a continuous basis ... Efforts of the various groups to consolidate their forces or to recruit new or youthful adherents must be frustrated.[59]

On March 4, 1968, Hoover expanded the COINTELPRO. One of the reasons was to "prevent the rise of a Black 'messiah' who would unify and electrify the militant Black nationalist movement." "Malcolm X might have been such a 'messiah'; he is the martyr of the movement today. Martin Luther King, Stokely Carmichael, and Elijah Muhammed all aspire to this position."[60]

While no one in the Black community knew specifically about the existence of COINTELPRO, nor about these internal communications, the hostility of the FBI toward Black activists and their leaders was well known. The stage was set for tragedy. On April 4, 1968, King was murdered. President Lyndon Johnson said, "If I were a kid in Harlem I know what I'd be thinking right now ... I'd be thinking that the whites have declared open season on my people and they are going to pick us off one by one unless I get a gun and pick them off first."[61]

The explosion did not happen immediately.

A large group of students from Marshall high school watched a klatch of militant speakers in Garfield park … " Go out and get Whitey!" one speaker yelled. "Go out and burn." Leaving the park and heading west on Madison the students encountered police who ordered them to scatter. When they didn't, an officer fired his gun into the air. … Soon the students were running East along Madison, breaking windows and pulling fire alarms as they went.[62]

By the time the guard arrived on Chicago streets in force, however, it was too late to stop the worst of the looting. Between 4:00 p.m. and 10:00 p.m. there were thirty-six major fires, including the entire 3,300 block of Madison.

Throughout the weekend, police in the Lawndale and Austin neighborhoods on the West Side and in the Woodlawn neighborhood on the South Side rushed from emergency call to emergency call as mobs of men, women and children moved from store to store, breaking plate-glass windows and taking what they found. Television sets, clothing, food and liquor were carted away from largely white-owned businesses that lined Madison Street and Homan and Kedzie Avenues. Fires blazed out of control across the West Side.[63]

By evening the military had arrived.

Not long after sunset Friday, Army units and the first of 3,000 Illinois National Guard troops arrived to back up police, who had no training for such a civic catastrophe. Military units and fire department crews were greeted by sniper fire, but no soldiers, police or firefighters were killed or seriously hurt. By Saturday afternoon, soldiers in Jeeps bristling with machine guns had secured the overpasses along the Eisenhower from downtown almost to the city's western edge.[64]

Things We Lost in the Fire

The riots heralded both an end and a beginning. Liberalism in a real sense died in the fires of the long hot summers of the late 1960s. "When the smoke cleared, and the sirens ran down, an invisible wall went up between urban and suburban America, every bit as real as the one in Berlin. Many would argue it is still standing today."

Liberalism rested on the narrative that Blacks were innocent victims of white racism. "[U]ntil the riots happened ... theirs had been the aggrieved, the just, the righteous cause."[65] In the eyes of whites, after the riots, that narrative of victimhood was gone.

"[B]lacks before [the riots] were all innocent victims; afterward they were all ungrateful looters." According to Risen, they made a "chronological dichotomy" as if "every Black in America marched with SCLC until 1965, when they signed up with the Panthers."

There were two key stereotypes which defined race for the dominant majority. One stereotype was that of Sambo, a childlike figure of inferior intelligence. The other was Nat, a beast, poisoner of white men, a rebel. The ghetto, the stratification of Blacks in the worst jobs, the social separation could be explained by the notion that Blacks were viewed as an inferior order of human life. Since the riots, the notion of race was more closely knitted together with crime. It has been that way ever since. Concomitantly the inner city itself was viewed increasingly as a place of criminality and violence. "[A] new domestic militarism that saw the inner city as an alien territory within American cities, a cancer that had to be isolated from the rest of the body politic."[66]

In the aftermath of the riots the inner city was no longer merely a foreign county; it was a war zone.

Disinvestment

White-owned business fled the ghetto.

> To make matters worse, scores of stores were forced out of business or pushed out of the neighborhoods by insurance companies in the wake of the 1968 riots that swept through Chicago's West side after the assassination of Dr. Martin Luther King, Jr. Others were simply burned or abandoned. It has been estimated that the community lost 75 percent of its business establishments from 1960 to 1970 alone.[67]

> Faced with skyrocketing security costs, high city taxes, and an aging local physical infrastructure, numerous businesses abandoned the neighborhood for safer, more spacious outlying suburbs.[68]

The panorama of burned-out houses and buildings with plywood streets for eyes traces back in many instances to the riots of 1968. After the riots, businesses in Garfield Park and North Lawndale were forced to close or burned down and never recovered. An abundance of vacant lots remain in the area from shops and homes that were burned down and never rebuilt.

White flight intensified. In 1966, Chicago had 200 schools with white enrollment in excess of 90 percent. By 1980, there were fewer than ten. New York City lost 139,000 white pupils between 1968 and 1976. By 1980, the public schools had Black or Hispanic majorities.

Backlash

A backlash had been building against the perceived encroachment by Blacks on "white rights." Segregation was a caste system. But it was a caste system that was held in place traditionally by statutes and laws. Racial order and legal order were intertwined in the minds of whites. The riots were a collective cry for structural change. This was not to be. When Congress passed equal opportunity laws altering the racial status quo, this was already perceived as a threat. Blacks were trying to take what was rightfully theirs. Whites conflated their fears of change with their fears of violence in the street into a single narrative associating Black demands for equality with a threat to the existing social order.

> [T]his call for massive, structural reform coincides with a broadening anti-civil rights backlash. No longer a southern phenomenon, resistance to civil rights reform took hold across the nation.

The response to unrest would not be along the lines of the Kerner commission report. What was to some a rebellion against unjust conditions was to others simply a matter of "crime in the streets." Law and order, not social change, was demanded by many Americans. Into this new political cauldron stepped Richard Nixon. The Republican presidential nominee would be particularly effective at tapping backlash politics and marshalling the law and order rhetoric that now appealed to so many voters.

[J]ust as Vietnam has eclipsed civil rights as a defining issue affecting U.S. prestige abroad, law and order had eclipsed social justice as a politically popular response to racial conflict.[69]

This conflation of white fears of violence and white fears of social change is evident in the language of Fair Housing legislation passed in 1968. "Fair housing legislation was defeated in 1966 in part because whites were shocked by racial violence and afraid their neighborhoods would be overrun and devalued by Black residents. When fair housing measures did become reality in 1968, it was accompanied by an anti-rioting provision."[70]

Enter Richard Nixon, candidate for president in 1969. The very foundation of his campaign was an appeal to this politics of racial fear, deepened by the recent urban unrest. Nixon famously stated, "Doubling the conviction rate in this country would do more to cure crime in America than quadrupling the funds for [the]war on poverty."[71] Race and crime, not inequality, were at the root of the urban crisis.

> We live in a deeply troubled and profoundly unsettling time. Drugs, crime ... racial discord ... on every hand, we find standards violated, old values discarded, old precepts ignored ... As a result, all of our institutions in America today are undergoing what may be the severest challenge in our history.[72]

The answer was law and order.

> Law and order were dog whistle racism. It was a code word for "keep blacks in their place." As Michelle Alexander writes, "Proponents of racial hierarchy found they could install a new racial caste system without violating the law of the new limits of acceptable political discourse, by demanding 'law and order,' rather than 'segregation forever.'"[73]

As Harry Robins "Bob" Haldeman, Nixon's Chief of Staff, wrote in his diary, "The president emphasized that the whole problem is really the Blacks. The key is to devise a system that recognized this while not appearing to."[74] A corollary to this narrative was that crime really meant "Black crime." As written, "Crime then was not about fear, but racial fear. Emphasizing it enabled Nixon to tap visceral prejudices that had divided Americans before the birth of the republic."[75]

Conclusion

White racism created the ghetto and white racism maintains it. As in the case of Ossian Sweet in the 1930s, when whites rioted at the sight of a Black family moving into a white neighborhood, the racism here is rooted in a narrative of Blacks as harbingers of crime, immorality. This narrative drove a policy of containment and quarantine. It was as if Blacks carried a virus which was contagious in their bodies or in their skin.

The narrative was so strong that white real estate agents could mobilize it for purposes of blockbusting—a rumor that Blacks were moving in was enough to make many white families sell their home. It was so deeply assumed it became the official policy of the federal government. It was so othering that the practice of consigning Blacks from birth to death to precincts of squalor and poverty was accepted as a public good.

This narrative transcends individual fear or hate. This was collective fear. The traits of deviance associated with Blacks were common knowledge or common sense, part of the received meaning of race that comes down in apostolic succession for slavery. It was this ideology that blinded white society from seeing the need for structural change. The failure of white society to deliver this led to the urban rebellion. It was this ideology that limited the process of change to formal changes in law, rather than real change, which would have required a transfer of wealth and power. These equal opportunity laws did enable the talented tenth to move out of the inner city to the ghetto. Millions did so between the 1970s and the year 2000. During the late fifties and sixties, a post-war liberalism struggled to be born. In place of liberalism was racial fear, which took the oxygen from the room of social discourse. White flight was only the beginning.

A darker, more violent picture of Blacks emerged in the minds of whites. The government massively invested in the suburbs to build idyllic spaces of comfort for whites escaping the ghetto. Concomitantly, they would shut down the great society programs of Lyndon Johnson and increasingly disinvest in the inner city. The white flight and disinvestment would combine with de-industrialization. The result of this convergence would produce the post-industrial ghetto we know today: a ghetto where factories have closed, there are blocks and blocks of boarded-up homes, and hope is a lottery ticket.

At the root of this are the narratives we have identified, first a narrative of Blacks as harbingers of immorality and later the narrative of Blacks as harbingers of crime. These narratives over time have crystallized into a presumption: a presumption of deviance or criminality. It was this presumption at bottom that shaped the second ghetto and which led to the post-industrial ghetto we have now.

Notes

1   Count Basie Orchestra, "Goin' to Chicago Blues", Track no. 2 on *Sing Along with Basie*, Roulette Label, 1958, Studio Album.

2   Stephen Thermatron and Abigail Thermatron, *America in Black and White* (New York: Touchstone Books, 1997).

3   Dominick A. Paeyga, *Chicago: A Biography* (Chicago, IL: University of Chicago Press, 2009).

4   Ibid.

5   Douglas S. Massey and Nancy A. Denton, *American Apartheid: Segregation and the Making of the Underclass* (Cambridge, MA: Harvard University Press, 1993), 30.

6   Arnold R. Hirsch, *The Making of the Second Ghetto: Race and Housing in Chicago 1940–1960* (Chicago, IL: University of Chicago Press 1998).

7   Thomas J. Sugrue, *The Origins of the Urban Crisis, Race and Inequality in Postwar Detroit* (Princeton, NJ: Princeton University Press 1996), 33.

8   Darlene Hine and John McClusky, *The Black Chicago Renaissance* (Champaign, IL: University of Illinois Press).

9   Hine and McClusky, *The Black Chicago Renaissance*.

10   Ibid.

11   Ibid.

12   Hirsch, *The Making of the Second Ghetto*.

13   Ibid.

14   Ibid.

15   Ben Austen, *High Risers, Cabrini Green and the Fate of American Public Housing* (New York: Harper Publications, 2018), 7.

16   Hirsch, *The Making of the Second Ghetto*, 55.

17   Ibid.

18 Ibid.

19 Ibid.

20 Sugrue, *The Origins of the Urban Crisis.*

21 347 U.S. 483 (1954).

22 Kevin Mumford, Newark: *A History of Race, Rights and Riots in America* (New York: New York University Press, 2007).

23 James David Dixon, "Is Detroit Different? All Together Now: Metro Detroit Is in a Period of Unprecedented Diversity," *Journal of Law & Society* 15 (Fall 2013), 63, 67.

24 Murray Forman, *The Hood Comes First : Race, Space and Place in Hip-Hop* (Middletown CT: Wesleyan University Press, 2002), 47.

25 John F. Bauman, Roger Biles, and Kristen M. Szylvian, *From Tenements to the Taylor Homes: In Search of An Urban Housing Policy in Twentieth Century America* (Harrisburg, PA: Pennsylvania State University Press, 2000), 164.

26 Dario Lasario, *America's Many faces* (Morrisville, NC: Lulu.com. 2014).

27 Hirsch, *The Making of the Second Ghetto*,100.

28 Ibid., 104.

29 Ibid.

30 Ibid.

31 Ibid.

32 Ibid.

33 David T. Greetham, *Chicago's Wall: Race, Segregation and the Chicago Housing Authority* (Wooster, OH: Senior Independent Study Thesis, 2013).

34 Greetham, *Chicago's Wall.*

35 Ibid.

36 Ibid.

37 David Wilson, *Cities and Race: America's New Ghetto* (New York: Routledge, 2007).

38 Wilson, *Cities and Race*, 25.

39 Daniel Patrick Moynihan, *The Kerner Report: The National Advisory Commission on Civil Disorders* (Princeton, NJ: Princeton University Press, 2016).

40 Sugrue, *The Origins of the Urban Crisis.*

41 Ibid.

42 Ibid.

43 Ibid.

44 Norman Whitfield and Barrett Strong, "Ball of Confusion (That's What the World is Today)," Temptations Greatest Hits II. Motown, 1970.

45   W. E. B. Dubois, *Dusk of Dawn* (New York: Oxford University Press 2014), 66.

46   See Gerald Horne, *Fire This Time: The Watts Uprising and the 1960s* (Charlottesville, VA: The University Press of Virginia, 1995), 555.

47   Horne, *Fire This Time.*

48   There were a number of underlying problems. Education in Newark was unequal.

49   Tabitha Wang, "Newark Riot" (1967), "Black Past" (June 17, 2008) https://www.blackpast.org/african-american-history/newark-riot-1967/.

50   Steven Gillon, *Separate and Unequal: The Kerner Commission and the Unraveling of American Liberalism* (New York: Basic Books, 2018).

51   Samuel Harris, "Shepherds of the Passaic," June 25, 2009, https://pen.org/shepherds-of-the-passaic/.

52   Steven N. Gillon, *Separate and Unequal: The Kerner Commission and the Unraveling of American Liberalism* (New York: Basic Books, 2018).

53   Gillon, *Separate and Unequal.*

54   Gary Younger, *The Speech: The Story Behind Dr. Martin Luther King Jr's Dream* (Chicago, IL: Haymarket Books, 2013).

55   Tony Cappacio, "MLK's Speech Attracted the FBI's Attention," *Washington Post,* August 27, 2013, https://www.washingtonpost.com/.

56   David J. Garrow, *MLK: An American Legacy: Bearing the Cross, Protest at Selma* (New York: Open Road Media, 2016).

57   Lewis V. Baldwin, *To Make the Wounded Whole: The Cultural Legacy of Martin Luther King Jr.* (Minneapolis, MN: Fortress Press, 1992).

58   National Archives, "Findings on MLK Assassination," p. 433, https://www.archives.gov/research/jfk/select-committee-report/part-2e.html#security.

59   Brian Glick, *War at Home: Covert Action Against U.S. Activists* (Boston, MA: South End Press, 1989).

60   Jonathan David Farley, "Preventing the Rise of a Messiah," *The Guardian,* April 4, 2008, https://www.theguardian.com/commentisfree/2008/apr/04/preventingtheriseofamessi.

61   Peter Levey, *The Great Uprising: Race, Riots in Urban America during the 1960s* (Cambridge, UK: Cambridge University Press, 2018).

62   Clay Risen, *A Nation on Fire* (Hoboken, NJ: John Wiley & Sons, 2009).

63   James Coates, "Riots Follow Killing of Martin Luther King Jr.," *Chicago Tribune,* December 19, 2007.

64   Stevenson Swanson, *Chicago Days: 150 Defining Moments in the Life of a Great City* (New York: Contemporary Books/McGraw Hill, 1997).

65   Clay Risen, *A Nation on Fire: America in the Wake of the King Assassination* (Hoboken, NJ: John Wiley & Sons, 2009).

66   Risen, *A Nation on Fire*, 5.

67   William Julius Wilson, *When Work Disappears: The World of the New Urban Poor* (New York: Alfred A. Knopf, 2011).

68   Sean Zielenbach, *The Art of Revitalization: Improving Conditions in Distressed Inner-City Neighborhoods* (New York: Routledge, 2002).

69   Mary L. Dudziak, *Cold War Civil Rights: Race and the Image of American Democracy* (Princeton, NJ: Princeton University Press, 2011).

70   Garth E. Pauley, *The Modern Presidency & Civil Rights: Rhetoric on Race from Roosevelt to Nixon* (College Station, TX: Texas A & M University Press, 2001; see also, D. Marvin Jones, *Fear of a Hip-Hop Planet: America's New Dilemma* (Santa Barbara, CA: Praeger, 2013).

71   William R. Kelly, *Criminal Justice at the Crossroads* (New York: Columbia University Press, 2015).

72   Kevin L. Yuill, *Richard Nixon and the Rise of Affirmative Action: The Pursuit of Equality in an Era of Limits* (Lanham, MD: Rowman & Littlefield, 2006), 100.

73   Jones, *Fear of a Hip-Hop Planet*.

74   Richard Reeves, *President Nixon: Alone in the White House* (New York: Simon & Schuster, 2002), 110.

75   Robert Parkinson, *Texas Tough: The Rise of America's Prison Empire* (London: McMillan, 2009), 297.

4

The New Black Codes: The Presumption and the Drug War

Figure 4.1 Convicts leased to harvest timber, around 1915, Florida.

Source: Alamy.

The Thirteenth Amendment of the U.S. Constitution, ratified January 31, 1865, formally abolished slavery throughout the United States. In addition, under the Fourteenth Amendment, all Blacks born in the United States became citizens of the United States and the states in which they were born. But in cruel contradiction to the promise of these constitutional guarantees, the South created Black codes in which "freed slaves" were re-enslaved in all but name.

> Negroes were liable to a slave trade under the guise of vagrancy laws and apprenticeship laws; to make the best labor contracts, Negroes must leave the old plantations and seek better terms; but if caught wandering in search of work, and thus unemployed and without a home, this was vagrancy, and the victim could be whipped and sold into slavery. In the turmoil of war, children were separated from parents, or parents unable to support them properly. These children could be sold into slavery and "the former owner of said minors shall have preference."[1]

Under the infamous Black codes, "freed slaves" were forced to work the land of their former masters under labor contracts.

> Louisiana passed an elaborate law in 1865 to regulate labor contracts for agricultural pursuits … The law required all agricultural laborers to make labor contracts for the next year within the first ten days of January, the contracts to be in writing, to be with heads of families, to embrace the labor of all the members, and to be "binding on all minors thereof."[2]

If they failed to make a written contract for employment, Blacks were subject to a fine: "failure to make a written contract" was a misdemeanor punishable by a fine of $5.00 to $50.00. Once they signed the labor contract, former slaves were subject to arrest and fines if they tried to leave the land before doing the contracted work.

> Mississippi provided that "every civil officer shall, and every person may arrest and carry back to his or her legal employer any freedman, free or negro, or mulatto who shall have quit the service of his or her employer before the expiration of his or her term of service without good cause."[3]

If they refused to work or disobeyed orders they were punished as criminals. In Florida, for example,

It is provided that when any person of color shall enter into a contract as aforesaid to serve as a laborer for a year or any specified term on any farm in this state, if he shall refuse or neglect to perform the stipulations of his contract by willful disobedience of orders ... failure or refusal to perform work assigned to him, idleness, or abandonment of the ... employment ... he or she shall be liable, upon the complaint of his employer ... to be arrested and tried before the criminal court for the county.[4]

These labor contracts created a host of no-win choices.

This latter law almost compelled many southern blacks to choose between two choices which would lead to the same answer. Either accept an unfair labor contract with your former owner (or on a former plantation) or commit the crime of being unemployed. However, if you accept the labor contract, you will have to go into debt to afford the tools to till the land; you likely will not be able to pay this debt off—and guess what—that's a crime.[5]

Black Codes also typically contained Apprenticeship laws that forced Black children, orphans, or those whose parents were deemed unable to support them by a judge into unpaid labor for white planters: "In the turmoil of war, children were separated from their parents, or parents unable to support them properly. These children could be sold into slavery, and the former owner shall have preference."[6]

The most oppressive laws of the Black codes were laws against vagrancy. In Georgia it was ruled that

All persons wandering or strolling about in idleness, who are able to work, and who have no property to support them; all persons leading an idle, immoral, or profligate life, who have no property to support them and are able to work and do not work; all persons able to work having no visible and known means of a fair, honest, and respectable livelihood; all persons having a fixed abode, who have no visible property to support them, and who live by stealing or trading in, bartering for, or buying stolen property ... shall be deemed and considered vagrants ... they shall be fined and imprisoned or sentenced to work on the public works, for not longer than a year.[7]

Blacks were also subject to arrest by "any person present" upon view of a misdemeanor. "Upon view of a misdemeanor committed by a person of color any person present may arrest the offender and take him before a magistrate to be dealt with as the case may require." By contrast, "In the case of a misdemeanor committed by a white person toward a person of color, any person may complain to a magistrate."[8]

Misdemeanors were broadly defined to include anything in the mind of whites that was offensive to them. Thus, for a Black to make an "insulting gesture" (in context: "to a white person") was a crime. Mississippi declared:

> [A]ny freedman, free Negro, or mulatto committing riots, routs, affrays, trespasses, malicious mischief ... seditious speeches, insulting gestures, language or acts, or assaults on any person, disturbance of the peace ... vending spiritous or intoxicating liquors, or committing any other misdemeanor, the punishment of which is not provided for by law, shall, upon conviction thereof, in the county court, be fined not less than ten dollars, and not more than one hundred dollars, and may be imprisoned, at the discretion of the court, not exceeding thirty days.[9]

The laws were designed to criminalize Blacks and systemically herd them into prison. Once in prison they could be forced to work as slaves through the "convict lease system."

Hence the language of the 13th Amendment, which states "Neither slavery nor involuntary servitude, *except as a punishment for a crime whereof the party shall be duly convicted*, shall exist in the United States." This system functioned efficiently and effectively to achieve its goal of effectively re-enslaving thousands of Blacks in the antebellum south.

> At the end of the 1880s, thousands of black men across the south were imprisoned in work camps only for violations of the new racial codes, completely subjective crimes, or no demonstrable crime at all. Among the "felons" sold to the Pratt mines in 1890, seven men were working for the crime of bigamy, four for homosexuality, and six for miscegenation— an offense almost solely prosecuted against black men who engaged in sex with white women. Many others had been arrested and sold for ostensible crimes that explicitly targeted blacks' assertions of their new civil rights: two for "illegal voting" and eleven on a conviction for "false pretense," the euphemism for laws aimed at preventing black men from leaving the employ of a white farmer before the end of a crop season.[10]

The true crime in all of these instances under the Black codes was Blackness itself. This system mirrored slavery as a system of cruel, systemic exploitation of Black labor: The massive number of "freed slaves" sentenced to prison did not sit idle. They were, all according to law, leased out.

> Black convicts were leased to private companies, typically industries profiteering from the region's untapped natural resources. As many as 200,000 black Americans were forced into back-breaking labor in coal mines, turpentine factories and lumber camps. They lived in squalid conditions, chained, starved, beaten, flogged and sexually violated. They died by the thousands from injury, disease and torture.[11]

For both the state and private corporations, the opportunities for profit were enormous.

The system of Black codes mirrored slavery in another way: it was a police regime. A police regime does not punish; it is a means of intimidating and controlling a dangerous population. Norms of equal justice, due process, and all individual rights do not apply. There is an inside/outside dichotomy. They are, despite the 14th Amendment, outside of the circle of community and humanity and, while nominally citizens, persons without rights.

This reinscribed the mark of lower-cast status. This caste system was premised on a presumption. In slavery it was a presumption of inferiority attached equally and reciprocally to Blackness or their status as slaves. For the Black codes it was a presumption of criminality attached to Blackness itself.

The past is prologue; armed with this background we will consider both the drug war and the war on crime and how each of these police regimes echo back to the nineteenth century and, more specifically, the era of the Black codes. If the Black codes made it a crime to be Black in the post-bellum south, the drug war and the war on crime similarly imposed a badge of criminality on the Black poor and those in the post-industrial ghetto.

Search and Destroy: A Social History of the Drug War

Richard Nixon's presidency was built on an appeal to fear (Figure 4.2). In a 1969 speech he stated, "We live in a deeply troubled and profoundly unsettling time. Drugs and crime ... racial discord ... on every hand we find standards violated, old values discarded, old precepts ignored. ... As a result of all this, our institutions in America today are undergoing what may be the severest challenge of our history."[12]

Figure 4.2 Richard Nixon.

Source: Library of Congress, https://lccn.loc.gov/96522669

Crime was a civilizational threat to America. The answer was law and order. This was, of course, dog-whistle racism: driving this civilizational threat of crime were Black people. The issue of crime was not merely about fear but racial fear. Nixon's reference to "racial discord" was in context a transparent effort to evoke images of the recent urban rebellions which were occurring at the time. But Nixon sought to tap into deeper sources of this "racial fear." As Robert Perkinson wrote, "Emphasizing it allowed Richard Nixon to tap into visceral prejudices that had divided Americans before the birth of the Republic."[13] By 1971, Nixon's law and order campaign crystalized into a crusade against drugs. Nixon, who by now had become president, officially declared a "War on Drugs," on June 18, 1971, calling drugs public enemy number one.

> Drugs are among the modern curse of youth just like the plagues and epidemics of former years. And they are decimating a generation of Americans. [My administration] will accelerate the development of tools and weapons … to fight illegal drugs … a tripled Customs Service, more federal drug agents, massive assistance to local police, and antidrug operations abroad.[14]

War is a condensation symbol. Such symbols "condense into one symbolic event, sign, or act patriotic pride, anxieties, remembrances of past glories or humiliations, promises of future greatness." Such symbols "silence debate, shifting society from thought to action."[15] Spending on the drug war climbed steadily from $3 million in 1971 to $321 million in 1975.

Ronald Reagan, doubling down on the initiative of Nixon, declared his own war on drugs on October 14, 1982 (Figure 4.3).

> The mood toward drugs is changing in this country, and the momentum is with us. We're making no excuses for drugs—hard, soft, or otherwise. Drugs are bad, and we're going after them. As I said before, we've taken down the surrender flag and run up the battle flag. And we're going to win the war on drugs.[16]

Wars must have enemies. Reagan defined drugs as "the dark evil enemy within." Nixon's association of crime and disorder with African Americans had already created a prevailing consensus among the American public in which Blackness became ultimately linked to immorality, disorder, criminality, and

Figure 4.3 Ronald Reagan.

Source: Library of Congress, https://lccn.loc.gov/96522678

drugs.[17] Reagan's declaration of war on drugs was not, in context, a war on an inanimate object, it was a war on drug dealers and users who had already been defined as Black. The "dark evil enemy" was Black. Desmond and Emirbayer write, "Americans so often comprehend crime through Blackness, and Blackness through crime, Blackness, as conceived by non-Black America, is itself a crime."[18]

This process of criminalization of Blackness would reach new orders of magnitude with the emergence of crack cocaine. As early as 1985, Ronald Reagan began a propaganda campaign to "publicize" its emergence and build a "more elaborate racial narrative." As Michele Alexander writes, his demagogic strategy worked flawlessly. "The media campaign was an extraordinary success. Almost overnight, the media was saturated with images of Black 'crack whores,' 'crack dealers,' and 'crack babies'—images that seemed to confirm the worst negative racial stereotypes about impoverished inner-city residents."[19]

On June 17, 1986, the narrative linking race and crack cocaine was given a face. It was then that Len Bias, whose talent was compared to Michael Jordan's, was selected as the National Basketball Association's second overall draft pick. He was going to play for the Boston Celtics—the previous year's NBA champions. The night of the 18th, after whistle-stop publicity to pose for the press, he returned to his college to celebrate with friends. By the next morning he was dead. "Dr. John E. Smialek attributed Bias's death last Thursday morning directly to cocaine, 'which interrupted the normal electrical control of his heartbeat, resulting in the sudden onset of seizures and cardiac arrest.'"[20] But the 22-year-old Len Bias "was a very healthy individual who showed no signs of heart disease." "The lesson of Bias' death," reported Newsweek, "is that cocaine kills." The article was titled "Cocaine Is a Loaded Gun."[21] In his study of the War on Drugs, *Smoke and Mirrors*, Dr. Baum would write, "Len Bias was a terrific basketball player. In death he would become the Archduke Ferdinand of the Total War on Drugs."[22]

It did not matter that there was no evidence that Bias had ingested crack cocaine. Bias's death occurred in the midst of a crack epidemic. His story fit neatly, seamlessly, into the building political narrative about the surge of crack use in the inner city. While there was no evidence that Bias's death was due to crack, the connection was deeply assumed.

Nor did it matter that Bias was not "from the ghetto." Len Bias came from a two-parent household in Landover, Maryland, a suburb of Washington, DC, just down the road from University of Maryland's College Park campus.[23] In the early 1980s, the framing of the purported "cocaine epidemic" in sports drew automatic associations with the drug trade in Black inner cities, and not surprisingly, Black athletes bore the brunt of this criminalization. Given this context, it is hardly surprising that Drug Enforcement Agency (DEA) Chief John C. Lawn automatically connected Bias's death to the supposed pathology of the Black ghetto. "He grew up in an environment where drug use is pervasive," Lawn stated. "Peer pressure killed him."[24]

Moral panic is a mass expression of fear and concern over something or someone perceived to threaten the values and norms of society. In his 1972 book *Folk Devils and Moral Panics*, Stanley Cohen wrote that a moral panic occurs when

> [a] condition, episode, person or group of people … emerges to become defined as a threat to societal values and interests; its nature is presented in a stylized and stereotypical fashion by the mass media; the moral barricades are manned by editors, bishops, politicians, and other right-thinking people.[25]

This received story that crack killed Len Bias escalated the fear of drugs whipped up by Nixon to free-wheeling moral panic about crack epidemics in the urban ghetto. The media painted a picture of an urban nightmare.

> In July, ABC News broke new ground by sending a cameraman to accompany a police raid on a crack house …. On 2 September 1986, viewers tuned into CBS to hear a sombre Dan Rather (CBS's news anchor) announce: "Tonight, CBS takes you to the streets, to the war zone, for an unusual two hours of hands-on horror." The programme was *48 Hours on Crack Street*, and … it attracted a total of 15 million viewers—one of the highest viewing figures for any documentary in US history.[26]

Most cocaine users were undoubtedly white. Even former federal drug czar William Bennett admitted that "[T]he typical cocaine user is white, male, a high school graduate employed full time and living in a small metropolitan area or suburb."[27] "The image of the Black—or at least ethnic minority—crack user was perpetuated by almost every TV report. Crack-house busts showed decrepit houses in Black neighborhoods containing Black people."[28] The media branded a stereotype of Black crack users and dealers into the public's mind despite the fact that the vast majority of Blacks are not involved with drugs or the drug trade. To this stereotyping the media added a narrative of potential infestation of suburbs by this urban epidemic.

By the end of 1986, the media had labeled crack the most dangerous drug and had decried the outbreak of a national "crack epidemic." The media exacerbated white fears by warning of the potential for crack to seep out of the inner city and into their neighborhoods, thereby spreading into the "higher social ranks of the country." "Crack has captured the ghetto," Newsweek declared, "and is inching its way into the suburbs."[29]

The crack epidemic was also associated by the media with extreme violence. One article, cited by Democratic Senator Lawton Chiles in support of the Anti-Drug Abuse Act of 1986, recounted how a drug-addicted teenager brutally murdered his own mother "with a butcher knife in a fight over crack."[30]

Reagan channeled this hysteria and moral panic in a 1986 speech: "Today there's a new epidemic: smokable cocaine, otherwise known as crack. It is an explosively destructive and often lethal substance which is crushing its users. It is an uncontrolled fire."[31]

The stitching together of the images of smokable cocaine, crack houses, and Blacks added a new layer of racism to the war on drugs campaign. Whites use and used powdered cocaine at rates statistically equal to Blacks; but it is smokable cocaine which is demonized as the source of the epidemic or infection.

Ronald Reagan signed the The Anti-Drug Abuse Act of 1986 into law on October 27, 1986. The act included both mandatory minimum sentences and enhanced penalties for crack cocaine addiction. "The Anti-Drug Abuse Act of 1986, establish[ed] for the first time mandatory minimum sentences triggered by specific quantities of cocaine."[32]

However, it also established a 100-to-1 disparity between distribution of powder and crack cocaine. For example, distributing just five grams of crack cocaine carries a minimum five-year federal prison sentence. This is the same penalty for distributing 500 grams of powdered cocaine.

This massively increased the funding of the war: the budget for fighting illegal drugs increased from slightly more than 1 billion in 1980 to 9.4 billion in 1989.[33]

There were actually two wars taking place. One was a war in which the U.S. government brought to bear local police, sometimes armed with tanks and assault vehicles, the DEA, CIA, courts, and Coast Guard to wage both a national and international fight to interdict the flow and sale of drugs. But the more important war was a war of words, mobilizing a mix of facts and myth to shape an image of drug crime in ways that amplified racial fears. Race would come to define the crime involved and the focus and nature of "the war."[34] It became a war against the Black community. In the 1990s, two factors converged to escalate the war: further rising crime rates and a media campaign to focus the crisis on urban Black youth. The theme of this media campaign was the prediction that a generation of urban thugs would be more vicious than any before. The Central Park Jogger case was a catalyst for the narrative.

In April 1989, a young, white female jogger was brutally beaten, raped, and left to die in Manhattan's Central Park.[35] Within hours, police arrested and charged a group of seven African American and Latino teens, ranging in age from 14 to 16, with rape, assault, and attempted murder. Local politicians seized on the incident. In the summer of 1989, New York City Mayor Edward Koch called for the death penalty for "wilding,"—the new term coined for what allegedly happened in the park—called the seven suspects "monsters," and complained that the juvenile justice system was too lenient.[36] But the *coup de grace* was not a case, nor an executive order, but an article written by a professor at Princeton.

In an article entitled "The Coming of the Super-Predators,"[37] John Dilulio, a former Princeton political science professor, predicted the rise of a class of criminals: radically impulsive, brutally remorseless youngsters. He noted that

> Since 1985, the rate of homicide committed by adults age 25 and older has declined by 25 percent, from 6.3 to 4.7 per 100,000 as the baby boomers matured into their middle aged years. At the same time, however, the homicide rate among 18–24 year olds increased by 61 percent from 15.7 to 25.3 per 100,000. Even more alarming and tragic, homicide is now reaching down to a much younger age group—children as young as 14–17. Over the past decade the rate of homicide committed by teenagers, ages 14–17 has more than doubled.[38]

Reading these statistics as gospel, Dilulio argued that he had discovered a demographic crime bomb: he warned that by the year 2000 an additional 30,000 young murderers, rapists, and muggers would be roaming America's streets, sowing mayhem. A generation of "super-predators" was coming.

On the horizon, therefore, are tens of thousands of severely morally impoverished juvenile super-predators. They are perfectly capable of committing the most heinous acts of physical violence for the most trivial reasons (for example, a perception of slight disrespect or the accident of being in their path). They fear neither the stigma of arrest nor the pain of imprisonment. They live by the meanest code of the meanest streets, a code that reinforces rather than restrains their violent, hair-trigger mentality. In prison or out, the things those super-predators get by their criminal behavior—sex, drugs, money—are their own immediate rewards. Nothing else matters to them. So for as long as their youthful energies hold out, they will do what comes "naturally." Murder, rape, rob, assault, burglarize, deal deadly drugs, and get high.[39]

At the root of the problem was a class of criminals which was "morally impoverished." This term was both a counterpoint to a narrative that economic poverty caused crime and a shorthand for a notion that these were not merely juvenile delinquents but sociopaths. "We're talking about elementary school youngsters who pack guns instead of lunches. We're talking about kids who have absolutely no respect for human life and no sense of the future. In short, we're talking big trouble that hasn't yet begun to crest."[40]

Dilulio was invited by then-President Bill Clinton "to attend a working dinner on juvenile crime" at the White House. Hillary Clinton's remarks a few months after that dinner make clear that his ideas had resonated. In her remarks at Keene State College in New Hampshire, she talked about "the kinds of kids that are called 'super-predators'—no conscience, no empathy."[41]

The "super-predators," like so many other scary media concoctions, were given Black faces: the Black rapist, the Black crack-cocaine-using pregnant woman, the Black babies addicted to crack, the free-loading Black welfare mother, the Black, gun-toting, drug-dealing gang member, and the "Black male criminal" in general.[42]

While Dilulio's book did not emerge until 1996, his "super-predator" narrative, which he had circulated much earlier, was largely responsible for the *Violent Crime Control Act and Law Enforcement Act of 1994*.[43] Called the crime bill, it "expanded the school-to-prison pipeline and increased racial disparities in juvenile justice involvement by creating draconian penalties for so-called *super predators*—low-income children of color, especially Black children, who are convicted of multiple crimes."[44]

Driven by this hysteria—stoked by an evolving set of urban myths ranging from the crack babies to super-predators—the war against drugs and zero-tolerance programs resulted in massively disproportionate incarceration of Blacks in prisons and jails.

> Throughout the drug war, African Americans have been disproportionately investigated, detained, searched, arrested and charged with the use, possession and sale of illegal drugs. Vast numbers of African Americans have been jailed and imprisoned pursuant to the nation's tough drug trafficking laws, implemented as part of the War on Drugs. Indeed, in some jurisdictions, the majority of African American men age thirty-five and under are within the grip of the criminal justice system.[45]

In absolute numbers the number of Black men in prison grew five-fold between 1980 and 1990.[46] In 1980 there were 143,000 Blacks in prison. By 2000, there were 791,000. This resulted from an incredible disparity in arrest and incarceration rates.

Arrest Rates

In every year from 1980 to 2007, Blacks were arrested nationwide on drug charges at rates relative to population that were 2.8 to 5.5 times higher than white arrest rates.[47] State-by-state data from 2006 show that Blacks were arrested for drug offenses at rates in individual states that were 2 to 11.3 times greater than the rate for whites.[48]

Incarceration Rates

There are 4,630 Black men in prison nationwide per 100,000 Black men in the population, whereas the rate for white men is 482. In ten states and the District of Columbia, Black men are incarcerated at staggeringly high rates that range from 5,740 to 7,859 per 100,000. In contrast, the range among the ten states with the highest rates of white male incarceration is 620 to 1,151. The highest rate of white male incarceration (1,151) is lower than the lowest rate of Black male incarceration (1,195).

African Americans constituted 53.5 percent of all persons who entered prison because of a drug conviction; a Black man was 11.8 times more likely than a white man to enter prison for drug offenses.[49]

To appreciate the scope and prevalence of incarceration, I note with interest that in 1980 there were 143,000 Black men in prison but 463,700 enrolled in colleges or universities. By the year 2000 the proportions were reversed: there were 791,600 Black men in prison and 603,032 enrolled in colleges and universities.[50] Today the lifetime chances of a Black male going to prison are one in three.[51]

Moreover, in the context of the drug war—despite popular misconceptions—Blacks and whites use cocaine and marijuana at statistically identical rates. Moreover, when whites are arrested, they receive sympathy and disproportionately some alternative to incarceration. Blacks do not get sympathy; they get prison. The single explanation of these astonishing racial disparities is race.

Criminalization of the Urban Poor

But in the aftermath of formal equality, it is not all Blacks who are directly targeted by the "drug war." Within the pattern of systemic racial disparity, there is another pattern. In his book *Code of the Street: Decency, Violence and the Moral Life of the Inner City*,[52] Elijah Anderson spoke of how when he walked down Germantown Avenue, the deeper he went into the inner city, the more he observed a deepening of socio-economic isolation. In the urban core, the concentric circles of social disadvantage reach their ultimate intensity. The deployment of police, the foot soldiers of the drug war, concentrates in a similar way. While under Jim Crow systemic racism was focused on all Blacks, the drug war systemically targeted inner-city areas as a primary theater of war and reached its ultimate intensity there.

This flowed inexorably from the fact that "disadvantaged urban Blacks" were convenient scapegoats. They were already the main characters in the media narrative about the "crack epidemic" as a national crisis. According to Michael Tonry, in light of our history of scapegoating "minority groups," the targeting the urban poor was foreseeable:

Given what we know about past periods of intolerance of drug use and the tendencies to scapegoat minority groups, and that disadvantaged urban Blacks are the archetypal users of crack cocaine—and therefore the principal possessors, sellers, and low-level distributors—anyone who knew the history of American drug policy could have foreseen that this war on drugs would target and mostly engage young disadvantaged members of minority groups as the enemy. And it has.[53]

Ronald Reagan doubled down on this stereotyping. President Reagan hired staff dedicated to publicizing the emergence of crack cocaine in inner-city neighborhoods—specifically in poor, Black communities—to perpetuate the nation's moral panic and secure the passage of War on Drugs legislation.[54]

The drugs primarily targeted by the drug war—cocaine and more recently crack—are notoriously used and distributed in the inner city. Second, the focus on smokable crack cocaine rather than powdered cocaine, which had indeed become epidemic in inner-city areas, represented a tacit strategic focus on the urban ghetto Black poor.[55]

It was this targeting of crack cocaine and, in effect, the targeting of inner-city neighborhoods—what Judge Sheindlin calls indirect racial profiling—that resulted in the vastly disproportionate arrest and incarceration of Blacks.

Three-quarters of the drug arrests were crack-related even though only an estimated one-third of the city's drug transactions involved crack. Whites constitute the majority of those who deliver methamphetamine, ecstasy, powder cocaine, and heroin in Seattle; Blacks are the majority of those who deliver crack. Not surprisingly then, seventy-nine percent of those arrested on crack charges were Black. The researchers could not find a "racially neutral" explanation for the police prioritization of the downtown drug markets and crack.[56]

But how is it possible that America could wage a war against Blacks in the urban ghetto with the support of Black mayors, Black prosecutors, and Black judges, particularly in places like D.C., where, ironically, incarceration rate of Blacks reached astonishing levels? There are two narratives which intervene to invisibilize the systemic racism of the drug war. The first is a narrative that the urban ghetto is a "war zone," a place of violence and mayhem populated by criminals. We have criminalized the Black poor. We have for years conceptualized the problem as one of mass incarceration of Blacks. Vast though it is, mass incarceration is an effect. It flows in the first instance from the mass criminalization of the Black poor of the urban ghetto.

A parallel narrative is that in attacking these areas we are simply going where the crime is, focusing on high-crime areas. Between these narratives, Black police, prosecutors, and Black presidents—like Obama—see themselves as arresting and incarcerating criminals.

The Master Narrative of the Drug War: The Ghetto Is a War Zone

> As soon as this high crime rate is emphasized through the press, then people begin to look upon the Negro community as a community of criminals. And then any Negro in the community can be stopped in the street. "Put your hands up," and they pat you down. You might be a doctor, a lawyer, a preacher, or some other kind of Uncle Tom. But despite your professional standing, you'll find that you're the same victim as the man who's in the alley. Just because you're Black and you live in a Black community, which has been projected as a community of criminals.[57]—Malcolm X

Violent crime rates skyrocketed beginning in 1960 until 1990 (Figure 4.4).[58,59]

As the great Malcolm X noted, the Black community was frequently scapegoated as the source of crime—and implicitly its rise. The narrative of Black criminality became more particularized during the long hot summers of the 1960s as Blacks in inner cities from Watts to Washington D.C. erupted in urban rebellions. Dr. King noted that riots are the voice of the unheard.

But whites consumed by racial fears did not see these urban rebellions as urgent calls for change. They saw them only as a threat to themselves. White politicians like Nixon poured gasoline on these fears with his dog-whistle rhetoric of "crime in the streets"—he gave these racial fears an urban focus. Enter Edward C. Banfield. Building on nineteenth-century notions of the urban poor as a "dangerous class" (see e.g. Charles Loring Brace), Banfield wrote his infamous work, *The Unheavenly City*.[60] In his book he theorized the existence of a "dangerous class" of people who lived in inner cities. He starts with the premise linked to a popular theory referred to as "the logic of urban

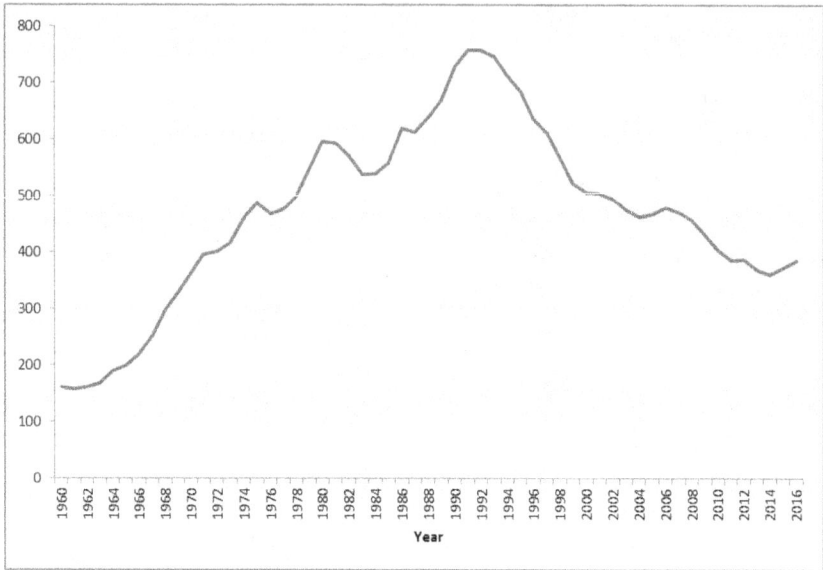

Figure 4.4 National Violent Crime Rate, 1960–2016.

Source: Figure 1, *Recent Violent Crime Trends in the United* States, Congressional Research Service, June 20, 2018. From *Sourcebooks of Criminal Justice Statistics, Table 3.106.2012;* Federal Bureau of Investigation, *Crime in the United States 2016,* Table 1.

growth." This theory holds that the poorest of a city's population will live in the urban core. The violence and squalor of this urban core was not fixed by economic forces but cultural or "class pathology."

At the core of this "class pathology" was an inability to "sacrifice the present for a future satisfaction because he has no sense of the future." The least future-oriented member of this lower class lives from "moment to moment" and is radically improvident as well as violent and mentally ill. Banfield went on to associate the urban crisis not with lack of opportunity or inequality but "a startling absence of values—and inherent violence—of this dangerous class." Applying his dangerous class stereotype to Blacks during the urban rebellions of the 1960s, Banfield argued these Blacks were not rioting because of social conditions—"by any conceivable measure of material welfare the present generation of urban Americas is, on the whole, better off than any other large group of people has ever been anywhere"—but simply for "fun and profit."

A later generation of sociologists, epitomized by Dilulio, portrayed Blacks in the inner city as the epitome of Banfield's dangerous class. In their reiteration of Banfield's thesis, they renamed the dangerous class "the ghetto underclass"—the dangerousness was implicit in the signifier of the ghetto itself. Popular culture relentlessly portrayed urban Blacks through this dangerous/underclass lens. Television shows like *COPS* began each show with photos of Blacks spreadeagled over a police car. In turn, by the 1990s, a cottage industry of films from *Boyz in the Hood* to *Menace 2 Society* to *Training Day* painted a picture that echoed the violent portrayal of the Black community on *COPS* and the evening news. These films marked the ghetto as an evil, deviant, even criminogenic space, a breeding ground for crime.

Constitutional Legitimacy: The High-Crime-Area Frame

The criminal justice system has two functions. One of them is to apprehend and punish criminals. The other is ideological. This ideological function occurs on two stages. There is a front stage, a stage that exists in presidential speeches and judicial opinions. This is a stage of formalism in which we put a face on discriminatory practices, which coincides with constitutional ideals. The back stage is the stage of the real world, a stage of unvarnished action—the everyday functioning of the system. On the front stage, Ronald Reagan targeted smokable crack cocaine. But on the back stage, the stage of action, Blacks, particularly the Black poor, are targeted. How was this rationalized by the courts?

On September 8, 1995, Sam Wardlow was standing on a corner at 4035 Van Buren in Chicago holding an opaque bag.[61] A police caravan of four cars approached. Wardlow looked in their direction and began to run "inexplicably." In the last car of the four-car caravan were two officers, Nolan and Harvey. According to the court, Nolan and Harvey turned their car southbound, watched him as he ran through the gangway and an alley, and eventually cornered him on the street. Nolan then exited his car and stopped Wardlow. Under the famous case of *Terry v. Ohio*,[62] this "stop" constituted a seizure within the meaning of the 4th Amendment. As such, under *Terry*, the police needed specific articulable facts to justify the stop. But Wardlow had committed no criminal act. Running itself is an innocent act. The government argued, however, that running is the consummate act of evasion. But the court found significant the place where the "act of running" occurred. Wardlow ran in an area "known for heavy narcotics trafficking."

> An individual's presence in a "high-crime area," standing alone, is not enough to support a reasonable, particularized suspicion of criminal activity, but a location's characteristics are relevant in determining whether the circumstances are sufficiently suspicious to warrant further investigation. Accordingly, we have previously noted the fact that the stop occurred in a "high crime area" among the relevant contextual considerations in a *Terry* analysis. ... We conclude Officer Nolan was justified in suspecting that Wardlow was involved in criminal activity, and, therefore, in investigating further.[63]

If Wardlow had been running in the suburbs of Chicago, no suspicious inference would apply to that locale. Location becomes an operative element in the calculus of determining whether "reasonable suspicion" exists. There is nothing to limit this "high crime area" notion to drug crimes. It transfers effortlessly to crimes involving the possession of guns and many other types of investigations. But mere presence in a particular neighborhood in an urban context may reflect less individual choice than socio-economic circumstances. The court reasons in a formalistic way. It does not take socio-economic context into account. But from a realist point of view—taking socio-economic context into view—making mere presence in a neighborhood an operative fact in the determination of whether the police have the right to seize an individual is in tension with a social contract–based notion that an individual should be judged on their conduct, not on the socio-economic circumstance, i.e. that he or she may live in the ghetto.

This shifts the focus from an individualized evaluation of the facts of a case to a categorical approach in which one's mere presence in "a place associated with crime" becomes in part the arbiter of who is to be seized. One law professor calls this "fourth-amendment apartheid."

Between these two interpenetrating narratives, i.e. the narrative of the inner city as a "war zone" and the legitimating thesis that mere presence in a high crime area carries with it a degree of suspicion, the criminalization of the urban poor has been normalized and legitimated.

Tragically, the tactics of targeting Black communities for military-style campaigns was not limited to the war on drugs. Given the popularization of hyper-aggressive policing during the drug war in the 1980s and 90s and concomitant popularization of the inner city as the source of violence and crime by 1992, new military-style campaigns were launched using the drug war's philosophy and tactics as a template.

New York's War on Guns

In one of the first policy documents issued by Bratton's New York Police Department (NYPD), "Police Strategy No. 1: Getting Guns off the Streets of New York," the department announced a series of initiatives aimed at reducing gun violence.[64] The document emphasized that between 1960 and 1992, the number of murders committed in New York City with a handgun increased by almost 2,000 percent, growing from one-quarter to three-quarters of all murders.[65] Guns are the most iconic symbols of violent crime.

This war on guns, like the war on drugs, combined a military mindset with specialized units and hyper-aggressive tactics, focused on certain areas of town.

Deployment of Special Forces

Police Strategy No. 1 did not refer to "stop-and-frisk" or related approaches to finding guns, but it did announce the expansion of the elite Street Crimes Unit (SCU) and its deployment "in a concentrated approach" to high-crime areas to "increase firearms-related arrests." In 1997 Commissioner Saffir took the baton from Bratton. The street crimes unit was augmented by 300 officers to a total complement of 400.[66]

A key aspect of the war on guns was the use of arrest quotas, which were frequently obtained by ignoring due process guarantees.

Officer Noel Leader testified about how this pressure was corrosive to civil rights. He stated that where pressure is applied to the commanding officers of the Street Crime Unit, officers will engage in unlawful and illegal practices. They are pressured to produce numbers since the management has a number fixation of percentage gained, a fixation on coming up with numbers and statistics and not dealing with people and human beings and emotions and feelings.[67]

By 2002, Commissioner Raymond Kelly took over the reins and increasingly escalated the war: between 2002 and 2011 stops rose sharply from 97,000 to 686,000 a year in New York.[68] Altogether, the NYPD conducted over 4.4 million stops. The racial disparities which resulted were summed up by the Center for Constitutional Rights.

From 2005 to 2008, approximately 80 percent of total stops made were of Blacks and Latinos, who comprise 25 percent and 28 percent of New York City's total population, respectively. During this same time period, only approximately 10 percent of stops were of whites, who comprise 44 percent of the city's population.

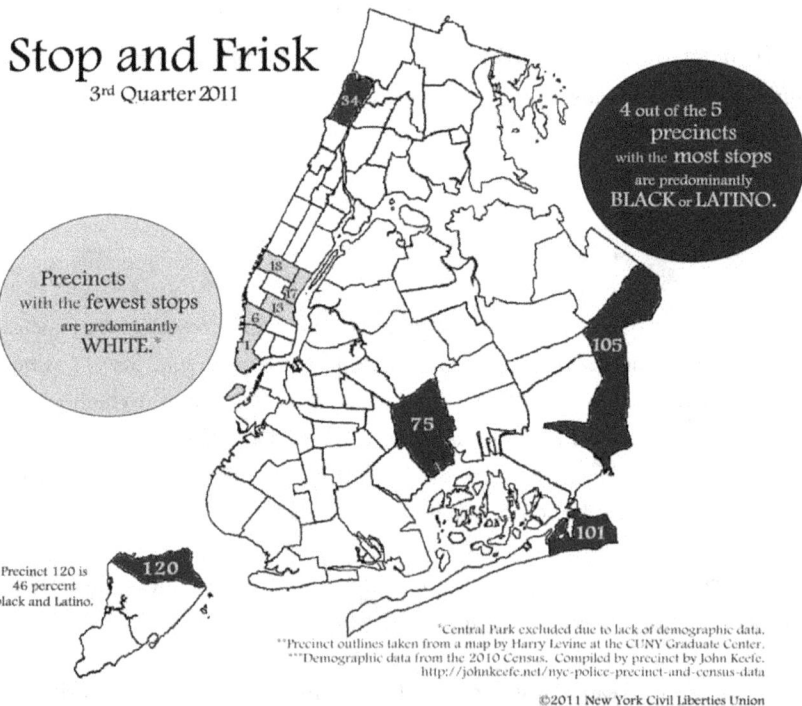

Figure 4.5 Stops per Precinct 2003–2011.

Source: New York Civil Liberties Union.

The Center for Constitutional Rights report also stated that "Blacks and Latinos are more likely to be frisked after a NYPD-initiated stop than whites" and that "Blacks and Latinos are more likely to have physical force used against them during a NYPD-initiated stop than whites."[69]

These disparities were not, as many imagine, the result of individual officers enacting their stereotypes of Blacks. This was the result of strategic deployment of police in so-called high-crime areas (see Figure 4.5), which were almost always Black or brown.[70]

The Decline of the Right of Locomotion

It was virtually inevitable from the military mindset hardwired into the basic concept of the drug war, amplified by an "us versus them" narrative, and amplified further by the pressure, that the police would use aggressive and, too often, hyper-aggressive tactics in carrying out the war. The 4th Amendment in this case was the first casualty.

The astonishing statistical disparities are not happening simply because Blacks are committing more crimes, or even because Black communities are more targeted—i.e. overpoliced. Targeting is a critical element, but the most criminalizing aspect is that they are—as documented in several cities—stopped and arrested *systemically* in violation of 4th Amendment guarantees. In prosecuting the drug war there is wide recognition that in the inner city, reasonable suspicion and probable cause were thrown away. "Driving while Black." "Walking while Black." These terms take their meaning from police harassment in the context of the drug war. But the most egregious example of police hyper-aggression is the street sweep.

"Drug sweeps" or "street sweeps" occur when the police simply close off a neighborhood and indiscriminately detain or arrest large numbers of people without lawful justification. Police conduct street sweeps in order to subject those caught in the dragnet to questioning and searches in the absence of probable cause or reasonable suspicion. One such drug sweep, which occurred in New York City, was described in the following account:

In a publicized sweep on July 19, 1989, the Chief of the Organized Crime Control Bureau (OCCB), led 150 officers to a block in upper Manhattan's

Washington Heights. Police sealed off the block and detained virtually all of the 100 people who were present there for up to two hours, during which time the police taped numbers on the chests of those arrested, took their pictures and had them viewed by undercover officers. By the end of the operation, police made only 24 felony and two misdemeanor arrests … which strongly suggests there was no probable cause to seize those who were arrested.[71]

I personally witnessed police conducting a raid on an apartment building in Miami in which everyone coming out or going into the apartment building was made to lie down and turn their pockets inside out at gunpoint.

The same military-style hyperaggressive policing so characteristic of the drugs war—as it was waged in the inner city—reappears in New York's "stop and frisk" campaign. In *Floyd v. New York*, Judge Sheindlin found that police engaged in a pattern and practice of routinely and systemically stopping Black and brown New Yorkers without reasonable suspicion.[72]

Ferguson is another example. The Department of Justice found that police officers systemically violated the rights of Black citizens in Ferguson. "Our investigation showed that Ferguson police officers routinely violate the Fourth Amendment in stopping people without reasonable suspicion, arresting them without probable cause. One case will serve as an example.

In 2012 a 32-year-old African American man sat in his car cooling off after playing basketball in a Ferguson public park. An officer pulled up behind the man's car blocking him in, and demanded the man's social security number and identification. Without any cause, the officer accused the man of being a pedophile referring to the presence of children in the park … the officer also asked to search the man's car. The man objected citing his constitutional rights. In response the officer arrested the man, reportedly at gunpoint, charging him with eight violations of Ferguson's municipal code.[73]

The report went on to note that the program cynically exploited the Black community like an ATM.[74]

Yet another example is the City of Baltimore, which officially adopted zero-tolerance policing in 2000. By 2005, the number of arrests jumped to over 100,000, approximately 76,500 of which were warrantless. Overwhelmingly, these arrests were concentrated in the inner city. The Office of the State's Attorney took issue with these mass arrests for minor crimes and did not file charges in approximately one-third of the cases that originated with warrantless arrests. Through this mechanism, police officers arrest individuals, put them through the booking process, detain them in cramped, dirty cells, and eventually release them from central booking. They are not formally charged and do not see a judge. One journalist observer refers to this as "catch and release."[75]

These practices of stopping, frisking, and arresting Blacks in the inner city without probable cause has produced a maddening dualism.

The Kerner Commission prophecy that we were becoming two Americas has come true. In one America, driving with a broken tail light means a possible ticket; in another America, the America of Philandro Castile, it may mean a fatal encounter with police. In one America, jogging in your own neighborhood risks running into and possibly having to run from a stray dog. In the America of Ahmaud Arbery, it risks being perceived as a fleeing felon and shot by a white wannabe vigilante. In one America, jaywalking, while a crime on the books, has been decriminalized for the mostly white populations of the suburbs, but in the America of Michael Brown, merely jaywalking subjects you to confrontation and possibly being shot by police.

There are two Americas here—one America in which people are treated like citizens, the America of us, and one in which they are treated like people without rights (at least not 4th Amendment rights), the America of them. But the dichotomy is no longer captured by a dividing line between Blacks and whites. The line between the ghetto and the suburbs has replaced the color line. Whether one is treated as a second-class citizen is no longer a matter of how much melanin is in one's skin, but more so the zip code one lives in.[76].

Race has become a spectrum. Blackness may mean one thing for those who have made it out of the ghetto, an Obama, a Kamala Harris, even a doctor or lawyer or Ph.D. But for those in the ghetto, the significance of being Black in that context means something very different. I am reminded of Commissioner Kelly's remarks that "We want these kids to know that we are on them from the time they leave the house." The constant targeting of Blacks in the ghetto—for surveillance, for stops, for arrest—creates a sense not merely that everything you do, from walking, to driving, to sitting on the steps, is suspect, but that *your identity itself is suspect*. Blacks in the inner city have been criminalized.

When we combine this with the fact that there are currently 465,000 Blacks in prison, 877,000 on probation and 280,000 on parole (as of 2018), the pervasiveness of this as a great stigma flows from this. The stigma, while directed at Blacks in the ghetto, transcends its boundaries. Why in the midst of the twenty-first century are Blacks still facing massive discrimination in housing when they apply for a loan? Why are Blacks with the same education systemically at a disadvantage with their counterparts? Incarceration *due to the drug war* and its companion racial projects becomes, like the Black codes, "practically a brand upon" us—all of us, even if we make it out of the ghetto (as we see in our next chapter). Our nation's drug laws, together with local zero-tolerance programs, though facially neutral, have become the new Black codes.

The Black codes re-enslaved Blacks, both criminalizing them and exploiting their labor in a manner reminiscent of slavery. What is happening here is analogous in many ways.

First, the drug war occurs at the same time as the prison building boom. In addition, cash-strapped cities reap billions in federal funds for police departments who show efficiency in fighting drug crimes, a metric often measured by the number of stops or arrests. Even more important, politicians reap great political capital for leading these so-called wars against drugs and crime. But more important than any of this is that criminalizing masses of Black people perpetuates a presumption. Blacks are prone to crime, or violence, or deviance, or all of the above. There is a feedback loop here. The more the presumption is reinforced, the more Blacks will be arrested and jailed. Conversely, the fact that whites are overwhelmingly absent among the ranks of those seen spread-eagled over the police car or walking in handcuffs and leg irons perpetuates a counter-presumption of white innocence or moral superiority. Dubois talked about the "wages of whiteness." Does not the criminalization in the twenty-first century of massively disproportionate numbers of blacks continue to pay whites a similar kind of wage?

Notes

1   W. E. B. Dubois, *Black Reconstruction in America: Toward a History of the Part of Which Black Folk Played in the Attempt to Reconstruct Democracy in*

America (1860–1880) (New Brunswick, NJ and London: Transaction Publishers, 2013), 18.

2   Dubois, *Black Reconstruction in America*, 150.

3   Ibid., vi.

4   Ibid., 155.

5   https://contemporarybeacon.com/about/ Contemporary Beacon. Last visited January 10, 2021.

6   W. E. B. Dubois, *Black Reconstruction in America*, 18.

7   Ibid., 174.

8   Ibid., vi.

9   Ibid., 153.

10 Douglas A. Blackmon, *Slavery by Another Name: The Re-Enslavement of Black Americans from the Civil War to World War II* (New York: Doubleday, 2008).

11 Kathy Roberts Forde and Bryan Bowman, *The Conversation: Exploiting Black Labor after the Abolition of Slavery, February 6, 2017*, https://theconversation.com/exploiting-black-labor-after-the-abolition-of-slavery-72482.

12 Louis Filler, *The President in the 20th Century: The Presidency in Crisis* (Englewood Cliffs, NJ: Jerome S. Ozer, 1990), 57.

13 Robert Perkinson, *Texas Tough: The Rise of America's Prison Empire* (New York: Picador, 2010).

14 Rudolph Joseph, *Legalizing Marijuana: Drug Policy Reform and Prohibition Politics* (Westport, CT: Praeger, 2008), 21.

15 Murray Edelman, *The Symbolic Uses of Politics* (Urbana, IL: University of Illinois Press), Chap. 6.

16 Steven Belenko, Cassia Spohn, *Drugs, Crime and Justice* (Thousand Oaks, CA: Sage, 2015).

17 Kenneth B. Nunn, "Race, Crime, and the Pool of Surplus Criminality: Or Why the 'war on Drugs' was a War on Blacks," *Journal of Gender, Race, and Justice* 6, no. 6 (2002), 381.

18 Matthew Desmond and Mustafa Embirbayer, *Racial Domination, Racial Progress: The Sociology of Race* (New York: McGraw-Hill, 2009).

19 Alexander, Michelle. *The New Jim Crow* (The New Press. Kindle Edition), 6.

20 Susan Schmidt and Tom Kenworthy, "Bias' Death, Autopsy Reveals: Dose Said to Trigger Heart Failure; Criminal Inquiry to Be Pressed," *The Washington Post*, June 25, 1986.

21 Dominick Streatfeild, *Cocaine: An Unauthorized Biography* (New York: St. Martin's Press, 2001), 297.

22   Streatfeild, *Cocaine.*

23   Theresa Runsteedtler, "Racial Bias: The Black Athlete, Reagan's War on Drugs and Big-Time Sports Reform," *American Studies* 55, no. 3 (2015) 98–117.

24   Bill Wood, "The Cocaine Related Death of Basketball Star Len Bias Should ...", *UPI Archives*, June 26, 1986.

25   Stanley Cohen, *Folk Devils and Moral Panics: the Creation of the Mods and Rockers* (New York, London: Routledge, 1972), 9.

26   Streatfeild, *Cocaine*, 297.

27   Clarence Lusane and Dennis Desmond, *Pipe Dream Blues: Racism and the War on Drugs* (Boston, MA: South End Press, 1991).

28   Streatfeild, *Cocaine*, 303.

29   Jason A. Gillmer, "*United States v. Clary*: Equal Protection and the Crack Statute," *American University Law Review* 45, no. 2 (1995) 497.

30   132 Cong. Rec. 7637 (daily ed. June 17, 1986) (statement of Sen. Lawton Chiles). See also "16-Year-Old Confesses to Killing His Mother," *New York Times*, May 5, 1986, http://www.nytimes.com/1986/05/05/nyregion/16-year-old-confesses-to-killing-his-mother.html ("A [sixteen]-year-old boy walked into a Manhattan police station yesterday morning and confessed to having stabbed his mother to death two days earlier, apparently in a fight over his use of cocaine.").

31   Campaign Against Drug Abuse, Ronald Reagan, September 14, 1986, from PBS American Experience https://www.pbs.org/wgbh/americanexperience/features/reagan-drug-campaign/.

32   Cracks in the System: 20 Years of the Unjust Federal Crack Cocaine Law (American Civil Liberties Union), October 2006.

33   Eric E. Sterling, U.S. Drug Policy, Institute of Policy Studies, November 1, 1999. https://ips-dc.org/us_drug_policy/.

34   Kenneth B. Nunn, "Race, Crime and the Pool of Surplus Criminality."

35   Aisha Harris, "We Were Just Baby Boys," *New York Times*, May 30, 2019; *When They See Us*, Directed by Ava DuVernay (2019); see also D. Marvin Jones, *Race, Sex, and Suspicion: The Myth of the Black Male* (London: Bloomsbury Academic, 2005), 41–54.

36   See Jay Maeder, "Wild Thing Turning Out Koch, Spring 1989," *Daily News*, 35, December 4, 2001.

      "WILDING," the game was called. That meant running in packs and beating up everyone in sight.

      ...

Quickly jailed, the punks whooped and hooted and swaggered and strutted and loudly sang a street corner hit called "Wild Thing"—That's what happen when bodies start slappin'/Doing' the wild thing … I get paid to do that wild thing.

Michael Welch, Erica A. Price, and Nana Yankey, "Moral Panic over Youth Violence: Wilding and the Manufacture of Menace in the Media," *Youth and Society* 34, no. 1 (September 2002) 3–30.

Wilding had been added to a growing roster of crimes associated with urban culture, along with mugging, looting, gang banging, drive-by shootings, and carjacking. Moreover, those buzz words generally are racially biased because they are introduced to describe Black (and Latino) lawbreakers more so than white offenders.

37 John Dilulio, "The Coming of the Super-Predators," *The Washington Examiner*, November 27, 1995.

38 John Dilulio, *Body Count* (New York: Simon & Schuster, 1996), 21.

39 Dilulio, *Body Count*, 16.

40 Dilulio, "The Coming of the Super-Predators."

41 User Clip: Hillary Clinton on "super predators" in 1996, C-Span, Remarks by Hillary Clinton at Keene State College in New Hampshire on January 28, 1996, https://www.c-span.org/video/?c4582473/user-clip-hillary-clinton-superpredators-1996.

42 J. A. Scully, "Examining and Dismantling the School-to-Prison Pipeline: Strategies for a Better Future," *Arkansas Law Review* 68 (2016) 966.

43 Ranya Shannon, "3 Ways the 1994 Crime Bill Continues to Hurt Communities of Color," Center for American Progress, May 10, 2019.

44 Shannon, "3 Ways."

45 See Kenneth Nunn, "Race, Crime, and the Pool of Surplus Criminality"; A. James Fisher and Jim Fisher, *SWAT Madness and Militarization of the American Police: A National Dilemma* (Santa Barbara, CA: ABC-CLIO, 2010).

46 Fox Butterfield, "Study Finds Big Increase in Black Men as Inmates since 1980," *New York Times*, August 28, 2002.

47 Human Rights Watch U.S.: Drug Arrests Skewed by Race, March 2, 2009 https://www.hrw.org/report/2009/03/02/decades-disparity/drug-arrests-and-race-united-states.

48 Human Rights Watch, *Decades of Disparity: Drug Arrests and Race in the United States* (New York: Human Rights Watch, 2009), https://www.hrw.org/sites/default/files/reports/us0309web_1.pdf.

49   Human Rights Watch, *Targeting Blacks: Drug Law Enforcement and Race in the Unites States* (New York: Human Rights Watch, 2008), 3.

50   Since 2000 Dr. Ivory Tolson states that the ratio has been reversed. He states that there are 1.4 million Black men in college right now. He goes on to say, what's transpired since then is there's been more than a 100 percent increase in the number of Black men in college. He does not actually dispute the figures for the year 2000.

51   https://www.drugpolicyfacts.org/chapter/race_prison.

52   Elijah Anderson, *Code of the Street: Decency, Violence, and the Moral Life of the Inner City* (New York: W. W. Norton, 1999).

53   Michael Tonry, *Race and the War on Drugs*, University of Chicago Legal Forum, volume 1994, Issue 1. See also Nunn, "Race, Crime and the Pool of Surplus Criminality": "Whether the issue is the drug war, street crime, welfare fraud, or sexual violence, African Americans will be targeted as the likely cause of the problem," 5.

54   Dylan Tureff, "Securing White Votes by Incarcerating Black Bodies: The Criminalization of Blackness and the Perpetuation of Moral Panic in the American Carceral State," *Georgetown Public Policy Review*.
     http://www.gpprspring.com/securing-white-votes-by-incarcerating-black-bodies-tureff.

55   While recognizing the hysteria too often focused on disadvantaged minorities Tonry offers a race neutral explanation rooted in social disorganization of Black communities, less stable social networks which lead Blacks to engage in activities out of doors—like drug selling—that whites engage in indoors.

     First, more of the routine activities of life, including retail drug-dealing, occur on the streets and alleys in poor neighborhoods. In working-class and middle-class neighborhoods, many activities including drug deals are likelier to occur indoors. This difference means that it is much easier for police to find dealers from whom to make an undercover buy in a disadvantaged urban neighborhood than elsewhere. Second, because of social disorganization in poor urban minority neighborhoods, it is easier for undercover narcotics officers to penetrate networks of friends and acquaintances than in more stable and closely knit working-class and middle-class neighborhoods. The stranger buying drugs on the urban street corner or in an alley is commonplace

     ...

A stranger trying to buy drugs in the working-class Highland Park neighborhood around the Ford plant in St. Paul, Minnesota, or in Highland Park, Illinois, a middle-class suburb of Chicago, is likely to have much less success. Drugs are used and sold in both places, but seldom in the streets and not to strangers.

Michael Tonry's observations are obviously true but have little to do with why Blacks are so disproportionately imprisoned. Even when whites are caught, their crimes are seen as individual frailty where Black offenders are seen as "typical" of Black people.

56 Human Rights Watch, *Race, Drugs and Law Enforcement in the United States* (New York: Human Rights Watch, 2019).

     https://www.hrw.org/news/2009/06/19/race-drugs-and-law-enforcement-united-states (last visited 6/24/2022.

57 George Breitman, *Malcolm X Speaks: Selected Speeches and Statements* (New York: Grove Weidenfeld, 1990).

58 Between 1960 and 1969 violent crime increased from 288,640 violent crimes in 1960 to 1,932,000 in 1992. United States Crime Rates 1960–2019. https://www.disastercenter.com/crime/uscrime.htm.

59 Lauren-Brooke Eisen and Oliver Roeder, "America's Faulty Perception of Crime Rates," *The Huffington Post* (March 16, 2015).

60 Edward C. Banfield, *The Unheavenly City Revisited* (Boston, MA: Little, Brown & Company, 1968).

61 392 U.S. 1 (1968), 121.

62 Ibid.

63 *Illinois v. Wardlow*, 528 U.S. 119 (2000), 124.

64 New York City Police Department, 1994, "Getting Guns Off the Streets of New York," Police Strategy No 1. New York: New York City Police Department.

65 Ibid.

66 D. Marvin Jones, *Dangerous Spaces: Beyond the Racial Profile* (New York: Praeger, 2016), 67. See also Peter K. Manning, *Theorizing Policing: The Drama and Myth of Crime Control* (Thousand Oaks, CA: Sage, 2001), 322.

67 Police Practices and Civil Rights in New York City: A Report of the United States Civil Rights Commission (Washington, D.C.: United States Civil Rights Commission, August 2000).

68 Matthew Lippman, *Law and Society* (Thousand Oaks, CA: Sage, 2020).

69 CCR Reports: Racial Disparity in NYPD Stop and Frisks, Executive Summary, Last modified January 11, 2010. www.ccrjustice.org/.../ccr-reports-racial-disparity-nypd-stop-and-frisks.

70 *Floyd v. New York* 283 F.R.D. 153, 165 (2013); see also Ta-Nahesi Coates, "Ending Michael Bloomberg's Racist Profiling Campaign," *The Atlantic* (August 12, 2013).

71 Kenneth Nunn, "Race, Crime and the Pool of Surplus Criminality."

72 *Floyd v. New York.*

73 Investigation of the Ferguson Police Department, United States Department of Justice, March 4, 2015, p. 3.

74 Stephen Dere, Chick Raasch, and Jeremy Kohler, "DOJ finds Ferguson targeted African Americans, used courts mainly to increase Revenue," *The Times and Democrat* (March 5, 2015).

75 Edward Dickerson, "Where Murderers Reign, It's Catch and Release for Low-Level Crimes," Courthouse News Service, April 12, 2021.

76 See D. Marvin Jones, *Fear of a Hip-Hop Planet: America's New Dilemma* (New York: Praeger, 2013); Jones, *Dangerous Spaces.*

5

Strangers in Paradise: The Presumption in White Spaces

And then—the veil. It drops as drops the night on southern seas—vast, sudden, unanswering. There is Hate behind it, and Cruelty and Tears. As one peers through its intricate, unfathomable pattern of ancient, old, old design, one sees blood and guilt and misunderstanding. And yet it hangs there, this Veil, between Then and Now, between Pale and Colored and Black and White—between You and Me. Surely it is a thought-thing, tenuous, intangible; yet just as surely is it true and terrible and not in our little day may you and I lift it.[1]

Figure 5.1 Lunch Counter protest in North Carolina.

Source: Bettmann/Getty Images.

So, what is the veil, then? As Michael Homi asks, "Is it a barrier or a defense, a curse or a blessing? Is it a flimsy and rent fabric, or a rigid, imprisoning cage? Is it a mark we wear or a role we play? Is it the demands we make for our freedom or the restriction of our freedom brought about by the racial policy of the state?"[2] Stanley Brodwin equated the color line with the Dubosian notion of the veil—with the customs, practices, and legal statutes that enforced racial caste.

There were separate hospitals, separate swimming pools, and even separate brothels in New Orleans for Blacks and whites. Courts maintained separate Bibles for white and Black witnesses to kiss. Restaurants had separate plates for Blacks and whites. Blacks could ride on the same bus as whites but famously had to sit in the back. It was not all separate, of course; Black maids could ride in the same car as their mistresses. In a formal sense these were separate societies. But the social meaning of this color line, as it was called, was that Blacks had to know their place and stay in it. The color line is popularly associated with the notion of "separation of the races." But Blacks worked as maids, butlers, and nannies in intimate contact with whites. Coming down "in apostolic secession from slavery,"[3] the color line enforced racial hierarchy, not separation.

Dubois believed the veil could not be lifted. He describes it as an immovable wall.

> The shades of the prison-house closed round about us all: walls strait and stubborn to the whitest, but relentlessly narrow, tall, and unscalable to sons of night who must plod darkly on in resignation, or beat unavailing palms against the stone, or steadily, half hopelessly, watch the streak of blue above.[4]

But a "shift" would occur which caused this "sturdy structure" of oppression to tremble. Howard Winant writes:

> Starting after World War II and culminating in the 1960s, there was a global shift, a "break," in the worldwide racial system that had endured for centuries. The shift occurred because many challenges to the old forms of racial hierarchy converged after the war: anticolonialism, antiapartheid, worldwide revulsion at fascism.[5]

Howard Winant is talking about a shift created by political movements. But there was another shift created by changes in the way "race" was understood.

A paradigm shift. This shift began a decade earlier. Segregation rested in part on a notion that racial inferiority was a result of nature, not nurture. Thus, in context, "Blacks were poor ... because of their natural inferiority."[6] This racist premise was confirmed in the minds of whites by the inferior social conditions that defined Black life.

> The degradation into which the African America had fallen since his release from bondage ... was viewed as continuing proof of black inferiority ... Other minorities had coped with ignorance and poverty and managed to prevail. The continuing derelict state of colored people in America, the story-book land of opportunity, had to be their own fault.[7]

If Blacks were poorly educated and poorly paid, and living in slums, the fault was in their bloodline. This was circular, but accepted as fact.

The first crack in the foundation of segregation occurred here among the intellectual elite, as some began to question the significance of race. Anthropologists like Franz Boas in 1926, writing in *Psychological Review*,[8] sociologists like John Dollard in his famous study *Caste and Class in A Southern Town*,[9] Gunnar Myrdal in *An American Dilemma*,[10] and others argued that "so-called natural" differences between the races were really environmental. By the 1950s, these arguments were widely accepted as true among the academic elite. Another reason was World War II. The United States had fought a war against racism and Nazi ideology—and Blacks who had bled alongside whites in the struggle were less willing, as former soldiers, to accept the same degradation as before. Finally, there was the politics of the Cold War. The United States was engaged in a contest with Russia for the hearts and minds of people in the Third World in both Africa and Asia.

The convergence of these historical forces produced *Brown*.[11] In *Brown v. Board of Education*, the Supreme Court famously ordered the desegregation of public schools with all deliberate speed.[12] With this decision over sixty years ago, the Court heralded a new era of racial politics, which Derrick Bell called the Second Reconstruction.

> During two brief moments of history the United States experienced major social movements which, at their core, expressed a powerful vision of multicultural democracy and human equality. The first was developed before the seminal conflict in American history, the Civil War (1861–65),

and came to fruition in the twelve-year period of reunion, reconstruction and racial readjustment which followed (1865–77). Almost a century later, a "Second Reconstruction" occurred. Like the former period, the Second Reconstruction was a series of massive confrontations concerning the status of the African American and other national minorities.[13]

This transformation of racial politics was midwifed as well by civil rights battles fought at lunch counters and bus terminals. "The Second Reconstruction actually began in earnest on the afternoon of 1 February, 1960. Four young Black students from North Carolina Agricultural and Technical College, Joseph McNeil, David Richmond, Franklin McCain and Izzell Blair, sat at a drugstore lunch counter in the 'whites only' section."[14] By 1968, the federal courts and Congress struck down laws which permitted or required segregation, sweeping aside the massive resistance of the Southern politicians. The dismantling of laws which required or permitted segregation had dramatic sociological effects. Between 1970 and 1995, 7 million Blacks moved out of the inner city to the suburbs.[15] This late-twentieth-century great migration occurred about the same time that globalism, technological change, and the federal disinvestment in the ghetto also took place.

> Disaster struck more than four decades ago in the form of an American polity's decision to go global, restructuring the nature of work inside the country's traditional borders and outsourcing millions of American jobs abroad. ... Work has disappeared, and with its disappearance, hope became a lottery ticket.[16]

The inner cities took on the appearance of war-torn areas with burned out houses, others with plywood sheets for eyes, and still others with abandoned cars in their yards. The inner city, in its increasing social isolation, became a place where failure in public schools was normalized and violence was so rampant one urban poet called it "concrete Vietnam." The conditions of this post-industrial ghetto drew some to compare them to Third World countries within the United States.

For the talented tenth who were able to make it out of the ghetto, they crossed a line much like that crossed by other immigrants into the United States; they were in another country. As Richard Wright says in *Twelve Million*

Black Voices (1941), "Water flows because of gravity. People flow because of symbols and hope."

This hope that the suburbs represented a higher level of dignity and empowerment is reflected in the classic late-'70s television show about a Black businessman who becomes successful enough to move from Queens to a deluxe apartment in Manhattan's upper East Side, *The Jeffersons*. The show's theme song is aptly named "Movin' On Up." "Beans don't burn in the kitchen, fish don't burn on the grill, it took a whole lot of tryin' but we finally made it up that hill." In *The Wire*, McNulty, a Baltimore police detective, takes Bubbles, his C.I., and a homeless resident of the ghetto to his home in the suburbs. Bubbles says "there is a thin line between heaven and here."[17] This image of the suburbs as heaven and the ghetto as the other place reflects a powerful narrative of ascent[18] that drove the move of the talented tenth out of the inner city.

In the minds of the newcomers to suburbs, where there were beautiful homes with tree-lined streets: they had moved not merely a physical distance, but a moral distance, elevating them from second-class to first-class citizens. Moreover, many of us believed that the civil rights gains that propelled the talented tenth and opened the door to suburban homes and jobs in corporate America were permanent gains.

Their hope, my hope, was naïve. History is not always linear. As William Faulkner wrote, "The past is never dead. It's not even past."

> In two historic instances, Negro Americans have been beneficiaries—as well as victims—of the national compulsion to level or blur distinctions. The first leveling ended the legal status of slavery, the second the legal system of segregation. Both abolitions left the beneficiaries still suffering under handicaps inflicted by the system abolished.[19]

In 1877, during the first Reconstruction, in an effort to win a disputed election, the Northern Republicans agreed to remove Northern troops from the South in exchange for the Democrats' acquiescence in a Southern election. After the Hayes-Tilden compromise in the nineteenth century came an era of redemption in which the South used the law to create "Segregation." Since at least 1988, we have seen a similar pattern of retreat and abandonment on the part of the federal government for dismantling racial caste.

The modus operandi of the Jim Crow era was overt, official decrees which excluded Blacks from schools and housing. But increasingly today, the social isolation of Blacks, whether in schools or housing, is carried forward by private action.

Increasingly in the midst of an era of formal equal opportunity, many whites prefer to live in neighborhoods where there are few or no Blacks. The Supreme Court has immunized decisions made by "private actors" under the doctrine of state action: official discrimination of Blacks, whether in housing or schools, requires one to identify discrete decisions made by identifiable government officials with discriminatory intent. Neither the social phenomenon of white flight nor the individual choice to move into or out of a neighborhood because of race is subject to court legal or legislative intervention. Laissez faire!

At the same time, "Even when Black households try to cross color boundaries, they are not always met with open arms: Studies have shown that white people prefer to live in communities where there are fewer Black people, regardless of their income."[20] These choices are enabled by an increasing wealth gap. "The median white family held 13 times as much net wealth as the median Black family in 2013 … and 10 times as much wealth as the median Latino family. Just a decade earlier, the disparity was 7 to 1 for Black families."[21]

The result of this dynamic interplay is a plethora of schools and neighborhoods which are racially homogenous—"white." Increasingly, whites "suspect" that the Blacks entering these enclaves are "out of place", a designation which carries with it an indicia of suspicion. Thus a Black shopper entering a department store in one of these neighborhoods using a credit card he or she legitimately owns may be suspected of credit card fraud; Black youths driving an expensive car in one of these neighborhoods may be suspected of having stolen the car. Driving this suspicion is the narrative that these "out of place" Blacks are in essence "trespassers." Of course these unfortunate Blacks have typically engaged in no conduct which would constitute trespass in a legal sense. This is not necessary: their real crime seems to be one of "racial trespass."

There is a resurgence of a "segregationist" mentality here.[22] This reflects the deeper meaning of the veil. As Stephanie Shaw writes, "To find the metaphor we should think about the veil that is literally a caul—the membrane (a 'skin') that encloses a fetus in the womb, part of which still covers the head of some babies at birth."[23] The veil represents a mask; through the veil whites could not see the humanity of Blacks. It is the ideology of segregation which constitutes the veil. We are experiencing a Gramscian moment, when, although the formal structure of segregation has been dismantled, the ideology or mentality of segregation—the ghost of segregation—still haunts us in the post-civil rights era of the twenty-first century.

Let Us Consider the Story of Henry Louis Gates Jr

In his book, *Colored People*,[24] Henry Louis Gates notes he grew up in Miner's County in Piedmont, West Virginia. His father worked in a paper mill and his mother cleaned houses.

But Gates's brilliance and hard work propelled him beyond Piedmont, over the mountains, to become the Alphonse Fletcher University Professor at Harvard. In sports there are athletes who, because of their great fame, become powerful personalities: a LeBron James, Tiger Woods, Venus Williams. They transcend the game. Gates did that as a teacher and historian, becoming by 2009 someone many held as the leading African American intellectual in the United States. Commensurate with his success, Gates lived on Ware Street two blocks from Harvard Square in an expensive, exclusive area of town.

On July 16, 2009, he returned from China by taxi-cab and found his front door jammed. Gates and his driver pushed against the door to open it. Enter Lucia Whalen.

> 911 Call Dispatcher: Tell me exactly what happened. Caller [Ms. Whalen]: Umm, I don't know what's happening. I just have an elder woman, uh, standing here, and she had noticed two gentlemen trying to get in a house at that number, 17 Ware St., and they kind of had to barge in. And they broke the screen door and they finally got in, and when I had looked, I went further, closer to the house a little bit, after the gentlemen were already in the house, I noticed two suitcases, so I'm not sure if these are two individuals who actually work there, I mean who live there.[25]

Notice that Whalen never identifies the men as Black, never claims that she believed this was criminal activity. "I don't know if they live there and just had a hard time with their key."[26]

With this nebulous tip, Sgt. James Crowley responded to the radio run of a possible burglary in progress. Crowley first approached the door and asked Gates to step outside, and Gates refused. Crowley then asked for Gates's ID. As Gates went to retrieve the ID, Crowley boldly entered Gates's house. "In response to Sgt. Crowley's request, Professor Gates turned around to get his Harvard ID and his Massachusetts driver's license. At that moment, to Gates' surprise, Crowley followed Gates into his home."[27] The fourth amendment guards the boundary between a private space in which the citizen has a right to be free and left alone, and public space in which the state is free to investigate crime. The home is at the center of this zone of privacy in fourth-amendment terms. Crowley needed a warrant to enter Gates's home, or at the very least probable cause. Crowley had neither.

What are the grounds for this warrantless intrusion? It is not probable cause, much less exigent circumstances: it is a sense that Gates does not fit into the upscale neighborhood—he is presumptively out of place, incongruent.

Blacks moving to the suburbs' white spaces are in many ways like immigrants moving to a foreign country. This reflects the gulf between the inner city and Greater America. They are allowed to come in, but they are never completely in. Mexicans, for example, stereotyped by Trump as rapists and drug dealers, carry their border with them. They are presumptively criminal. Ossian Sweet was, and the immigrants of the first migration were targeted by these suspicions when they tried to buy houses in white neighborhoods in the north. The fear was that they brought criminal values with them as they migrated to cities like Detroit from the South. In this late-twentieth-century migration, Blacks meet a similar presumption; the ghetto follows them. They may be educated, erudite, and accultured, but they are presumed otherwise. They are culturally alien, citizens of this other country that the ghetto represents. This is true regardless of whether they ever lived in the ghetto or how long it has been since they resided in the suburbs.

According to Gates, he then gave Crowley both his driver's license and his Harvard identification card. Objectively this was enough. But Crowley radioed the dispatcher he was "up with a guy who says he resides here but uncooperative." Animated by unanchored suspicions, Crowley called for back-up and the Harvard police.

Crowley "Keep the cars coming"

Male patrol 1: "Copy"

Crowley: "Can you send the Harvard police this way."

Crowley then insisted that Gates step outside. And when he did, Crowley said, "thank you for honoring my request. You are under arrest." Crowley arrested Gates on a charge of disorderly conduct.[28] To sustain a charge of disorderly conduct, there must be some conduct which creates a threat of violence or public disruption.[29]

But Crowley never articulates any concern for violence or threat of violence. Crowley states, "Gates began to yell over my spoken words, accusing me of being a racist police officer." And when Crowley asked Gates to step outside, Gates, according to Crowley, replied "[Y]a, I'll speak to your mama outside."[30] In this characterization of Gates's speech Crowley paints Gates as a Sambo-like character—or a ghetto-like character—who cannot speak proper English. In defending Crowley, Officer Justin Barrett makes explicit the Sambo narrative that Crowley deployed: he explicitly refers to Gates to as a "banana-eating jungle monkey."[31]

But Gates was charged with disorderly conduct. This makes no sense. Disorderly conduct is a crime that can only be committed in a public place. One cannot commit the crime of disorderly conduct in a private home. Yet the conversation referred to by Crowley occurred inside his private home. The charge of disorderly conduct was pretextual: Gates was arrested for disrespecting Crowley. One writer calls this "contempt of cop."

> "Contempt of cop," as it's sometimes called, isn't a crime. Or at least it shouldn't be. It may be impolite, but mouthing off to police is protected speech, all the more so if your anger and insults are related to a perceived violation of your rights. The "disorderly conduct" charge for which Gates was arrested was intended to prevent riots, not to prevent cops from enduring insults. Crowley is owed an apology for being portrayed as a racist, but he ought to be disciplined for making a wrongful arrest.[32]

This analysis is correct with respect to the pretextual nature of Gates's arrest, but it misses the racial subtext. Gates did not violate the norms of legal order but the norms of racial order, in Crowley's mind.

Sambo often appeared with big eyes and his mouth open showing fear. Interestingly, the media famously portrayed Gates in handcuffs with his mouth open going to jail as a "Sambo figure." This mirrored Justin Barrett's portrayal of Gates as a "banana-eating monkey."

Monster: Horror in Stanford

In the film *Get Out*,[33] Chris, an innocent Black youth, is lured by his girlfriend Rose Armitage to the countryside to meet her parents. It is symbolically a different world, a world of affluence, privilege, and demographic homogeneity—it is virtually all white. The traditional Hollywood horror films are situated in a place remote from civilization, following the hero's journey through a jungle or, in the case of the hood-horror films, the urban ghetto. But here in the Afro-centric horror film, the journey through the jungle has been replaced with a journey to a place remote from the urban ethos and from Black people. The idyllic pastoral setting, however, is a smokescreen hiding an insidious conspiracy taking place behind the curtain of tranquility, rural charm, and respectability. The Armitages are really monsters, in a moral sense. They plan to drug Chris, take out his brain, and replace it with the brain of an aging white man.

The unsuspecting Chris has tea with Rose's mother, a psychiatrist, who talks to him about his smoking addiction. As she talks, the mother stirs her tea with a silver spoon. The silver spoon symbolizes white privilege.[34] She uses it ironically as a controlling device. The rattle of the spoon against the porcelain cup hypnotizes Chris and puts him under. Chris sinks into the chair, falling into "the sunken place." The "sunken place" represents the social predicament of Blacks, symbolized by powerlessness. Chris wakes up just in time to escape.

In many ways, *Get Out*, intended as far-fetched fantasy, is a metaphor for a real-life horror which occurred in Sanford, Florida.

Trayvon Martin was an "A or B student who majored in cheerfulness," said his English teacher, Michelle Kypriss, of Dr. Michael M. Krop Senior High School in Miami.[35]

Trayvon lived with his mother in Miami Gardens. Miami Gardens was created in 2003 as a suburban enclave for middle-class Blacks displaced by urban renewal.[36] But despite its suburban location, the city's socio-economic characteristics are comparable to those of an inner-city neighborhood: 73.3 percent of the city is Black, 25 percent Hispanic.[37] The per capita income is about $17,000. The unemployment rate in 2014 was about 11 percent.[38] The violent crime rate for Miami Gardens in 2016 was higher than the national violent crime rate average by 68 percent.[39] Trayvon was a still innocent but at-risk teenager who had been suspended from school when officials found an empty plastic baggie in his book bag that contained traces of marijuana.[40]

On February 21, Trayvon left on a Greyhound bus for a five-hour ride to Orlando,[41] the closest stop to Sanford, Florida. Trayvon was going to visit his father at the Retreat on Twin Lakes, a 260-unit gated community. Orlando was the closest stop. Tracy Martin would later say he invited his son Trayvon to his home "to disconnect and get his priorities straight."[42]

The Retreat at Twin Lakes is a socio-economically different world from Miami Gardens. In some ways it is as much a contrast to the Miami Gardens "ghetto" as the fictional community of the Armitages contrasted with Chris Washington's urban neighborhood. While Miami Gardens is 98 percent populated by people of color, the Retreat is 90 percent white. As both a predominantly white and gated community, the Retreat is precisely the kind of community caricatured by Rich Benjamin as "Whiteopia."[43]

The act of building walled communities in the suburbs is popularly understood as something done to enhance security. But the building of boundaries, particularly the building of walled fortress communities in the suburbs, is a political act as well; the rise of these gated communities coincidentally occurred as suburbs were potentially becoming more racially (and culturally) diverse. Gated communities sky-rocketed between 1970 and 1996, when Blacks began their flight from the inner city.[44]

At the same time, in the speeches of politicians like Nixon and later Reagan, Black people were coded as welfare queens, drug dealers, and criminals.[45] Television and film used a similar coding.

The forting up of these communities—the walls, security cameras, guards, and racial homogeneity—reflect a response to the influx of Blacks, coded as harbingers of violence, crime, and social malaise. For the whites who live behind the gated community walls, security and whiteness are intertwined. Fear of crime and fear of cultural contamination by Blacks have been fused.

The people who move here are united by their fears. As Richard Benjamin writes, "Gated communities churn a vicious cycle by attracting like-minded residents who seek shelter from outsiders and whose physical seclusion then worsens paranoid groupthink against outsiders."[46] The seclusion and group think are reminiscent of the white enclave in *Get Out*.

At the time Trayvon was visiting, the anxiety level on the surface, about crime, was particularly high. From January 1, 2011, to February 26, 2012, police were called to the Retreat 402 times.[47] The community had experienced eight burglaries, nine thefts, and a shooting.[48] Real crime, of course. But the large disparity between the reported and actual crimes has led many to speculate that many of the calls were false alarms. Zimmerman, the neighborhood watch captain, had a history of reporting sightings of Blacks as suspicious activity.

> On April 22, 2011, Zimmerman called to report a black male about "7–9" years old, four feet tall, with a "skinny build" and short black hair. There is no indication in the police report of the reason for Zimmerman's suspicion of the boy.
>
> ...
>
> And on Oct. 1 he reported two black male suspects "20–30" years old, in a white Chevrolet Impala. He told police he did "not recognize" the men or their vehicle and that he was concerned because of the recent burglaries.[49]

Trayvon Martin was innocent—as innocent as Chris Washington in *Get Out*—of the dangers lurking in the countryside. He thought he was going to an idyllic setting of peace and relaxation. In fact, he was crossing into "Whiteopia."

On the fateful night of his encounter, Tracy, Trayvon's father, had left for dinner with his fiancée Brandy Green. Trayvon stayed home playing video games with Green's son.[50]

After his father left, Trayvon took a walk to the 7-Eleven to buy Skittles and iced tea.[51] Trayvon wore a hoodie to fend off the rain. Trayvon's teenage face still stares back at us from the surveillance camera photo of the teenager as he buys the candy and the tea. The horror begins when Zimmerman sees him walking back to Brandy Green's house.

Zimmerman: Yeah, a dark hoodie, like a gray hoodie, and either jeans or sweat pants, and white tennis shoes. He's[unintelligible], he was just staring. [0:42]
Dispatcher: OK, he's just walking around the area?
Zimmerman: … looking at all the houses.
Dispatcher: OK …
Zimmerman: Now he's just staring at me.[52]

Of course, as with Henry Louis Gates, Zimmerman never actually sees Trayvon. Trayvon was, in Ellison's words, invisible. The cognitive problem here stems from the fact that race is the ultimate sticky metaphor and that race and crime have become "stuck" together. "Race" quintessentially invokes dichotomies of them and us.

> Race is sticky with respect to all other categories of otherness. In *Tar Baby*, Morrison is focusing on the stickiness between race, class and gender. But the category of criminal is also sticky with respect to race. The racial other is the quintessential other. The criminal is also quintessentially, the other. The two categories, race and criminal, are already close together—stuck together in a sense—in a signifying chain.[53]

In popular culture, "crime" is personified by the urban gangbanger or thug usually dressed in a hoodie and saggy pants. The image of race and the urban gangbanger has been fused. In turn, race, Black men dressed in hoodies, and crime form another link in the signifying chain. Each of these three images now invokes and references each other. The same metaphoric substitution which occurs in our discourse occurred in Zimmerman's mind in his perception of who Trayvon was. He simply conflated an image of the urban gangbanger in his mind with a real person.

Ostensibly Zimmerman suspected Trayvon of looking for homes to burglarize. These suspicions were unanchored. But in the mentality of racial paranoia exhibited by Zimmerman, no criminal conduct is necessary. Trayvon's mere presence, or more specifically, the incongruence of his presence, is presumptively a threat. This harkens back to the case of *Chicago v. Morales*.

In May 1992, the city of Chicago held hearings on youth gangs in the city. Testimony revealed that street gangs are responsible for a variety of criminal activity, including drive-by shootings, drug dealing, and vandalism.

But the philosophy of the city council was that gangs were dangerous populations. Dangerous populations are thought of as toxic quantities that must be efficiently controlled. Famously, they crafted an anti-loitering ordinance which read.

> Whenever a police officer observes a person whom he reasonably believes to be a criminal street gang member loitering in any public place with one or more other persons, he shall order all such persons to disperse and remove themselves from the area. Any person who does not promptly obey such an order is in violation of this section.[54]

The Chicago ordinance explicitly targeted nothing more than innocent activity referred to vaguely as loitering. While occasionally an "adjunct" to illicit behavior, people standing around, or sitting on steps with their friends, is no crime. The point of the ordinance was a shift from policing conduct to status. It was more specifically an explicit attempt to target the status of being or merely appearing to be a gang member. Nonetheless, the 4th Amendment generally requires individualized suspicion. Moreover, the criminal law requires both a criminal act and a guilty person. The individual must engage in conduct. To arrest a person because of mere status or his appearance would violate due process of law.

The City of Chicago justified this status scheme by arguing that the mere presence of these groups in public was a threat. "A large collection of brazen, disorderly, and lawless gang members and hangers on the public ways intimidates residents ... That, in turn, imperils community residents' sense of safety and security, detracts from property values, and can ultimately destabilize entire neighborhoods."[55]

The notion of visible lawlessness assumes that one can identify these dangerous alienated youths by their appearance. There is a race/class subtext here. This ordinance and ordinances like it imposed disproportionate burdens on minorities. "With no criminal conduct to go by, police officers probably used race as a critical factor in judging whether an individual might be a gang member."[56]

Zimmerman borrows this reasoning, substituting appearance as an urban thug for gang member. The urban youth targeted by the Chicago police were visibly lawless because of their dress and attitude. While the Chicago ordinance was merely tacitly racist, Zimmerman's mentality was virtually explicit: in Zimmerman's mind, Black plus hoodie equaled threat. Trayvon was the quintessential outsider. He was an urban savage inside the gates—of Whiteopia—where he did not belong. His presence was seen not merely as a trespass but as a criminal invasion.

So, Zimmerman followed him.

> Dispatcher: He's running? Which way is he running?
> Zimmerman: Down toward the other entrance of the neighborhood.
> Dispatcher: Which entrance is that he is heading towards?
> Zimmerman: Toward the back entrance—Fucking punks. These assholes, they always get away …
> Dispatcher: Are you following him?
> Zimmerman: Yeah.[57]

Underneath the hoodie was an innocent child. We can imagine how his heart raced in terror as he realized he was being followed—stalked by a strange white man. On the phone with his girlfriend, he shared his final moments of fear.

> I asked him how the man looked like. He just told me the man looked "creepy." "Creepy, White. I just told him to run," Rachel told the court, adding that she heard a "hard-breathing man" in the background.[58]

In *Get Out* Chris Washington sinks into a chair and finds himself trapped, in a waking nightmare of powerlessness. This is a metaphor for Trayvon's plight in Sanford. It was if Trayvon had gone into a 7-Eleven to get some Skittles and emerged into a waking nightmare where he was trapped and powerless. This was Trayvon's sunken place.

Zimmerman stalked Trayvon and later shot the unarmed youth in the chest. He nonetheless claimed he was merely "standing his ground."

In criminal law there is a familiar doctrine that one cannot create the conditions of one's own defense. Said another way, self-defense is available only to those who did not initiate the aggression. In addition, traditionally, in public (outside of the home) *one has a duty to retreat* in the face of a threat before resorting to deadly force. Stand-your-ground laws are based on a kind of code, the "code of the West" narrative that a "true man does back down." They eliminate the duty of a person attacked in public to back down. But this right to "stand your ground" assumes that you did not initiate the conflict. Zimmerman had initiated aggression by following, stalking, and seeking to detain/arrest an innocent child.

For the jury to acquit Zimmerman on these facts was an act of jury nullification. I would compare the Sanford jury to the jury in Money, Mississippi, that acquitted two white men in the killing of Emmet Till. Of course, in the midst of the racial fear that permeates our screens, our newspapers, and our jury rooms, it was never Zimmerman who was really on trial. Trayvon was on trial. He was already guilty. The jury made the same claims of knowledge about Trayvon as Zimmerman. Trayvon was guilty not based on any conduct or criminal act. He was a Black man in a hoodie in a white space. His mere presence signified "visible lawlessness" and "incipient crime."

Trayvon was not only presumed guilty; he was presumed to be disposable. These two presumptions combined to create a "sunken place" in our criminal justice regime. The travesty of justice which occurred in Sanford flows from this.

"A Mosaic of White Spaces"

The city's public spaces, workplaces, and neighborhoods may now be conceptualized essentially as a mosaic of white spaces, black spaces, and cosmopolitan spaces (racially diverse islands of civility) that may be in various stages of flux, from white to black or from black to white ... Accordingly, the racially mixed urban space, a version of which I have referred to elsewhere as "the cosmopolitan canopy," exists as a diverse island of civility, located in a virtual sea of racial segregation.[59]

In his book *The Great Good Place*,[60] Ray Oldenburg argues that the "third place" is critical to civil society for democracy. Home is the first place. Work is the second place. Churches, parks, coffeehouses, and bars are the third place. These third places are formally public, inviting, and appear accessible to all. But while physically open, access to these spaces is ideologically constrained.

The source of these ideological constraints can be traced back to segregation. The notion was that race was a natural line of demarcation between communities. This notion was colorfully expressed by Florida

Supreme Court Justice William Glenn Terrell, in the of *Virgil Hawkins v. State Board of Control*. In this case Virgil Hawkins, a Black man, was expressly denied admission to Florida State University law school because of his race. Denying there was any violation of equal protection the court stated:

> I might venture to point out in this connection that segregation is not a new philosophy generated by the states that practice it. It is and has always been the unvarying law of the animal kingdom. The dove and the quail, the turkey and the turkey buzzard, the chicken and the guinea, it matters not where they are found, are segregated; ... the fish in the sea segregate into "schools" of their kind; when the goose and duck arise from the Canadian marshes and take off for the Gulf of Mexico and other points in the south, they are always found segregated; and when God created man, he allotted each race to his own continent according to color, Europe to the white man, Asia to the yellow man, Africa to the black man, and America to the red man, but we are now advised that God's plan was in error and must be reversed.[61]

In tandem with the notion that segregation was "natural" and ordained by God in public spaces like schools, the Southern/segregationist mentality had long held that restaurants, bars, steamships, theaters, and churches—*owned by whites*—were private spaces—extensions of the home. Thus, during the debate over the civil rights act of 1975, Joshua Hill, a Senator from Georgia articulated this idea, in effect arguing that property rights—and the individual's freedom to associate with whom he or she pleased—created a zone of autonomy in which the owner of a hotel or theater had as much right as a homeowner to decide whom to invite in.

> I must confess, sir, that I cannot see the magnitude of this subject. I object to this great Government descending to the business of regulating the hotels and the common taverns of this country, and the street railroads, stage-coaches, and everything of that sort. It looks to me to be a petty business for the government of the United States ... What he may term a right may be the right of any man that pleases to come into my parlor and to be my guest. That is not the right of any colored man upon earth, nor of any white man, unless it is agreeable to me.[62]

Charles Sumner, in advocating for the passage of an equal public accommodations law, provided an eloquent reply:

The Senator may choose his associates as he pleases. They may be white or black, or between the two. That is simply a social question, and nobody would interfere with it. The taste which the Senator announces, he will have free liberty to exercise, selecting always his companions; but when it comes to rights, there the Senator must obey the law, and I insist that by the law of the land all persons without distinction of color shall be equal in rights. Show me, therefore, a legal institution, anything created or regulated by law, and I show you what must be opened equally to all without distinction of color.[63]

Sumner's civil rights act passed but was held unconstitutional by the Supreme Court in what are known today as the civil rights cases. This was only the first shoe to fall. Under *Plessy v. Ferguson*, the ideology of race as a natural boundary to community crystalized into law.

We officially dismantled the formal legal framework of Jim Crow, root and branch. But again, it was only an outer ditch; behind it, deeper and stronger, was the notion that race still defines a natural boundary, drawing a line between "us" and "them." The ideology of Senator Joshua Hill is very much alive. Hill essentialized Blacks based on the racial methodology of the time that Blacks were biologically inferior. Now we have largely erased race but we have "raced" culture. Black culture, particularly ghetto culture, is stereotyped as criminogenic. Hill rationalized racial exclusion using property baselines. The baselines have shifted from property/privacy to crime.

Sitting While Black

There is a well-known stereotype of a particular kind of coffee-shop patron—an aspiring screenwriter or freelancer, scrupulously cobbling together their pitches or book proposals, courtesy of their favorite local haunt's free Wi-Fi, electrical outlets, and comfortable furniture, paying for their mobile home office with just a $2 cup of bottomless coffee. This patron, of course, is usually white.[64]

Starbucks takes its name from Starbuck in *Moby Dick*. Starbuck, the young chief mate of the Pequod, is a thoughtful and intellectual Quaker from Nantucket. Founded in Seattle, Washington, by three students who met at the University of San Francisco, Starbucks has grown to over 28,000 locations nationwide. I visited Starbucks scores of times when, after a bike ride on Sunday morning, we would stop for a coffee break. Starbucks has an atmosphere reminiscent of the pub in Cheers, a place where everyone knows your name. It is the quintessential place where people, students, entrepreneurs, professors, nurses, doctors, and others who can afford expensive coffee can go to meet their friends or go by themselves and drink in the communal atmosphere along with their coffee. It is communal with a yuppie connotation. The urban dictionary, in defining "yuppie," says yuppie culture revolves around "Starbucks and the experience of foreign restaurants." Within this implicit class-based limitation, selling a "culture of community" is part of their brand.

Enter Donte Robinson and Rashon Nelson. Both were 23-year-old entrepreneurs who happened to be Black. They walked into Philadelphia's upscale Rittenhouse Square area, at 18th and Spruce, to meet a business associate about a potential business deal.

They walk in at 4:35 p.m.—10 minutes early for the meeting. Nelson immediately asks to use the restroom but is told it's only for paying customers. He sits down with Robinson, and the manager comes over to ask if they want anything. They explain they're fine and are just waiting for their friend.

4:37 p.m.—Police are called.

4:41 p.m.—Officers arrive.

According to Holly, the manager, when talking to the police, "I have two gentlemen at my cafe that are refusing to make a purchase or leave." According to Robinson, he calmly told police they were there for a business meeting: "It's a real estate meeting, O.K.," said Robinson. "We've been working on this for months. We were days away from changing our whole entire situation."[65]

But the officers ultimately placed both men in handcuffs in front of a large crowd, iPhone cameras snapping.

Holly blamed what she claimed was a corporate policy at City Center Philadelphia locations which prohibits excessive loitering in their stores. I assume there is such a policy on paper. However, the law in discrimination cases looks past what is on paper to the actual implementation of the so-called policy. An under-enforced policy, for our purposes, is no policy at all. Whites routinely "loiter" at Starbucks for hours. CEO Kevin Johnson has apologized repeatedly for how the incident was handled, saying "Starbucks was built as

a company that creates a warm, welcoming environment for all customers."
For privileged whites, this has led to a culture of whites using Starbucks as an
office away from home, a place to meet friends, to use free Wi-Fi and order
nothing. In essence, the company is saying: "Starbucks offers itself up as a
public space, right? Come, stay as long as you want." In substance, there was
no anti-loitering policy.

Though the two men were arrested for trespassing, there was no objective
basis for the arrest. Under Pennsylvania law, trespassing occurs when someone
enters a building or establishment, "surreptitiously, breaks into a building,
stays in a building after someone in authority gives him notice he is no longer
welcome."[66] The young Black entrepreneurs walked through an open door,
they never refused to order anything, and they were never asked to leave.

Racial Trespass

In a 2017 report conducted by the ACLU on stop and frisk in Philadelphia,
statistics in the Rittenhouse Square neighborhood where this Starbucks
is located showed that 68 percent of stops by the PPD were conducted on
black residents, despite having a neighborhood black population of merely 3
percent. This is a phenomenon referred to as "out-of-place policing," which
not only ties blackness to criminality, but views the presence of black people
in white neighborhoods as suspicious.[67]

Perhaps what they were guilty of is a "racial trespass." In the past, white
spaces, white neighborhoods, and white towns were often marked by "whites
only" signs. Today these spaces are marked in part by demographics, by
conspicuous affluence, but mostly by a border constituted by a sense of the
culture of a space or social context as somehow particularly white. Blacks don't
belong in upscale coffee houses, tony neighborhoods, or in predominantly white
suburbs baby-sitting white kids. From the standpoint of the law, these racial
boundaries are imaginary. But from inside the ideology of those who believe
the stereotypes about Blacks—particularly Blacks in hoodies with gold teeth—
it is natural that we must police "our communities" to keep out these criminal
types. For them the lines are very real. In high school I worked as a dishwasher
on some evenings. Some of the restaurants were in white neighborhoods. I

remember taking the bus to a restaurant in a white neighborhood. A resident of the neighborhood yelled out, "What are you doing here nigger, this ain't Baltimore Street." I don't know where the invisible boundary line was, but I had apparently crossed the line.

In many ways Donte Robinson and Rashon Nelson were like Trayvon. Donte Robinson was wearing a hoodie and twisty braids. Rashon Nelson was wearing a jogging suit and a James Harden-like beard. A hundred hood movies and a thousand news segments of Black men spread-eagled over the police car have fused the image of Black men in twisty braids and hoodies with images of gangbangers. They were profiled as surely as Trayvon Martin or Michael Brown.

While Blacks cannot become white, they must develop public identities that conform to white middle/upper-class norms. They must reject ghetto values, dress, and appearance. This is the new race. Had Donte and Rashon worn business suits, perhaps Holly would have coded them differently. But the combination of their race, dress, and appearance equated in her mind to "racial other" on the spectrum that race has become. In Morales, the presence in public of three or more gang members represented disorder. This case mirrors Morales as well: their mere presence in that space was incongruous, disorderly, and threatening. The threat in Morales was that the mere presence of gang members in public spaces made residents afraid to come out of the house. Here, it was the threat that the mere presence of these interlopers would frighten away customers: they might feel uncomfortable with individuals who represented a class or culture—both class and culture have been racialized— which was alien to the upper-class elitist ethos of the Starbucks space.

The intimacy of the space compounds the sense of racial imposition. The coffee house, no less than a bus or church pew, is a place where customers are in physical proximity to each other. As in the days of Senator Joshua Hill, while the law formally sees these spaces as public, through the lens of whiteness, these spaces are remapped as part of the private sphere, extensions of the home. Race again is a metaphor of kinship. It continues to draw a line between them and us. While the line is no longer drawn based on biological difference, we have racialized culture. The hoodie coat, the urban wear, the twisty braids all come together at the intersection of race and space to anchor a presumption that these urban, inner-city types don't belong here.

Finally, coffee houses, like elite universities, represent a quintessential site for social discourse. They are at the center of what Habermas calls the public sphere. They are a space where, as Professor Carl Boggs says, "public opinion is formed ... a realm mediating between the larger society and the state, and allowing for democratic control of the state."[68]

Sleeping in the Dorm While Black

As CNN reported, on May 8, 2018, "a Black Yale University graduate student was interrogated by campus police officers early Tuesday after a white student found her sleeping in a common room of their dorm and called police."[69]

It is after 1 a.m. at Yale university. Lolade Siyonbola, a 34-year-old Black graduate student, "was working on a paper in the hall of graduate studies when she fell asleep in a common room." She was awakened by Sarah Brash, a philosophy Ph.D. student, who turned on the lights and stated, "you're not supposed to be sleeping here. I'm going to call the police."

"I deserve to be here. I pay tuition like everybody else," an annoyed Siyonbola told responding officers in one video after they asked for her ID. "I'm not going to justify my existence here."[70]

But she had to.

The stereotypes of Sambo and Nat form an arc that reaches from the nineteenth century to the twenty-first, connecting with the narrative that Blacks are not fit to be in elite educational institutions, and with a related notion that the only natural place for Blacks "is that destitute and fearsome locality so commonly featured in the public media, including popular books, music and videos, and the TV news—the iconic ghetto."[71]

Lolade Siyonbola opened the door of her dorm room with her own key, but police still demanded to see ID. But even when she produced ID, this was not enough. The police checked to see if the ID card matched a database on student records. They repeatedly told Siyonbola, "We need to make sure you belong here," even after she opened the doors to her apartment with her own keys.

Other racially charged incidents have been reported. In 2015, the son of *New York Times* columnist Charles Blow was held at gunpoint by campus police officers because he supposedly fit the description of a burglary suspect. Later in 2015, Yale students took to the street to protest a number of racist incidents, including a Black girl being denied entrance to a "white girls only" party at Sigma Alpha Epsilon, and administration downplaying or outright defending racist speech on campus.

The recent incidents take on huge significance because of a proliferating pattern: as of this writing, there is a virtual epidemic of whites calling the police on Blacks for engaging in innocent activities in "white spaces." In Memphis, Tennessee, a property manager called the police on a Black man, Kevin Yates, for sitting by the pool "with socks on."

> Porter said Yates was sitting poolside, dangling his feet in the water with socks on when Walker approached him, telling him repeatedly to take his socks off. Walker identified herself as the property manager.

> At this point, Porter said she intervened to ask what the problem was, and Walker responded that "no socks, t-shirts, hats, or things of that nature are allowed in the pool."

> Porter then asked for identification, and Walker told her she and her guests needed to leave. She refused, and Walker called the police.[72]

Conclusion

It was Abraham Lincoln who wrote, "As I would not be a slave so I would not be a master; what differs from this to the extent of the difference is not a democracy." Lincoln's goal was not merely to abolish slavery but to eradicate what he termed the Dred Scott philosophy on which it rested: the notion that Blacks were an inferior order of human life. The project of Reconstruction was to make Blacks full-fledged citizens in substance as well as name. The first Reconstruction ended in 1877. *Brown* inaugurated the Second Reconstruction, a second effort at achieving Lincoln's vision of equal citizenship. The Second Reconstruction foundered on the same shoals which wrecked the first experiment. While the laws that upheld segregation were dismantled, the ideology of segregation which anchored those laws remained intact.

Our situation is captured by Gramsci who wrote, "When the state trembled, a sturdy structure of civil society was at once revealed." The state was "only an outer ditch, behind which there stood a powerful system of fortress and earthworks."[73]

Segregation was a kind of racial state. The Jim Crow laws which propped up the racial state were like the "state that trembled" (that Gramsci and his followers had confronted and overthrew). Our Jim Crow laws—like the laws that upheld the fascist state in Gramsci's life—were only an "outer ditch" as well.

Behind the Jim Crow laws, deeper and stronger was the ideology that upheld segregation. The color line that Dubois called the veil was constituted by this system of ideology and belief; the laws mandating or permitting segregation were only its manifestation.

That ideology led first during the 1950s and '60s to white flight. In the twenty-first century, to paraphrase Professor Kruse, white flight has led to white fight: the incidents at the home of Henry Louis Gates, the horror in Sanford, the eviction of would-be Black entrepreneurs from Starbucks, the arrest of a Black undergraduate at Yale for sleeping in the common areas of the dorm—while Black—and the many other instances are all expressions of the fact that in the minds of whites there still is an invisible color line.

It is no longer anchored by law; it is anchored by images of Blacks either as criminals, thugs, or intellectually inferior entities who presumptively do not belong in proximity to whites in their upper-class neighborhoods, upscale coffee houses, and private schools. The same logic that says it is common sense that three Blacks wearing baseball caps driving a Mercedes in an expensive neighborhood equals reasonable suspicion says that a Black youth in a hoodie in a gated community is likely a burglar. The same logic holds that two Blacks sitting at a table in Starbucks—who decline to order for over two minutes—is an arrestable offense. They are either thugs, homeless men, or simply urban trash and must be ejected. This implies that many whites have remapped social space so that places that are intimate to them or vital to their security are *ipso facto* private spaces (read white spaces) which they—following the logic of Senator Joshua Hill—have a right to exclude Blacks from.

But why now? For decades, public displays of racial hostility were rare. While on the backstage at the dinner table, for example, whites may have expressed open hostility to Blacks, whites seldom displayed racial hostility overtly.

In essence, whites wore a mask created by an ethos or atmosphere that racial hostility could not be expressed openly. Forrest Whittaker, in the film *The Butler*, states that a Black butler had to have two faces. A subservient "Yasser boss" face for his white employer and a true face for himself. Whites wore two faces as well.

What has happened is that a set of forces have converged, which has reversed the sense that overt racial hostility is taboo. It is as if whites now feel it is ok to take off the mask and show their true face. Enter President Trump who was elected after stating, "When Mexico sends its people, they're not sending their best. They're sending people that have lots of problems, and they're bringing those problems with us. They're bringing drugs. They're bringing crime." Of course Trump is not the problem but a symptom. He tapped into a pre-existing fear.

> By 2050 … the population of European descent will be a minority … There will be as many Hispanics here—102 million—as there are Mexicans today in Mexico. Where Hispanics were 2.6 percent of our population in 1950 … by 2050 they will be 24 percent of a nation of 420 million.[74]

Many whites are afraid of a browning of America, the fear that people who are Black and brown will soon outnumber them in the polls and they will become politically powerless. As Richard Sundstrom writes, the "browning" connotes "a drying up of America's verdant lawns." Sundstrom goes on to say, "the drought related reference is entirely distinct from the demographic one as facts, yet as [a] metaphor [it] allude[s] to a fear that goes beyond the worry over demographic change, to a nationalistic terror of the loss of a nation and its culture."[75]

After Black President Obama, and now a Black woman, the Honorable Kamala Harris, as vice president, Blacks dominating certain sports—no longer merely basketball but tennis, with Serena and Osaka—increasing numbers of Black mayors, Black prosecutors, Black police chiefs, and Rashida Jones as the head of NBC News, there is a fear of cultural and political envelopment. This is amplified by the recent political ferment with Black Lives Matter and the debates over critical race theory. This creates a sense of invasion and a need to protect "what's theirs"—to evict the invaders.

Finally, racial hostility always intensifies in times of economic insecurity. "There is abundant historical evidence to demonstrate that in climates of economic scarcity, racism, misogyny, and various kinds of scapegoating are fueled. … General economic insecurity, then, is the triggering mechanism for racial … injustice."[76] While the recession lasted only from 2008 to 2009 (eighteen months), from 2000 to 2018 household income growth slowed to an annual rate of 0.3 percent. The stagnation produced anxiety.

The convergence of political narrative, fears of loss of white cultural identity, and widespread economic security have crystallized into deep racial polarization, which has produced a spectrum of racial militancy. On the one hand, there are Nazis, like those in Charlottesville and the Capitol who take to the streets. On the other, there are individual white vigilantes using their cell phones to call the police on individual Blacks for engaging in innocent activities in what they have marked as white spaces.

Dubois called the mentality and culture which upheld segregation the veil. We are living through a Gramscian moment in which we see that while the laws that enacted overt segregation have been lifted, the veil— the beliefs and ideas that upheld these laws—have not been lifted. The veil has crystallized into a presumption that Blacks don't belong in affluent— read white—spaces. The notion is that Blacks are culturally foreign, as if no matter how educated, outside of the ghetto they are out of place. We have raced culture. This presumption of incongruence is knotted together, intertwined with a presumption either of criminality (the Nat stereotype), as in the case of Trayvon, or of intellectual inferiority (the Sambo stereotype). The mere presence of Blacks in these so-called white spaces is a signal of disorder and, for a new generation of re-segregation-minded whites, a call to arms.

Notes

1   W. E. B. Dubois, *Dark Water: Voices from within the Veil* (San Diego, CA: Harcourt Brace, & Howe, 1920), 246.

2   Howard Winant, *The New Politics of Race: Globalism, Difference and Justice* (Minneapolis, MN: University of Minnesota Press, 2004).

3   Charles Black, "The Lawfulness of the Segregation Decisions," *Yale Law Journal* 69 (1960) 424–7.

4   W. E. B. Dubois, *The Souls of Black Folk* (Tampa, FL: Millennium Press, 2018), 5.

5   Howard Winant, *The New Politics of Race Globalism, Difference, Justice* (Minneapolis, MN: University of Minnesota Press, 2004).

6   Charles A. Gallagher and Cameron D. Lippard, *Race and Racism in the United States: An Encyclopedia of the American Mosaic* (Santa Barbara, CA: Greenwood Press, 2014).

7   Richard Kluger, *Simple Justice: The History of Brown v. Board of Education New York* (New York: Vintage Books, 1975), 305.

8   See Richard Kluger, *Simple Justice* (New York: Vintage Books, 2004).

9   John Dollard, *Cast and Class in a Southern Town* (New Haven, CT: Yale University Institute of Human Relations, 1932).

10 Gunnar Myrdal and Sissle Bok. *An American Dilemma: The Negro Problem and Modern Democracy* (New Brunswick, NJ: Transaction Publishers, 1996).

11 347 U.S. 483 (1954).

12 Ibid., 301.

13 Manning Marable, *Race, Reform, and Rebellion: The Second Reconstruction and Beyond in Black America* (Oxford, MS: University of Mississippi Press, 2007), 30.

14 Ibid., 59.

15 D. Marvin Jones, *Fear of a Hip-Hop planet: America's New Dilemma* (New York: Praeger, 2013), 18.

16 Houston A. Baker, *Betrayal: How Black Intellectuals Have Abandoned the Ideals of the Civil Rights Movement* (New York: Columbia University Press, 2008), 102.

17 David Simon (Producer), Clement Virgo (Director) *The Wire*, Old Cases, Season 1, Episode 4, September 10, 2006).

18 See from Robert Steptoe, *Behind the Veil: A Study of African American Narrative* (Champaign, IL: University of Illinois Press,1991). Robert Steptoe has identified two constituting patters in African American narrative from the slave narratives to the invisible man. One is the narrative of ascent in which the protagonist progresses toward … freedom and a narrative of immersion in which the protagonist returns to his /her cultural roots and reintegrates him/herself with the community.

19 Manning Marable, *Race, Reform, and Rebellion*, 3.

20 Christopher Petrella, *The Resegregation of America: The Consequences of Creeping Racial Segregation Constitute Nothing Less than a National Crisis*, Think, Opinion Analysis, MSNBC https://www.nbcnews.com/think/opinion/resegregation-america-ncna801446.

21 Rakesh Kochar and Richard Fry, *Wealth Inequality Has Widened Along Racial, Ethnic Lines Since the End of the Great Recession*, Pew Research Center, December 12, 2004.

22   See F. Michael Higginbotham, *The Ghosts of Segregation: Ending Racism in Post-Racial America* (New York: New York University Press, 2013). Professor Higgenbotham argues similarly that the racism we are seeing today is not new but "a re-run" of patterns of thinking and behavior that we witnessed in the era of segregation. He argues that segregation created a cycle of poverty and disparities in education etc. In turn these disparities reinforce individual attitudes of Black inferiority and white superiority. I heartily agree. However, I see the problem as something that has its roots within our language/culture, within the meaning of race itself. Thus, imagine our culture as a lake and individuals in society as those who drink from the lake. Our concept of race—a concept bound up with a presumption of inferiority or dangerousness—is a poison within the lake. Prejudiced attitudes of individuals are the result of drinking from the lake. It does become a problem of individuals but the "toxin" originates in the meaning making processes of our society, in the way in which Blackness has become a signifier of criminality.

23   Higginbotham, *The Ghosts of Segregation*.

24   Henry Louis Gates, *Colored People* (New York: Knopf Doubleday, 2011).

25   Charles Ogletree, *The Presumption of Guilt: The Arrest of Henry Louis Gates, Jr. and Race, Class and Crime in America* (New York: St. Martin's Press, Kindle Edition) 275–80.

26   Ogletree, *The Presumption of Guilt*.

27   Ibid.

28   The Massachusetts statute invoked is generally entitled Crimes against Chastity, Morality, Decency, and Good Order. As defined, the relevant section (53) applies to: "Common night walkers, common street walkers, both male and female, common railers and brawlers, persons who with offensive and disorderly acts or language accost or annoy persons of the opposite sex, lewd, wanton and lascivious persons in speech or behavior, idle and disorderly persons, disturbers of the peace, keepers of noisy and disorderly houses, and persons guilty of indecent exposure." Ogletree, *The Presumption of Guilt*, 176–80.

29   "The defendant engaged in fighting or threatening, or engaged in violent or tumultuous behavior, or created a hazardous or physically offensive condition by an act that served no legitimate purpose." Ogletree, *The Presumption of Guilt*, 432–4.

30   Cambridge Police Department, Incident Report f #9005127, Filed by James Crowley, 7-16-2009, https://ia803008.us.archive.org/9/items/files-all/henry-gates-arrest-report-2009_text.pdf.

31 Jason Kessler, "Jungle Monkey Email Jeopardizes Boston Officer's Job," CNN, U.S. section, July 29, 2009,https://www.cnn.com/2009/US/07/29/massachusetts. officer.email/index.html.

32 Radly Balko, "The Henry Louis Gates Teaching Moment: Put the Race Talk Aside: The Issue is Abuse of Police Power and Misplaced Deference to Authority," *Reason*, July 27, 2009, https://reason.com/archives/2009/07/27/the-henry-louis-gates-teaching.

33 Jordan Peele, *Get Out*, DVD, directed by Jordan Peele, Universal Pictures, Universal City, California, 2017.

34 Cameron Williams SBS, "Jordan Peele on the Origins of His Dark Satire/Thriller 'Get Out,'" SBS, May 4, 2017, https://www.sbs.com.au/movies/article/2017/04/21/jordan-peele-getting-make-his-favourite-film-didnt-exist-get-out.

35 *The Inquisitor*, "Was Trayvon Martin an Honor Student with a 3.7 GPA?, July 5, 2013, https://www.inquisitr.com/832039/was-trayvon-martin-an-honor-student-with-a-3-7-gpa.

36 Alejandro Portes, *The Global Edge, Miami in the Twenty-First Century* (Oakland, CA: University of California Press, 2018), 14–15.

37 American Factfinder, United States Census Bureau, American Community Survey, 2016, https://factfinder.census.gov/faces/nav/jsf/pages/community_facts.xhtml?src=bkmk.

38 Civic Dashboards, Unemployment Rate for Miami Gardens, Florida, http://www.civicdashboards.com/city/miami-gardens-fl-16000US1245060/unemployment_rate.

39 Reported Annual Crime in Miami Gardens, https://www.areavibes.com/miami+gardens-fl/crime/.

40 Sybrina Fulton and Tracy Martin, *Rest in Power: The Enduring Life of Trayvon Martin* (New York City: Random House, 2017), 209.

41 Fulton and Martin, *Rest in Power*, 16.

42 "Parents Seek Justice For Unarmed Son's Killing". CBS Miami. Associated Press, March 10, 2012, https://www.cbsnews.com/miami/news/parents-seek-justice-for-unarmed-sons-killing/, retrieved September 10, 2013.

43 Rich Benjamin, *Searching for Whiteopia: An Improbable Journey to the Heart of White America* (New York City: Hatchett Books).

44 Joao Pauloro Neves, "Chart Gated Communities in the United States, 1810–2010," in The Eradication of Public Space, January 2012, https://www.researchgate.net/publication/303913392_The_eradication_of_public_space_Dissolving_liminal_states.

45 See D. Marvin Jones, *Fear of a Hip-Hop Planet*, 18.

46 Rich Benjamin, "The Gated Community Mentality," *New York Times*, Op-Ed Section, March 29, 2012.

47 Matthew Deluca, "Did Trayvon Shooter Abuse 911?" *The Daily Beast*, March 22, 2012, https://www.thedailybeast.com/did-trayvon-shooter-abuse-911.

48 Deluca, "Did Trayvon Shooter Abuse 911?"

49 Ibid.

50 Fulton and Martin, *Rest in Power*, 234.

51 Ibid.

52 The Internet Archive, "Full Transcript of George Zimmerman's Call to the Police,"https://archive.org/stream/326700-full-transcript-zimmerman/326700-full-transcript-zimmerman_djvu.txt.

53 D. Marvin Jones, *Dangerous Spaces: Beyond the Racial Profile* (Santa Barbara, CA: Praeger, 2016), 12. See also Waheema Lubiano, *The House that Race Built: Original Essays by Toni Morrison, Angela Y. Davis, Cornel West, and Others on Black Americans and Politics in America Today* (New York: Vintage Books, 1998); see also Yvette Christiansë, *Toni Morrison: An Ethical Poetics* (New York: Fordham University Press, 2013), 216.

54 Chicago Municipal Code § 8–4–015 (added June 17, 1992). See also generally *City of Chicago v. Morales*, 527 U.S. 41 (1999).

55 Brief for Petitioner, *City of Chicago Petitioner v. Jesus Morales, et al.* Respondents, 1998 U.S. S. Ct. Briefs LEXIS 312.

56 Lawrence Rosenthal, "Gang Loitering and Race," *Journal of Criminal Law and Criminology* 91, no. 1 (2000) 100.

57 Internet Archive, "Full Transcript."

58 Ibid.

59 Elijah Anderson, "The White Space: Race, Space, Integration and Inclusion," *Sociology of Race and Ethnicity* I, no. 1 (2015), 10–21.

60 Ray Oldenburg, *The Great Good Place: Cafes, Coffee Shops, Bookstore's, Bars, Hair Salons* (Boston, MA: Da Capo Press, 1989).

61 *State ex rel. Hawkins v. Board of Control*, 83 So. 2d 20, 27–8.

62 50 Cong. Globe, 42nd Cong., 2nd Sess. 242 (1871) (remarks of Sen. Hill).

63 See 50 Cong. Globe, 42nd Cong., 2nd Sess. 242 (1871) (remarks of Sen. Sumner).

64 Shamira Abraham, "Black Loiterers, White Lingerers, and Starbucks Coffee," *New York Magazine*, April 24, 2018, http://nymag.com/intelligencer/2018/04/racism-at-starbucks-coffee-shop-illustrates-norms-are-racially-coded.html

65 ABC Nightline.

66   Pennsylvania Statutes, Annotated, 18 PaCS section 3503, Criminal Tresspass.

67   Abraham, "Black Loiterers, White Lingerers."

68   See Carl Boggs, "The Great Retreat: Decline of the Public Sphere in Late Twentieth Century America," *Theory and Society* 26, no. 6 (December 1997) 741–80.

69   Brandon Griggs, "A Black Yale Graduate Student Took a Nap in Her Dorm's Common Room. So a White Student Called Police," CNN, May 12, 2018.

70   Griggs, "A Black Yale Graduate Student."

71   Anderson, "The White Space."

72   N'dea Yancy-Bragg, "Woman Fired after Calling Police on a Black Man for Wearing Socks in Community Pool," *USA Today*, July 8, 2018.

73   Antonio Gramsci, *Selections from the Prison Notebooks of Antonio Gramsci* (Quintin Hoare et al., eds., 1st edn) (New York: International Publishers, 1971), 238.

74   Patrick J. Buchanan, *State of Emergency: The Third World Invasion and Conquest of America* (New York: St. Martin's Press 2006), 37.

75   Ronald Sundstrom, *The Browning of America and the Evasion of Social Justice* (Albany, NY: S.U.N.Y. Press, 2008).

76   Samuel L. Meyers and Bruce P. Corrie, *Racial and Ethnic Economic Inequality: An International Perspective* (New York: Peter Lang, 2006).

6

From Blackface to Sidney Poitier: The Presumption on Our Screens (Part I)

The release of D. W. Griffith's *The Birth of A Nation* defined ... the side that Hollywood was to take in the war to represent Black people in America. ... In other words, whenever Black people appeared on Hollywood screens, from *The Birth of a Nation* to *Guess Who's Coming to Dinner?* ... they are represented as a problem, a thorn in America's heel. Hollywood's Blacks exist primarily for white spectators whose comfort and understanding the

Figure 6.1 Sidney Poitier, Katharine Hepburn, Spencer Tracy, *Guess Who's Coming to Dinner*, 1967.

Source: Allstar Picture Library Ltd./Alamy Stock Photo.

films must seek, whether they thematize exotic images dancing and singing on the screen ... or images of pimps and muggers.[1]

There is an intimate relationship between racism in the social realm and denigrating, soul-killing images of Blacks in the social imaginary of television and film.

Hollywood's race films serve as a mirror of the racial attitudes in different eras of our history. From the image of Blackface performers shuffling and jiving on Black and white film, to the vivid technicolor images of *Shaft*[2] and *Foxy Brown*;[3] from the hyper-masculine images of Black *Gangstas in the Hood* films of the late twentieth century to the images of angry Black women in *Real Housewives of Atlanta*; in each era, the silver screen reflects the prevailing racial tropes of Blacks in each period. This stereotyping serves both psychological and political needs of whites.

Eduardo Bonilla Silva argues that stereotypes of Blacks in film, such as the Tom, the Coon, and the Mammy, create a "grammar of racial perception." This "structures cognition, vision, and even feelings about Blacks."[4] It is a mechanism which normalizes otherness. Thus, we speak of "Black crime" (but not white crime), and "historically Black colleges" (but not historically white colleges.)

But stereotypes affect our perception in ways that are even more profound. I see racial stereotypes as modern-day myths. The function of myth is to create a worldview which answers questions, for the people to whom the myths belong, about the what, how, and why of the world around them. In America the great "how question" is how to resolve a contradiction. Democracy is premised on a notion of equal justice for all. But the same constitution which promises democracy protected slavery. America went on after slavery to impose Jim Crow segregation. But the stereotyping/mythology of Hollywood's race films create a worldview in which American society is *ipso facto* a "just society" despite its racism. The stereotypes of Blacks in each era are premised on the archetypes of "Sambo" and "Nat" which we discussed earlier. But the dominant society makes variations on those themes to suit whatever the dominant society needs them to be to create an illusion which justifies their worldview.

In the era of segregation, the stereotypes of Blacks as dimwitted children explain why they are unfit to hold political office and why they are not allowed to vote. Stereotypes of Blacks as rapacious brutes explain why they must not attend white schools—"Not with my white daughter!" Stereotypes of the ghetto as a war zone or a community of criminals explain why Blacks are disproportionately the figures we see spread-eagled over the police car on the evening news. Finally, in the same vein, Tyler Perry movies portray Black women as angry and Black families as sources of conflict rather than nurturing. (I am guilty of having seen probably every Tyler Perry film.) These films support a narrative that the root of the problem of why Blacks are poor, live in ghettos, fail in school, or wind up in jail has to do with dysfunctional families and their own cultural pathology. Thus, the stereotyping of Blacks on screen—myth-reflecting and myth-making—is part of the machinery by which the dominant society legitimates racism.

The logic that drives these denigrating stereotypes and myths in each era is a presumption. In one era it is a presumption of inferiority. In another it is a presumption of criminality. In another a presumption of deviance.

The presumption of inferiority, criminality, or deviance that drives the racism in the films is not in my view separate from the same presumption that functions to drive racism in the courts, in housing, in schools, and in police departments. Rather, the stereotyping that happens in both realms is mutually entailed.

The process by which this happens is conflation. When massive numbers of people see, over and over, in film after film, Blacks portrayed as stereotypical figures—whether the Sambo figures of the early twentieth century or the urban thugs of the hip-hop era—people consuming these toxic images receive them as real, true, facts of life, common sense. They conflate real people with these denigrating images. They arrest, shoot, imprison real people reasoning from the facts-of-life, common-sense racial truths they have internalized. Denigrating images on the screen are not merely offensive, not merely a reflection of attitudes in society; the stereotyping accepted as fact legitimates and drives violence against Blacks. Recall the trial of the police officers who beat Rodney King. The disparity between crack cocaine and powdered cocaine is linked to a myth/stereotype about Blacks as super-predators. This reasoning from stereotypes, which takes place in the social imaginary of popular culture, shapes policy in the social real. The violence done to the image of Blacks on our screens is intimately connected to the violence that takes place outside the theater as well.

In the next two chapters I want to proceed historically. First, we will explore how Blacks were represented in film in the early twentieth century through the early 1960s, the Jim Crow era. Chapter Seven will focus on the blaxploitation era and beyond.

The Imagery of Jim Crow

Following the Civil War there was a new birth of freedom. The ratification of the 13th, 14th, and 15th Amendments represented a kind of second founding in which Blacks were formally included in "We the people." Blacks could not only vote, but that right was protected by thousands of federal troops stationed in the south. Blacks became judges, land owners, and members of Congress. This brief period of racial progress was called reconstruction. Reconstruction ended with the Compromise of 1877, when Northern Republicans agreed to remove federal troops in exchange for the South's concession of the disputed presidential election.[5]

The period that follows, roughly from the 1880s to at least the beginning of the Great War, is often referred to as the nadir of Black experience in America.[6] For whites in the South, the same period was called the period of Redemption. According to Woodward, segregation did not expand immediately when the federal troops departed. Separation of the races continued to be the rule in churches and schools in military life and public institutions as it had been before. But in the 1870s and 1880s Blacks could vote and own homes in proximity to whites. The "old heritage of slavery" and the "new heritage of legal equality" coexisted for a time.[7] Woodward writes, "Negroes still voted in large numbers, [and] held numerous political offices."[8]

This was not to last. Why is it still open to debate? Segregation is not rooted in Southern history or culture. Some argue that it was due to the emergence of white demagogues and their exploitation of race. Others argue it was due to the rise of pseudo-scientific racism, or economic frustration produced by declining cotton prices. But without question, the Jim Crow regime grew like kudzu in the last decade of the nineteenth century. Between 1890 and 1908 every state in the deep South adopted a new state constitution.[9] The explicit purpose in each case was to disenfranchise Blacks in each state.

Some states enacted literacy tests, others poll taxes, still others felony disenfranchisement schemes, resulting in the almost total disenfranchisement of all Blacks in the South. During the same period (1890–1908) there were race riots in Wilmington (North Carolina), New York City, New Orleans, Atlanta. Two thousand three hundred and forty-four people were lynched.[10] Sixty-two percent of them were Black.[11] Both Jim Crow laws and white violence were on the rise.

Galvanized by this, W. E. B. Dubois (Figure 6.2) and his supporters, like the runaway slaves of the ante-bellum South, crossed over into Canada in 1905 to meet at the Erie Beach Hotel in Fort Eire. They began the Niagara Movement there in that year.

Figure 6.2 W. E. B. Dubois (1868–1963), founder of the NAACP and the most important African American intellectual of the early twentieth century.

Source: Everett Collection Historical/Alamy Stock Photo.

Deriving its name from the proximity of their inaugural meeting place to Niagara Falls,[12] the Niagara Movement was the precursor to the National Association for the Advancement of Colored People (NAACP).

The NAACP, along with the National Equal Rights League (NERL) formed by Monroe Trotter, became catalysts for a new militancy for integration, a counterpoint to the accommodationist philosophy of Booker T. Washington.

Enter Woodrow Wilson (Figure 6.3). Wilson, ironically the leader of the "Progressive Movement," furthered the expansion of Jim Crow. As President of Princeton University, Wilson successfully encouraged Black applicants to withdraw their applications for admission.[13]

Figure 6.3 Woodrow Wilson.

Source: Library of Congress, Detroit Publishing Company 4a26353 //hdl.loc.gov/loc.pnp/det.4a26353.

Wilson's writings suggest that he did not believe in the equality of the races. A "son of the South," Wilson saw the two races "progressing at different rates" and on different evolutionary levels of civilization.[14] He spoke "without irony" of the South's "representative government" and its exalted "standards of liberty."[15] In spite of this, Wilson was elected president in 1912 with the support of Blacks—by promising Blacks he would be fair: "If elected I intend to be president of the whole nation, to know no white or Black, no North or South, East, or West."[16]

Prior to Wilson, the federal government had been a symbol of hope for negroes. But Wilson acquiesced as Secretary of the Treasury William McAdoo and Postmaster General Albert S. Burleson quietly introduced "federal segregation" into their departments. There was a "panoply of humiliations— separate bathrooms, segregated lunchrooms, and separation between white and Black employees doing the same work."[17] George Cox, a Black clerk who returned to his job after a leave of absence to attend school, "was suddenly reduced from clerk making $1,200.00 a year to a laborer making $500.00 a year."[18] "Black clerks like Cox were not simply fired or separated out: they suffered the pain of reduced status and income in a system that no longer valued their work. Discrimination in 1912 involved the erection of a ceiling above Black employees that capped economic and social mobility."[19]

The NAACP and the NERL both protested. Trotter (Figure 6.4), leader of the NERL, famously met with Wilson on November 12, 1914. Wilson defended segregation as a means of preventing "friction between white and Black employees and as a way of preventing employees of both races from feeling uncomfortable."[20] Wilson stated, "Segregation is not humiliating but a benefit, and it ought to be regarded so by you gentlemen." Trotter was unapologetic and confrontational: "Have you a new freedom for white Americans and a new slavery for your Afro-American fellow citizens?"[21]

It is on this stage of conflict between rising racism and the beginning of a new era of Black struggle that D. W. Griffith's film *The Birth of a Nation* made its debut.

Griffith's film was based on a 1905 novel by Thomas Dixon entitled *The Clansman: An Historical Romance*.[22] The film tells the story of two families, one Northern (the Stoneman's) and one Southern (the Cameron's), as they struggle physically and emotionally during and after the Civil War. The families are

Figure 6.4 Monroe Trotter.

Source: FLHC A2020/Alamy Stock Photo.

on opposite sides of the civil war. The eldest sons of each family die on the battlefield of the civil war. But the youngest sons fall in love with the girls of the other family "in a Romeo and Juliet story of gargantuan proportions."[23] In the background the era of reconstruction—according to Griffiths—unfolds. Reconstruction was roughly from 1865–1877. Griffith hyped his film as the "history." "My only regret is that it was all too true," he said. But as Bruce Chadwick describes the film, it was not history at all but an early example of "mythmaking" in film.[24]

According to Franklin, "the film portrays a [fictional] Black reign of terror that began with Appomattox and ended only with the withdrawal of the last northern troops from the South."[25] A returning Black solider, Gus, played by a white man in Black face, pursues Flora Cameron, an innocent white woman who jumps off a cliff rather than surrender to the Black brute. When

Flora jumps to her death, the title reads: "For her who had learned the stern lesson of honor, we should not grieve that she found sweeter the opal gates of death."[26]

The film goes on to portray the Ku Klux Klan as a sort of "SWAT team of righteousness restoring southern honor."[27]

Dixon called his novel a romance. It is rather a kind of racial pornography. The most grotesque fantasies and obscene stereotypes of Blacks are portrayed as true. Franklin calls the film "propaganda" presented as history.[28]

Birth of a Nation is the most racist film in history. It was also, in its day, a masterpiece of cinematic technique. The artistry of D. W. Griffith is illustrated by his innovative use of the camera.

> Before he walked on the set, motion pictures had been, in actuality, static. At a respectful distance, the camera snapped a series of whole scenes, clustered in the groupings of the stage play. Griffith broke up the pose. He rammed his camera into the middle of the action. He took closeups, crosscuts, angle shots and dissolves. His camera was alive, picking off shots; then he built the shots into sequences, the sequences into tense, swift narrative.[29]

Thus, at the climax of the film, Silas Lynch corners Elise the innocent daughter of the Camerons. "Lynch, drunk with wine and power, orders his henchmen to hurry preparations for a 'forced marriage.'"[30] But before he can succeed in his lustful designs, the Klan, in full regalia, ride to the rescue of "white womanhood, white honor in a head-on tracking shot."[31] In the "tracking shot" the camera is pointing backward in order to face the Klansmen front on, and so the Klansmen may appear to ride "at" rather than with the spectator. The shot evokes the sensation of a moving train found in the earliest days of cinema. D'Ooge writes,

> The horses, bearing members of the Ku Klux Klan, came at the audience straight out of the screen in a head-on tracking shot. The effect was electric. When the film was first released, audiences reportedly ducked to avoid being run over. Little did they know they had been hit already.[32]

Dixon had gone to school with Woodrow Wilson. That connection opened doors. The first screening of *Birth of a Nation* was at the White House in the East Room, on February 18, 1915. It was attended by President Wilson, members of his family, and members of his Cabinet. Wilson supposedly said, "It's like writing history with lightning, and it's all so terribly true."[33]

The NAACP led a national campaign against the film. However, the NAACP, led mostly by whites, sought to work through local censor boards as if cutting scenes would cure a film which was racist at its core. Monroe Trotter fought by direct assault on the showing of the film. "Trotter ... brought [protesters] to Tremont Theatre ... As Black people protested in the street, defiant Black viewers threw rotten eggs and vegetables at the screen as soon as the lights went down, then stood their ground against white viewers who hooted and shouted, 'kill the darkey! along with the images on screen.'"[34]

The film was never banned in Boston. It became the most successful film in America. After a ten-month run, "it had been viewed by a total audience of five million people."[35] In its first few years, the film made 18 million dollars, the equivalent of 238 million today.[36] The film was used as a recruiting tool for the Ku Klux Klan. In only three years, the 3,000-member club grew into a national force for bigotry and hatred with 3 million members, thanks to a propaganda campaign that featured sponsored screenings of "The Birth of a Nation."[37] The film has two other legacies. One legacy is the motion picture as we know them today. Griffith is the father of Hollywood.

But the darker legacy:

> *The Birth of a Nation* constitutes the grammar book for Hollywood's representation of Black manhood and womanhood, its obsession with miscegenation, and its fixing of Black people within certain spaces such as kitchens, and into supporting roles, such as criminals, on the screen. White people must occupy the center, leaving Black people with only one choice— to exist in relation to Whiteness.[38]

Thus, Blacks existed in film solely to provide "comfort" to whites, as thematized images of Blacks as entertainers, butlers, maids, or other images constructed to narrate a racial drama. While whites were portrayed as individual subjects with emotions, Blacks were "characterized by ... stereotypical behavior that emphasized otherness rather than a full spectrum of emotional and intellectual activities."[39]

They were instrumental characters who existed only for the service, pleasure, and affirmation of the racialist worldview of whites. This affirmed a subject–object or I–it relationship between Blacks and whites on film, mirroring their caste position in the social real. This erased their humanity and made them in a real sense invisible.

The Coon was "the most blatantly degrading of all Black stereotypes." During slavery, Blacks were stereotyped first as beasts. The beast image has two aspects. One is that a beast has little intelligence and no character to speak of. In the minds of the Master class, Blacks typified these bestial characteristics. They were called Blacks Sambos, representing this degrading stereotype.[40] The pure coon is the descendant of "Sambo," a "a no-account nigger, [one of] those unreliable, crazy, lazy, subhuman creatures good for nothing more than eating watermelons."[41] The classic coon figure was Stepin Fetchit. Stepin Fetchit was born Lincoln Theodore Matthew Perry in 1902.[42] He began his career in vaudeville. His partner won money betting on a horse named Stepin Fetchit, so they adopted the name for their act. When Perry won a contract in film, he took the name of his comedy team as his own, shortening it to Stepinfetchit. Perry danced his way to a film career that included forty-four films from 1927 to 1939, including *David Harum*,[43] *Judge Priest*, and *Steamboat Round the Bend*. Defined by the "grammar of race" set in place since 1915, Stepinfetchit was billed as the laziest man in the world.[44]

Other famous "coons" on the silver screen included Mantan Mooreland, *One Dark Night* (1939)[45] and *Mr. Washington Goes to Town*[46] (1941), famous for his bulging eyes and cackling laugh, and Willie Best who appeared in over one hundred films typically billed as "Sleep and Eat."[47] Bob Hope, who worked with him in *The Ghost Breakers*,[48] (1940) considered Willie one of the greatest talents he had ever met. By the 1950s, the television era, the Coon became a "trickster figure." This figure was "rascalish, loud, pushy, and conniving."[49] George "Kingfish" Stevens as the Kingfish was a classic example, "a scheming coon character whose chicanery left his pals distrustful and the audience laughing."[50] Descendants of the Coon figure include Richard Pryor's characters in *Silver Streak*[51] and *Which Way Is Up*,[52] George Jefferson in *The Jeffersons*,[53] J. J. Evans in *Good Times*,[54] Jar Jar Binks in *Star Wars*,[55] David Mann as Leroy S. Brown in Tyler Perry's *Meet the Browns*,[56] and Chris Washington in *Get Out*.[57]

A variation of the Coon figure, the "Pickaninny," appears in a series of Black and white shorts from 1922 to 1938 called *Our Gang*.[58] It was also known as *The Little Rascals*. The films started as silent, but converted to sound in 1929. There were four main characters: Chubby, Stymie, Buckwheat, and Farina. The "Pickaninny" is a buffoonish child, a harmless little screwball creation whose eyes popped, whose hair stood on end with the least excitement, and whose antics were pleasant and diverting. Buckwheat was the quintessential Pickaninny stereotype, appearing as a wide-eyed child, typically with his hair in plats. Descendants of the Pickaninny occur in Arnold from *Diff'rent Strokes*[59] (1978–1986), Webster on *Webster* (1983–1987), and Hushpuppy in *Beasts of the Southern Wild*.[60]

Happy Slaves

[I]f slaves were contented and happy, that fact alone should be the everlasting condemnation of slavery, and hunt the monster from human society with curses on its head. What! does it so paralyze the soul, subvert its instincts, blot out its reason, crush its upward tendings, and murder its higher nature, that a man can be "contented and happy," though robbed of his body, mind, free choice, liberty, time, earnings, and all his rights, and while his life, limbs, health, conscience, food, raiment, sleep, wife and children, have no protection[?][61]

A variation on the theme of Blacks as coons are Blacks as "happy slaves." This "happy slave" stereotype abounds in *Gone with the Wind* (Figure 6.5).[62]

Based on a book by Margaret Mitchell, *Gone with the Wind* was billed as a turbulent epic romance between Scarlett O'Hara, daughter of a wealthy plantation owner, and Rhett Butler, set against the backdrop of the Civil War and the subsequent era of reconstruction. Producer David O. Selznick originally conceived the film as a remake of "*Birth of A Nation*." The slaves were faithful, happy, and loved their masters. This was particularly true for the house slaves. They stayed on after emancipation. Mammy, the name of her archetype and her only descriptor, was the quintessential happy—and faithful—slave.

She has been described as "self-respecting ..., loyal, ... gentle, captious, affectionate, true, strong, just, warm-hearted, popular, fearless, brave, good, pious, capable, thrifty, proud, regal, courageous, superior, skillful, tender, queenly, dignified, neat, quick, competent, possessed with a quick temper, trustworthy, faithful, patient, tyrannical, ... careful, harsh, devoted, truthful."[63]

Figure 6.5 Hattie McDaniel, Olivia de Havilland, and Vivien Leigh in a publicity photograph for the film *Gone with the Wind*, 1939.

Source: Alamy.

Hattie McDaniel, who won the Oscar for best supporting actress for her performance, captured all of those qualities particularly her devotion. In *Gone with The Wind*, Scarlett, the headstrong daughter of O'Hara often turns to Mammy for affection and support as if she were her real mother. Mammy is not merely devoted to but also happy in raising Scarlett, and Scarlett's daughter Bonnie as her own. Mammy's total "happiness" in mothering the child of her slavemaster is consistent with the Mammy figure's character as the "supremely sacrificial slave." Dubois states she is "an embodied sorrow, an anomaly crucified on the cross of her own neglected children for the sake of the children who bought and sold her as a slave."

In *Imitation of Life*[64] the Scarlett figure is Bea Pullman, played by Claudette Colbert, and Mammy is her live-in maid Delilah Johnson played by Louise Beavers. As Salvador Murguía writes, "Like Scarlett, Bea is a beautiful woman struggling financially and flawed by selfishness."[65] Delilah, like Mammy, is sacrificially loyal, and tacitly and happily submits to economic exploitation by her employer. Delilah, like Aunt Jemima, has a special pancake recipe. Bea uses her business acumen to open a restaurant. Delilah cooks in the front window becoming the restaurant's mascot, "though it is in the form of an Aunt Jemima like caricature."[66] The restaurant is successful because of Delilah's recipe and cooking but Bea receives 80 percent and Delilah 20 percent. Despite the restaurant's surging success, Delilah is content to be Bea's maid. When Bea throws a lavish party at her house, both Bea and her daughter Peola must enter through the back door.

To the white gaze Delilah's character is a picture of devotion. But objectively Delilah is a portrait of a Black woman exploited by her employer:

> Bea owes her entire livelihood to Delilah, who helped raise Jessie [Bea's daughter], gave a family recipe out to the world, and cooked relentlessly in the restaurant for years, all for a measly 20 percent of the profits—yet, at a grand party celebrating the success of the business, the real person responsible for the achievement is relegated to the kitchen.[67]

Delilah's happy slave-like sacrifice of her own dignity at the altar of "devotion" to her mistress and her daughter comes at the cost of her own daughter's psyche. Peola, Delilah's daughter, is traumatized by the racism she sees her mother subjected to. In response Peola, who looks white, tries to pass with tragic results.

The "mammy" was a fixture of the Hollywood film industry through the postwar era up to the 1960s. Ethel Waters as Granny Dicey in *Pinky*, [68] and as Bernice Sadie Brown in *Member of the Wedding*[69] and Claudia McNeil as Lena Mama Younger in *A Raisin in the Sun*.[70] The romanticized mammy image survives in the popular imagination of the modern United States. Psychologist Shaniqua Walker-Barnes argues, "political correctness has led to the mammy figure being less prevalent in the twenty-first-century culture, but the mammy archetype still influences the portrayal of African-American women in fiction, as good caretakers, nurturing, selfless, strong, and supportive, the supporting characters to white protagonists."[71]

The most prominent survivals of the Mammy image occur in television—"Like the image of Aunt Jemima the image of the mammy was given a contemporary makeover as well as she appeared in television sitcoms." Ethel Waters and Hattie McDaniel, in succession, played memorable roles as a Mammy—here a maid—in the 1952 television show *Beulah*[72]—"a maid who catered to the needs wants and desires of her white employers but who also, in this updated Mammy version, hilariously, solves problems her bosses could not solve."[73]

More recent Mammy figures are Esther Rolle's character "Florida" in *Maude*,[74] as well as her character of the same name in *Good Times*,[75] Marla Gibbs as Florence in *The Jeffersons*,[76] Sheryl Hemphill as Shirley Wilson in *What's Happening !*,[77] Nell Carter as Nell Harper in *Grimmie a Break!*,[78] Martin Lawrence's character Big Momma in *Big Momma's House*,[79] Eddy Murphy's Rasputita Latimore in *Norbit*,[80] and Tyler Perry's character Madea in the famous *Medea* films. These sit-coms are updated cosmetically; they may wear afros, talk about Black history, or Black pride, but this was largely race porn. The Black sitcom is parasitic upon the happy slave's narrative. Blacks may live in the ghetto as in *Good Times* or *What's Happening* but they are happy and joyful. There is a sub theme in Tyler Perry's films which often focuses on adultery, incest, and the pathology of Black culture, particularly Black families headed by women.

Uncle Tom

"In the beginning there was an Uncle Tom"[81]

Tom originates in the epic novel *Uncle Tom's Cabin*[82] by Harriet Beecher Stowe. Stowe's Tom is a gentle, humble, Christian slave. His faith is simple, natural, and complete. Stowe uses Tom's character to show the perfect gentleness and forgiving nature which she believed lay dormant in all Blacks.

In 1903 Edwin S. Porter made a twelve-minute short motion picture entitled *Uncle Tom's Cabin*.[83] It is here that the stereotype of "Tom" or "Uncle Tom" appears on the screen. As Donald Bogle writes, "He was American Film's first Black character. The great paradox was that in actuality Tom was not Black at all. Instead he was portrayed by a nameless, slightly overweight white actor made up in Blackface."

The "Tom" is the socially acceptable good negro.[84] "Whether he is chased, harassed, hounded, flogged, or enslaved they keep the faith, n'er turn against their white Massas, and remain hearty, submissive, stoic … and oh so very kind."[85] The Tom will do also do almost anything, including sacrificing him or herself, to save the white protagonist. In Stowe's novel Uncle Tom is the classic example.

> At the Shelby Plantation, Uncle Tom demonstrates his power of faith and forgiveness. Tom even forgives Mr. Shelby for selling him, knowing that his master is in financial trouble. Tom is willing to sacrifice himself for the good of the plantation … Tom can be considered a Christ-like character. Like Christ, he is humble, pious and forgiving.[86]

In a later short film, *For Massa's Sake*, the slave sells himself back into slavery to help the master through a period of financial difficulties.[87]

The first production in which an actual Black man appears is the famous remake of *Uncle Tom's Cabin* in 1927 in which James Lowe plays the leading role. During this era Blacks could only play stereotypical roles. What distinguished their performances was the extent to which they humanized "their" character while staying within the stereotype. Lowe was celebrated for the artistry he brought to his performance. "So affecting was Lowe he was even sent to England on a promotional tour."[88]

Unlike the "Coon," the "Tom" was articulate, reliable, and could be a trusted friend or guardian for a child. While the Coon shuffled, the Tom could be light on his feet. Bill BoJangles Robinson is a smooth as silk Butler: calm, cool, and lighthearted as he dances up the steps with Shirley Temple. He danced his way through four films with Temple, in each playing her guardian and trusted friend.

The Tom could be a hero. A classic instance was "Big Sam" in *Gone with the Wind* who fights off two would-be rapists who attack Scarlett. While the Coon was "good for nothing," the Tom often playing the role of the butler could be indispensable. "Eddie Rochester Anderson is a bright, brisk, and clever manservant without whom Jack Benny would be lost."[89]

Modern day Toms frequently appear on screen as the Magical Negro. "The Magical Negro is a supporting stock character who comes to the aid of white protagonists in a film."[90] More specifically, K. Anthony Appiah (1993), defined the Magical Negro as "the noble, good-hearted Black man or woman" whose good sense pulls the white character through a crisis. Appiah labeled the helpful Black characters as "saints." Magical Negro characters, who often possess special insight or mystical powers, have long been a tradition in American fiction.[91] The character often has no past but simply appears one day to help the white protagonist.[92] In fact, helping the white protagonist is his *raison d'être*.

This "magical power" this character possesses varies greatly. Often his power is exhibiting folk wisdom that unleashes the white person's better instincts and helps them resolve dilemmas. Thus in Bagger Vance, Bagger uses his "wisdom" to guide Hardy and Junuh in improving their golf game by persuading them to rely on feeling instead of thinking as they play. Similarly Morpheus, "the wise demigod of the Matrix" uses his wisdom to guide and encourage Neo toward an awareness of self and his new role."[93]

However, Morpheus cannot use his superior talent and gifts to save himself from being captured by Mr. Smith. A female Magical Negro in the same film, in the guise of a chain-smoking Black grandmother played by Gloria Foster, uses a powerful "foresight" to warn and protect Neo in a life or death battle with the agents in The Matrix franchise.[94]

In their classic form both the Tom and the Mammy are relics of history. These classic stereotypes were characteristically uneducated or disheveled or simply obsequious, but marked in some conspicuous way as intellectually or socially inferior. These silver screen Black stereotypes reflected the doctrine of open supremacy. But this narrative of overt racism was unstable.

It is against this background that a new era for Blacks in American films begins. Perhaps the first dawning of this era of American film was Harry Belafonte in *Island in the Sun* (1957)[95] where Belafonte plays David Boyeur, an ambitious politician and radical. Boyeur "takes the election right out of the hands of a rich white candidate and woos and captivates a beautiful white woman."[96] In the 1959 version of *An Imitation of life*[97] Susan Kohner plays the mixed-race daughter of a Black widow, a Black girl who looks white and struggles with the dilemma of fitting in neither world. In both of these films the characters play central roles, express human emotions, and more importantly enact dramas, which in civil rights dilemmas are poignantly encoded. Most importantly, the characters play roles that have intrinsic value. In the Jim Crow era, the Black characters are typified by the fact that their only value was in relationship to white protagonists. Here they play central roles but they do so within the box of the *tragic mulatto* figure which reaffirms the notion Blacks are happiest when they stay in their place.

A Raisin in the Sun[98] is important here as well in that it poetically tells the story of conflict between the too often "deferred dream" of moving across the color line to a home in the suburbs and the white fears of Blacks doing so. But Walter Lee Younger's betrayal of his mother and his family by taking money for a down-payment and handing it over to con man he thought was his friend suggests Walter is an update of the stereotypical morally flawed, good for nothing Black man. A coon.

The watershed moment, which marks the transition between the Jim Crow film and the modern era is *Guess Who's Coming to Dinner*.[99]

In *Guess Who's Coming to Dinner* Sidney plays John Prentice, a Black doctor who falls deeply in love with Joanna "Joey" Drayton (Katherine Houghton) the beautiful headstrong daughter of Christina Drayton, art Gallery owner and Matt Drayton, publisher of a newspaper called *The Guardian*. They love each other deeply. But Prentice declares he will only get married if Joanna's parents approve.

The film dramatizes the collision between the centuries-old taboo against interracial marriage and the new world order of formal equality emerging in the aftermath of *Brown v. Board*. The taboo is driven by the concept of whiteness itself. Whiteness implies racial purity. Under the so-called "one drop rule" even a drop of Black blood corrupts the bloodline. Black blood is a contaminant. To maintain this white supremacist mythology historically, most states in the U.S. made interracial marriage a crime. In April 1967 the Supreme Court in a landmark decision ruled Virginia's anti-miscegenation law unconstitutional. *Guess Who's Coming to Dinner* was released in December of that year.

Another collision is taking place as well, between the old concept of race as something essential, a wall separating between a biologically inferior group and a superior one, and a new conception of race formed out the imperatives of cold war liberalism.

This liberalism was fed by a stream of social science discourse which, in academic circles had discredited traditional concepts of race. This in part led to *Brown*. But Cold War liberalism was primarily pragmatic. America could not compete with the Soviet Union for the hearts and minds of the newly emerged African nations while explicitly maintaining Jim Crow polices. In order to jettison the Jim Crow practices America had to jettison the biologic notion of race upon which that rested. A new liberalism arose which reflected this political necessity. This new liberalism rejected the idea that race in a biologic sense determined who one was.[100] Because it had to. Within this new paradigm race still represents a presumption of inferiority, and suspect moral character. But to be acceptable ideally, a Black man would have to be a kind of superman or super-negro whose accomplishments/character rebut the presumption of inferiority. Sidney demonstrates by what he has achieved that he is an exception to the stereotype of Black inferiority.

John Prentice came to dinner at Christine and Matt Drayton's house as the embodiment of Cold War liberalism's racial ideal. Prentice was an updated version of the Magical Negro. His special power was a combination of "achievement, moral character and charisma." He was so impeccably "accomplished, well-spoken, and aspiring"; a "mild-mannered Black man that America ought not to fear, that the Black middle class ought to be proud of, that racist white America would have trouble hating."

Sidney is a new Magical Negro. Like the old he exists entirely to fulfill the needs of whites—more specifically white liberalism of the 1960s. But his "magic" is his chameleon-like ability to slip between the categories of white and Black.

Sidney is a distinguished individual, a doctor, who happens to have Black skin. It was not Sidney's race or gender that defined him. It was his stature, and talent and exceptionalism as reflected by his Ivy League degrees and his Brooks Brothers suit.[101]

This is reassuring. He is precisely the answer to new liberalism's call for integration. He is so successful, a super-negro not merely a magic one, he can be accepted by elite whites like Christine and Matt Drayton as an equal and even as a son-in-law. But of course, the reason he can be accepted is not merely because of his achievements and character but what they represent.

The Magical Negro historically was a Tom. Sidney is as well. Donald Bogle calls him a super Tom. Characteristic of the Tom stereotype Sidney must make an ultimate sacrifice.

In the 1910 film *A Confederate Spy*,[102] a slave spies on the North for the Southern forces. Captured and shot he is content because he did it for Ol' Massa and Little Massa.

Sidney does not sacrifice his life; he sacrifices his Blackness. Blackness from the white perspective is bad. Those who are Black are merely Coons, Mammys, Tragic Mullatos etc. These images of Blackness articulate the various ways in which Blacks are presumed to be inferior. The presumption is so total that, in the words of Fanon, a "Black man is not a man."[103]

Sidney's problem is to become a man he must become as white as possible. He may be physically Black but to be fully accepted he must jettison his inferior Black identity. For postwar liberals this "Black identity," which was inferior, was simply a set of attitudes and values—analogous to a costume—which must be taken off and exchanged for an American business suit. For Prentiss it represents splitting off of a part of himself.

To make this transformation the Black person must look at himself through the eyes of whites, which creates a sense of splitting or doubling of consciousness. As Dubois writes, "it is a peculiar sensation, this double consciousness, this sense of always looking at one's self through the eyes of others, of measuring one's soul by the tape of a world that looks on in amused contempt and pity."[104] He is forced to privilege the white view of himself, and "inhabit an alienating fragmented reality."[105]

Fittingly, Sidney comes to dinner in a Brooks Brothers suit which represents not merely his sophistication or elite status but his whiteness, internalized assimilation. Here this may be read as cultural suicide.

The Bargain

Matt Drayton accepts Sidney in the film, welcoming him to his dinner table. But Matt is really embracing a man who culturally and politically is like himself. Whiteness is still supreme—there is simply a switch between whiteness as race and whiteness as American beliefs (worldview) or values. In his sacrifice—his assimilation—Sidney accepts a deal. Shelby Steele writes,

> The sixties stigmatized white Americans with the racial sins of the past—
> with the bigotry and hypocrisy that countenanced slavery, segregation, and
> white supremacy. Now, to win back moral authority, whites—and especially
> American institutions—must prove the negative: that they are not racist
> … Blacks—now fully acknowledged as America's long-suffering victims—

possess a largesse of moral authority that whites simply can never have. And this amounts to a currency of power in a society that now needs moral authority around race for the very legitimacy of its institutions.[106]

Through his act of assimilation Sidney relinquishes his claims: "I will not use America's horrible history of white racism against you, if you will promise not to use my race against me." The deal is this: I "grant whites the innocence and moral authority they need in return for their goodwill and generosity." He can never openly challenge white authority meaning he can never express his true beliefs. He must always wear a mask.

The dilemmas portrayed in the film mirror those faced by the talented tenth up to the present day. We still continue to wrestle with the choice between racial authenticity and acceptance, double consciousness and assimilation, and the choice of taking the deal and challenging the system. Michael Jordan, Tiger Woods, in sports, Clarence Thomas in law, Colin Powell, Condoleeza Rice, Candace Owens, Stacey Dash, Omorosa Manigault Newman, and Ben Carson are all individuals who politically have renounced any allegiance to Blacks. They have created public identities in which they only happen to be Black. They took "the deal." This identity becomes a prison in real life as on the screen. Obama is a hybrid. He consciously identifies with the plight of Blacks. But he was powerless to express any radical critique of racism. While Obama was campaigning, his enemies revealed his Pastor and Mentor Jeremiah Wright, who passionately denounced the U.S. for racism and hypocrisy.

> Not God bless America, God damn America. That's in the Bible, for killing innocent people. God damn America for treating her citizens as less than human. … [The United States] government lied about their belief that all men were created equal. The truth is they believed that all white men were created equal … The government lied about the Tuskegee experiment. They purposely infected African American men with syphilis. God damn America, for treating our citizens as less than human.[107]

At first Obama tried to defend Wright as a person while denouncing his comments. Later Obama stated he was "saddened" and "outraged" by Wright's comments and publicly resigned from the Church.

The images of Blacks on our screens do more than mirror and reflect— they teach and exert power (control) as models of what one must or must not be to succeed. The denigrating stereotypes represented in one pole of identity: a primitive set of attitudes, behaviors, and self-worth Black identity we would advance beyond. John Prentice represented an opposite pole of education, talent, and achievement. Within this there was the choice between "negritude"—what hip-hop artists call being a true "nigga" and the whitening required by a John Prentice-like choice of respectability.

A generation of Blacks navigated their path to adulthood in the shadow of these images or racial identity. James Baldwin describes the cultural synthesis that emerged among the talented tenth of his day:

> Aunt Jemima and Uncle Tom are dead, their places taken by a group of amazingly well adjusted men and women almost as dark and but ferociously literate, well-scrubbed, who are never laughed at, who are not likely ever to set foot in a cotton or tobacco field or any but the most modern kitchens.[108]

In college we were militants of various stripes, some of us wore dashikis, grew afros, celebrated Kwanza. Others were students of Malcolm X or Kwame Touré. We all clinched our fists in Black power salutes at rallies. We were going to confront racism and change the world. We rejected the bargain. We would not be Toms or slaves. But when we graduated from college and graduate school or medical school or law school our fists unclenched, we got haircuts and we put on the Brooks Brothers suits and went off to corporate America to work. Some of us became Republicans.

Race is no ordinary lake. It is a reservoir of images, narratives associated with slavery and Jim Crow.[109] These images continue to be controlling despite the fact we have achieved our Ph.D., Law degree, or M.D. The stereotypes follow us into board rooms, courtrooms, and corporate offices. The "acceptable Black" stereotype fixated on exceptionalism is a formula for tokenism. Blacks still make up 4.8 percent of the lawyers (and only 1.94 percent of equity partners), 5 percent of the doctors, 3 percent of the scientists and engineers, less than 5 percent of the judges, 5.4 percent of the legislators, 3.3 percent of the dentists, and 1 percent of Fortune 500 companies.

For Blacks with an advanced degree the wage differential between Blacks and whites is 18 percent. For the highest earners the wage gap differential is 33 percent.

But the most painful legacy of this stereotyping is the lack of respect. Race is an asset for the employer: the Black employee represents moral capital. But to the Black employee it is something that has to be overcome. Race carries with it a negative presumption. The employee carries the burden of proof: prove who you are. As Brent Staples writes,

> The fearsomeness mistakenly attributed to me in public places often has a perilous flavor. The most frightening of these confusions occurred in the late 1970s and early 1980s, when I worked as a journalist in Chicago. One day, rushing into the office of a magazine I was writing for with a deadline story in hand, I was mistaken for a burglar. The office manager called security and, with an ad hoc posse, pursued me through the labyrinthine halls, nearly to my editor's door. I had no way of proving who I was.[110]

I experienced a kind of profiling as well: "prove you belong here" was the question I felt from all the attorneys in each office I worked for and from each judge. I tried to answer this question through hard work. I still remember when I was trial attorney with the EEOC the office had about six attorneys. The last year I was there, 1988, I tried three cases in Federal court. I prevailed in each one. The other attorneys tried three cases between the five of them, but, with one exception, with very different results. Despite my outstanding success there was no recognition from my supervisor. My success was not sufficient to prove merit. It was not merit that establishes status for a professional Black but a sense of how well one "fits in to the group." "Fitting in" cannot be established merely by winning cases.

We inhabit a paradox. We may have cards that allow us access to enter the corporate suite, our own office, often a fancy title; we may become partners in law firms, win elections to the City council, even become a member of Congress, or the Mayor, or receive prestigious awards. But blacks are still, in most settings, most corporate suites, most law firms and court rooms, still eternal outsiders, almost always under a special kind of scrutiny. There are many exceptions, of course—an Oprah Winfrey, entrepreneur, billionaire, a Katanji Jackson, Supreme Court Justice, a Ben Crump, Esq., who has at least one law school named after him, a Tyler Perry, who at this writing purchased Black Entertainment Television, a Rashida Jones, President of MSNBC, a Donahue Peebles, a real estate entrepreneur and many, many others. But their relative rarity nonetheless results in a certain isolation. Some call them unicorns.

The plight of the Black talented tenth today is analogous to that of Marshall McLaurin who, although admitted to law school, had to sit apart.[111] He had to sit cordoned off in the library or in the classroom. Our isolation is no longer physical but psychological and social. We are always coming to dinner. But in the eyes of the dominant society, *as a class of people*, we never arrive. We are as Sartre described the Jew in Europe:

> [The Jew] accepts the society around him, he joins the game and he conforms to all the ceremonies, dancing with the others the dance of respectability. Besides, he is nobody's slave; he is a free citizen under a regime that allows free competition; he is forbidden no social dignity, no office of the state. He may be decorated with the ribbon of the Legion of honor, he may become a great lawyer or cabinet minister. But at the very moment when he reaches the summits of legal society, another society—amorphous, diffused, omnipresent—appears before him as if in brief flashes of lightning and refuses to take him in ... [H]e never encounters any particular resistance; people seem, rather to be in flight before him; a impalpable chasm widens out, and above all, an invisible chemistry devaluates all he touches ... Everything is accessible to him, and yet he possesses nothing; for he is told, what one possesses is not to be bought.[112]

Notes

1   Manthia Diarwa, *Black American Cinema: Aesthetics and Spectatorship* (New York: Routledge, 1993).

2   *Shaft*, directed by Gordon Parks (1971, Beverly Hills, CA: Metro-Goldwyn-Meyer, 2019).

3   *Foxy Brown*, directed by Jack Hill (1974, London: Arrow Video, 2015). DVD.

4   E. Bonilla Silva, "The Invisible Weight of Whiteness: The Racial Grammar of Everyday Life in Contemporary America," *Ethnic and Racial Studies* 35, no. 2, (2012) 173–94.

5   Comer Vann Woodward, *The Strange Career of Jim Crow* (Oxford, UK: Oxford University Press, 2002); Eric Foner, *Forever Free: The Story of Emancipation and Reconstruction* (New York: Vintage Books, 2006).

6   August Meir, *Negro Thought in America 1880–1915* (Ann Arbor, MI: The University of Michigan Press, 1988).

7   Woodward, *The Strange Career of Jim Crow*, 33.

8   Ibid.

9   Gary W. Burnett, *The Gospel According to the Blues* (Eugene, OR: Cascade Books, 2014), 33.

10 Lynching statistics by Year, UMKC School of Law, http://law2.umkc.edu/faculty/projects/ftrials/shipp/lynchingyear.html.

11 Ibid.

12 Robin D. G. Kelly, *Earl Lewis, To Make Our World Anew: A History of African Americans* (Oxford: Oxford University Press, 2000), 2379.

13 Progressivism was a movement which sought to address problems of economic inequality between the rich and poor through political reforms. Their defining belief was the perfectibility of democracy, and that this ideal transcended class divisions. Key strategic reforms included direct democracy and regulation of large trusts. Wilson, leader of the Progressive Movement in his day signed into law the Federal Trade Commission Act, lowered tariffs (which he believed created monopolies). He also advocated for direct democracy in the form of popular initiatives, referenda, and reform.

14 Henry Blumenthal, "Woodrow Wilson and the Race Question," *Journal of Negro History* 48, no. 1 (January, 1963) 1–21.

15 Eric Foner, *The Story of American Freedom* (New York: W.W. Norton, 1998).

16 Ross A. Kennedy, *A Companion to Woodrow Wilson* (Hoboken, NJ: John Wiley & Sons, 2013).

17 Eric Steven Yellin, *Racism in the Nation's Service: Government Workers and the Color Line in Woodrow Wilson's America* (Chapel Hill, NC: University of North Carolina Press, 2013), 114.

18 Yellin, *Racism in the Nation's Service*.

19 Ibid.

20 Ibid., 162.

21 Eric Foner, *The Story of American Freedom* (New York: W.W. Norton, 1998), 186.

22 Thomas Dixon, *The Birth of a Nation* (New Brunswick, NJ: Rutgers University Press, Robert Lang Editor, 1994), 7.

23 Robert Corliss, "D. W. Griffith's Birth of a Nation 100 Years Later: Still Great, Still Shameful." *Time Magazine* (March 3, 2015).

24 See "The Blue the Gray and Technicolor" in Bruce Vincent Chadwick, *The Reel Civil War: Mythmaking in American Film*(Topeka: Tandem Library Group, 2009).

25 Craig D'Ooge, "The Birth of a Nation: Symposium on Classic Film Inaccuracies and Virtues" (Washington D.C.: *Library of Congress Information Bulletin*, June 27, 1994).

26　Thomas Cleveland Holt and Laurie B. Green, *Charles Reagan Wilson, The New Encyclopedia of Southern Culture: Volume 24: Race* (Chapel Hill, NC: University of North Carolina Press, 2013), 191.

27　D'Ooge, "The Birth of a Nation," note 25.

28　Ibid., note 21.

29　Corliss, "D. W. Griffith's Birth of a Nation 100 Years Later."

30　Rogin, Michael. "'The Sword Became a Flashing Vision': D. W. Griffith's The Birth of a Nation," *Representations* 9 (1985) 150–95. Accessed September 18, 2020. https://doi.org/10.2307/3043769.

31　Tim Dirks, *The Birth of a Nation* (1915), http://144.214.21.63/CCS/film_culture/filmsite/birt3.html.

32　D'Ooge, "The Birth of a Nation."

33　There is a controversy as to whether Wilson said this. But it is troubling that Wilson's view of Reconstruction mirrored that of Dixon, who was Wilson's classmate at Johns Hopkins. Wilson wrote that the purpose of Reconstruction was "to put the white South under the heel of the Black South …. The white men were roused by an instinct of mere self-preservation until at last there had sprung into existence a great Ku Klux Klan, a veritable empire of the South to protect the Southern country." Wilson may never have made the statement. But it does disturbingly resonate with the worldview Wilson expressed in many his writings, particularly his view of reconstruction, and his tacit support for segregation in Federal departments.

34　Kerri K. Greenridge, *Black Radical: The Life and Times of William Monroe Trotter* (New York: Silverlight Publishing, 2019).

35　Melvyn Stokes and D. W. Griffiths, *The Birth of a Nation: A History of the Most Controversial Film in History* (New York: Oxford, 2007).

36　Stokes and Griffiths, *The Birth of a Nation.*

37　D'Ooge, "The Birth of a Nation," 24.

38　Manthia Diarwa, *Black American Cinema: The New Realism* (Abingdon-on-Thames, UK: Taylor & Francis, 1993).

39　Antony B. Pinn, *Understanding and Transforming the Black Church* (Eugene, OR: Wipf and Stock Publishers, 2010).

40　See Joseph Boskin, *Sambo: The Rise and Demise of an American Jester* (New York: Oxford University Press, 1986), 7–8.

41　Richard C. Keenan, "Review: Negative Image Black Actors in American Film," *Literature/Film Quarterly* 3, no. 4 (1975) 377, https://www.jstor.org/stable/pdf/43795485.pdf.

42 "Lincoln 'Stepin Fetchit' Perry, Biography," *The Library of Congress*, http://memory.loc.gov/diglib/ihas/loc.music.tdabio.138/default.html; see also Mel Watkins, *Stepin Fetchit: The Life and Times of Lincoln Perry* (New York: Pantheon Books, 2005).

43 *David Harum*, directed by James Cruze (1934, Fort Lee, NJ: Fox Films).

44 Miriam J. Petty, *Stealing the Show: African American Performers and Audiences* (Berkeley, CA: University of California Press, 2016).

45 *One Dark Night*, directed by Leo Popkin (1939, Hollywood, CA: Million Dollar Productions).

46 *Mr. Washington Goes to Town*, directed by Jed Buell and William Beaudine (1942, Atlanta, GA: Dixie National Pictures).

47 Nikki L. M. Brown and Barry Stentiford, *The Jim Crow Encyclopedia*: *Greenwood Milestones in African American History* (Westport, CT: Greenwood Press, 2008).

48 *The Ghost Breakers*, directed bydirected by George Marshall (1940, Hollywood, CA: Paramount Pictures).

49 Stephanie Greco Larson, *Media and Minorities: The Politics of Race in News and Entertainment* (Oxford, UK: Rowman & Littlefield, 2006).

50 Larson: *Media and Minorities*, 28.

51 *Silver Streak*, directed by Arthur Hiller (1976, Los Angeles, CA: Twentieth Century Fox).

52 *Which Way Is Up*, directed by Michael Shultz (1977, Universal City: Universal Pictures).

53 *The Jeffersons*, directed by Bob Lally, created by Don Nicholl, Michael Ross, Bernie West, featuring Isabel Sanford, Sherman Hemsley, and Marla Gibbs (January 18, 1975, to July 2, 1985, Los Angeles, CA: CBS).

54 *Good Times*, directed by Garren Keith, Herbert Kenwith, Bob LaHendro, Donald McKale, Perry Rosemand, created by Eric Monte and Mike Evans, featuring Esther Rolle and John Amos, CBS Television City in syndication (1922–27, Buffalo, NY; 1927–38 Beverly Hills, CA:Metro-Goldwyn Meyer).

55 *Star Wars*, directed by George Lucas (1977, Twentieth Century Fox, 1982—*A New Hope* on VHS).

56 *Meet the Browns*, directed by Tyler Perry (2008, Tyler Perry Studios) DVD.

57 *Get Out*, directed by Jordan Peele (2017, Los Angeles, CA: Blumhouse Productions).

58 *Our Gang*, directed by Robert F. McGowan, Gus Means, Gorgon Douglas, Edward l Cahn, George Sydney, Cy Enfield, Ray McCarey, James W. Horne, Robert A. McGowan, Fred C. Newmeyer, Nate Watt, written by Frank Capra, Charley

Chase, Walter Lance, featuring at different Times Norman Chaney ("Chubby") Matthew Beard ("Stymie") and Bill Thomas as Buckwheat and Ernie Morrison as "Sunshine" (1922–38). The short films were produced roughly from 1922 to 1938.

59 *Diff'rent Strokes*, directed by Herbert Kenwith, written by Ben Starr, Bud Grosman, Howard Leeds, Martin Cohan (1978–1985, Culver City, CA).

60 *Beasts of the Southern Wild*, directed by Benh Zeitlin (2012, Los Angeles, CA: Fox Searchlight Pictures).

61 Michael E. Woods, *Emotional and Sectional Conflict in the Antebellum United States* (New York: Cambridge University Press, 2014), 57, quoting Edmund Burke from the *American Anti-Slavery Almanac* published in 1839 (New York: Isaac Knapp 1839).

62 *Gone With the Wind*, directed by Victor Fleming (1939, Burbank: Warner Brothers, 2018) DVD.

63 Sybil de Gaudio, "The Mammy in Hollywood Film: I'd Walk a Million Miles-For One of Her Smiles," *Jump Cut* 28 (April 1983), 23–5.

64 *Imitation of Life*, directed by by John Stahl (1939, Universal City: Universal Pictures, 2012) DVD.

65 Daniel Bernardi and Michael Green, Eds., *Race in American Film: Voices and Visions that Shaped a Nation* (Santa Barbara, CA: Greenwood Press, 2017).

66 Salvador Jiménez Murguía, *The Encyclopedia of Racism in American Films* (London: Rowman & Littlefield, 2018).

67 Ibid.

68 *Pinky*, directed by Elia Kazan (1949, Los Angeles, CA: 20th Century Fox).

69 *Member of the Wedding*, directed by Fred Zinneman (1952, Los Angeles, CA: Columbia Pictures).

70 *A Raisin in the Sun*, directed by Daniel Petrie (1961, Los Angeles, CA: Columbia Pictures).

71 Chenequa Walker-Barnes, *Too Heavy a Yoke: Black Women and the Burden of Strength* (Eugene, OR: Cascade Books, 2014), 86.

72 *Beulah*, featuring Ethel Waters (1950–1), and Hattie McDaniel (April, 1952 to August 1952); Louise Beavers, (September 1952—September 1953 on ABC TV: New York: Biograph Studios (location), Roland Reed Productions).

73 Imani M. Cheers, *The Evolution of Black Women in Television: Mammies, Matriarchs and Mistresses* (Abingdon-on-Thames, UK: Routledge, 2018).

74 *Maude*, created by Norman Lear and Bud Yorkin, featuring Beatrice Arthur and Bill Macy (1972–78; Hollywood, CA: CBS Television City).

75 *Good Times*, directed by Gerren Keith, featuring Esther Rolle and John Amos (1974–79, Hollywood, CA: CBS Television City).

76   *The Jeffersons*, directed by Bob Lally, Oz Scott, Jack Shea, Tom Singletary, and Arlando Smith (January 18, 1975–July 2, 1985, Hollywood, CA: CBS Television City).

77   *What's Happening !!*, created by Eric Monte, featuring Ernest Lee Thomas, Haywood Nelson, Fred Berry, Danielle Spencer, Mabel King (August 5, 1976 to April 28, 1979, Culver City: Columbia Pictures Television).

78   *Gimme a Break*, directed by John Bowbab, Hal Cooper, Jim Drake, Linda Daye, Dick Harwood, featuring Nell Carter, Dolph Sweet, Lara Jill Miller, Lauri Hendler, Kari Michaelson, Howard Morton, John Hoyt, Joey Lawrence, Telma Hopkins (October 29, 1981, until May 12, 1987, Universal City: Universal Studios, 2010) DVD.

79   *Big Momma's House*, directed by Raja Gosnell (2000, Los Angeles, CA: 20th Century Fox Home Entertainment) DVD.

80   *Norbit*, directed by Brian Robbins (2007, Universal City, CA: Paramount Pictures) DVD.

81   Donald Bogle, *Toms, Coons, Mulattoes, Mammies, and Bucks: An Interpretive History of Blacks in American Films* (New York: Bloomsbury Academic Press 2016), 4.

82   Harriet Beecher Stowe, *Uncle Tom's Cabin* (Boston, MA: John P. Jewett, 1851).

83   Stephen Railton, "Readapting Uncle Tom's Cabin" in Salvador Jimenez Murguía, *The Encyclopedia of Racism in American Films*, 623.

84   Bogle, *Toms, Coons, Mulattoes, Mammies, and Bucks*, 4.

85   Ibid., 6.

86   Harriet Beecher Stowe, Uncle Tom's Cabin Thrift Study Edition (Minneola, New York: Dover Publications 2011) p. 409

87   Donald Bogle, *Toms, Coons, Mulattoes, Mammies, and* Bucks, 2.

88   Ibid., 4.

89   Ibid., 35.

90   John Christopher Farley, "That Old Black Magic," *Time Magazine*, May 27, 2000.

91   D. Marvin Jones, *Race, Sex and Suspicion: The Myth of the Black Male* (London: Bloomsbury Academic, 2005), 35.

92   Audrey Columbe, "White Hollywood's New Boogey Man," *Jump Cut: A Review of Contemporary Media*, http://www.ejumpcut.org/archive/jc45.2002/colombe/.

93   Cerise Glenn and Landra J. Cunningham, "The Power of Black Magic: The Magical Negro and White Salvation in Film," *Journal of Black Studies* 40, no. 2 (2007) 135–52, https://libres.uncg.edu/ir/uncg/f/C_Glenn_Power_2009.pdf.

94 The Wachowskis, *The Matrix* (1999, Hollywood, CA: Warner Brothers); *The Matrix Reloaded* (2003, Hollywood, CA: Warner Brothers); *The Matrix Revolutions* (2003, Hollywood, CA: Warner Brothers).

95 *Island in the Sun*, directed by Robert Rosen (1957, Century City: Twentieth Century Fox).

96 Bogle, *Toms, Coons, Mulattos, Mammies, and Bucks*, 190.

97 *An Imitation of Life*, directed by Douglas Sirk (1959, Chicago, IL: Universal Pictures).

98 *A Raisin in the Sun*, directed by Daniel Petrie (1961: Los Angeles: Columbia Pictures).

99 *Guess Who's Coming to Dinner*, directed by Stanley Kramer (1967, Los Angeles, CA: Columbia Pictures).

100 As Michael Omi and Howard Winant write: "With the advent of the vaguely egalitarian (racially speaking) vision of the new deal and of the anti-fascism of World War II … the ethnic paradigm definitively dislodged the biologic view in what appeared to be a triumph of liberalism." Michael Omi and Howard Winant, *Racial Formation in the United States* (New York: Routledge, 1986) 14.

101 Omi and Winant, *Racial Formation in the United States*, 929.

102 See Bogle, *Toms, Coons, Mulattos, Mammies, and Bucks*, 2.

103 Franz Fanon, *Black Skin, White Masks* (New York: Grove Press 2008).

104 W. E. B. Dubois, *The Souls of Black Folk* (New York: Gildan Media, 2019), 14.

105 Franz Fanon, *The Wretched of the Earth* (New York: Grove Press 2007), xix.

106 Shelby Steele, *A Bound Man: Why We Are Excited about Obama and Why He Can't Win* (New York: Simon & Shuster, 2007).

107 Reverend Jeremiah Wright, "The Day of Jerusalem's Fall," *ABC News*, April 27, 2008.

108 James Baldwin, "Many Thousands Gone," in *Notes of a Native Son*, (Boston, MA: Beacon Press, 1984), 27.

109 Jones, *Race, Sex, and Suspicion*, 89.

110 Al Smith, *African American: Readings on History and Identity* (2006) quoting Brent Staples, "Just Walk on By" originally published in Ms. Magazine, 1986

111 *McLaurin v. Oklahoma State Regents for Higher Educ.*, 339 U.S. 637, 60 S. Ct. 851 (1950), see also Jones, *Race, Sex, and Suspicion*, 81, discussing the case.

112 Jean-Paul Sartre, *Anti-Semite and Jew* (George G. Becker Trans. New York: Schocken Books, 1995).

7

From Blaxploitation to Hood Films: The Presumption on Our Screens (Part II)

Figure 7.1 Foxy Brown.

Source: Alamy.

The drug war and the mass incarceration of Blacks went hand in hand with the careful elaboration of a new set of racial stereotypes which helped to normalize and invisibilize systemic racism. The new racial stereotypes, like those that populated the films of the Jim Crow era, derive from plantation-era myths.

As we have noted, there were two major stereotypes of Blacks on the plantation. One was Sambo;[1] the other was Nat. Sambo "personified the mythology of Black inferiority." The Coon, the Tom, and the Pickaninny are all descendants of Sambo.

Nat was his violent twin. Blassingame, in his description of plantation stereotypes, describes Nat this way.

> Nat was the rebel who rivaled Sambo in the universality and continuity of his literary image. Revengeful, bloodthirsty, cunning, treacherous, and savage, Nat was the incorrigible runaway, the poisoner of white men, the ravager of white women who defied all the rules of plantation society. ... Nat retaliated when attacked by whites ... killed overseers and planters, or burned plantation buildings when he was abused.[2]

The stereotypes of Blacks in film from the latter half of the twenty-first century forward are primarily descendants of Nat.

In literature, Nat's most famous descendant is Bigger Thomas.[3] Bigger is a 21-year-old Black man with an eighth-grade education. He is forced by his circumstances to take whatever jobs he can find. He finds a job as a chauffeur for a rich family and spends an evening driving the daughter Mary and her boyfriend around while they drink and make out in the back seat. At evening's end Mary is drunk and Bigger must carry her to her bed. But while in her bedroom Bigger hears someone coming. Fearing he would be accused of sexual assault after being found in Mary's bedroom, Bigger places a pillow over Mary's head. He accidentally suffocates her. Richard Wright uses Bigger as a metaphor for the effects of white racism to limit the educational and employment options of Blacks and in turn to create "Black crime." Bigger is a sociopath, but his sociopathy is a product of dehumanizing ghetto conditions for which white society is to blame. I am reminded of the words of Tupac Shakur,

> Nightmare that's what I am
> America's nightmare
> I am what you made me
> The hate and evil that you gave me[4]

Tupac's comment that "I am what you made me / The hate and the evil that you gave me" applies to Bigger both because of the physical conditions in which Bigger was forced to live and because of the way he was perceived by whites. Bigger is for white society a kind of self-fulfilling prophecy. Bigger behaves like an animal precisely because the dominant white culture perceives him as an animal—a beast. Bigger/Nat appears in the taxonomy of Donald Bogle as "the brutal Black buck." The brute caricature portrays Black men as innately savage, destructive, and criminal—deserving punishment, maybe death.[5] This brute is a fiend, a sociopath, an anti-social menace. David Pilgrim wrote that "Black brutes are depicted as hideous, terrifying predators who target helpless victims, especially white women."[6]

In *Gone With the Wind*, Gus, who molests Flora and chases her to her death, is the archetypical Black buck.[7] In folk music the brutal Black buck is Stagolee. On Christmas night in 1895, Tommy Shelton and his acquaintance William "Billy" Lyons were drinking in the Bill Curtis Saloon.[8] Lyons was also a member of St. Louis' underworld and may have been a political and business rival to Shelton. Eventually, the two men got into a dispute, during which Lyons took Shelton's Stetson hat. Subsequently, Shelton shot Lyons, recovered his hat, and left. Shelton's nickname was Shack Lee.

The murder quickly entered folklore and became the subject of the famous song "Stagolee."

> Billy Lyons told Stagolee
> Please don't take my life
> I got two little babe and a darling, lovin' wif
> That bad man! Oh, cruel Stagolee[9]

While Jim Crow was rationalized through the image of Blacks as so many Sambos, in the era of the drug wars, the underclass status of Blacks was rationalized by the notion that Blacks were criminals and thugs—updated versions of Bigger Thomas or the "brutal Black buck." But there is a twist. Racial formations of the late twentieth century and the twenty-first century do not rely on the mythology of biological inferiority. Rather, they are based on the notion that Blacks have a pathological culture, or dysfunctional families, or are simply prone to crime. We are all Bigger Thomases. This combined in the mid-to-late nineties with local narratives about Blacks as super-predators.[10] Crosscutting the narrative that Blacks are prone to crime due to culture or family structure is the narrative that the inner city is a war zone. "Underclass" and "inner city" have become signifiers for Black criminality.[11] This allows whites an opportunity to project conditions of ghetto poverty, joblessness, and squalor onto Blacks themselves and to do so under the claim of colorblindness: "We are not opposed to Blacks; we are opposed to crime." The narrative changes to race-neutral terms. What remains the same or worse is that the majority of Blacks are trapped in inner cities or in prisons. The ghetto becomes like the prison; the prison like the ghetto.[12] The perpetuation of racial caste and the narrative of Black underclass criminality are intertwined.

It is against this background that we must understand the evolution of stereotypes in film of the post-civil rights era. From the blaxploitation films of the late sixties to the emergence of the urban gangster films of the hip hop era, stereotypes on the screen help to rationalize and normalize the violence and subordination taking place off screen.

The Blaxploitation Era

From the mid to late fifties to 1975, African backs bent under the yoke of colonialism straightened themselves out.[13] About the same time Stokely Carmichael led a generation of youth chanting "Beep-beep, bang-bang, Ungowa, Black power," Dashikis and Afros sprouted among Black youth, and a new breed of Black hero, no longer shuffling, grinning, or tap dancing appears. He, or she, is baadasssss.

> The term "baadasssss" is synonymous with Blaxploitation: it connotes a rebellious spirit in African-American thinking, of "sticking it to the man", of misbehaving. Baadasssss-ness permeates African-American culture, from the oral folklore of Brer Rabbit to the "toasts" made famous by the late Rudy Ray Moore, such as "The Signifying Monkey". Being a baadasssss doesn't just mean being a tough-guy—not all baadassssses are tough (or guys)—but they are all literally "outlaws"—beyond, or outside of, the law. They work in those liminal spaces between the law, between illegality and vice on the one side and harmless decadence … on the other.[14]

Black people since slavery encountered the law as explicitly an enemy: racial caste and legal order were explicitly intertwined. In the post-civil rights era, this tension continues. The law was not explicitly an instrument of this oppression, but police in the urban ghetto, on a day-to-day basis, in the minds of Blacks, still have their foot on Black necks. The baadasssss Black heroes embody the anger of those still trapped in the ghetto who still see the law as enemy—and their heroes as outlaws in the folk hero tradition of Stagolee. Donald Bogle notes that one of the original stereotypes of Blacks was the "brutal Black buck." The "baadasssss" represented a return of the Black buck but with a new agenda: "to stick it to the man." The celebration of violence in these films, from a ghetto-centric point of view, represents inversion, a cultural process in which top and bottom values are reversed. These so called "Blaxploitation Films" valorize the violence and rage of the new Black bucks. From the ghetto-centric point of view this is a kind of racial reckoning: It is no longer the Black man who is whipped, but rather it is he or she that does the whipping.

But how are the new Black heroes able to do this? To live in the ghetto is to live within a place of de-humanizing conditions with no way out. It is to be an American, but at the same time walled out of America.

> The dark ghetto's invisible walls have been erected by the white society, by those who have power, both to confine those who have *no* power and to perpetuate their powerlessness. The dark ghettos are social, political, educational, and—above all—economic colonies. … The objective dimensions of the American urban ghettos are overcrowded and deteriorated housing, high infant mortality, crime, and disease. The subjective dimensions are resentment, hostility, despair, apathy, self-depreciation, and its ironic companion, compensatory … behavior.[15]

The new "Black bucks" are also the new "Magical Negroes." They crash through the invisible walls of the ghetto that Blacks feel trapped within; they come through the screen to touch and inspire urban Black audiences with new hope. In discussing these films, I will characterize them from two perspectives. The first is from the ghetto-centric perspective, the second from the perspective of the dominant society, which, through a jaundiced gaze, reduces the figures in the film to modern versions of old stereotypes.

Sweet Sweetback's Baadasssss Song

"A baadasssss Nigger is coming back to collect some dues."
Poster for Sweet Sweetback's Baadasssss Song

The "original" "baadasssss" Black film hero of the so called blaxploitation era was Sweet Sweetback of Melvin Van Peebles 1971 action thriller *Sweet Sweetback's Baadasssss Song*.[16] For decades, Black leading men had been asexual. Sweetback was hypermasculine and prolifically sexual. But he is not animalistic, driven by sexual desire. "Unlike most white heroes ... Sweetback participates in sex not out of lust, but to survive."[17] And where the Coon was an easily frightened coward, and the Tom bowed his head to submit to the Massa's violence, Sweetback met violence with violence. The film heralded not merely a new Black hero but, with its sensational success, a new breed of Afro-centric films. Sweet Sweetback became the prototype for a cottage industry of films called the "blaxploitation" genre.

As Van Peebles tells it, the film tells the story of the "bad nigger" who challenges the white power structure and wins, thus articulating the main feature of the blaxploitation formula. *Sweetback* is "a tough pimp raised in a brothel."[18] The brothel is in Watts. When a murder takes place, the police are under pressure to find a suspect. They arrange with a brothel owner to take Sweetback down to the station as patsy. On the way, the officers arrest another Black suspect, a Black Panther named Mu, and handcuff him to Sweetback—whose destinies are now symbolically intertwined. When Mu insults one of the officers, they uncuff him from Sweetback to beat him. Sweetback, using the handcuff still limply hanging from his wrist, beats the two police officers senseless.

"By jeopardizing his life to oppose racist violence, Sweetback becomes a political outlaw."[19] From then on, Sweetback is on the run from police. Hiding from the police, Sweetback travels through the urban underworld, "the ruined landscapes of Black life."[20] He survives by "hiding among the seams of illegitimate commerce: in whorehouses, gambling dens, voodoo churches and halfway houses for Black revolutionaries." Along the way the disenfranchised in these strata of society are humanized "without isolating such [figures] along the margin of plot and action."

Eventually, as one Black person after another helps Sweetback in his run from the law—a theme that traces back to Richard Wright and Ellison—he makes it to Mexico, and the film ends with the message "A baadasssss Nigger is coming back to collect some dues." Peebles later stated, "I wanted a victorious film, a film where niggers could walk out standing tall instead of avoiding each other's eyes." It was.

Sweetback's story of a Black outlaw who overcomes the law is a metaphor for the historical moment of Black struggle at that time. The notion is that Blacks as a people had progressed from street consciousness to revolutionary consciousness. Black Panther leader Huey Newton declared Sweetback was "the first truly revolutionary Black film made." It became required viewing for Black Panther members.

Shaft

Directed by Gordon Parks, *Shaft*[21] burst upon the scene in 1971. Richard Roundtree's Shaft reprised the role of the defiant Black unintimidated by whites (see Figure 7.2). Sporting an iconic afro haircut with large sideburns, wearing a full-length leather coat, he strongly asserts his cool and his Blackness. But Shaft also displays a cunning mind—he is the Black James Bond. This unique combination makes him amphibian, able to move fluidly between the two worlds. Shaft's "magic," in Bogle's terms, is his ability to bridge these two worlds. Unlike Sweet Sweetback, John Shaft has gotten out of the ghetto and established himself as a detective and business owner. Shaft is native to the urban ghetto but lives in an upscale apartment in Greenwich village and keeps an office in Times Square. In an era in which Black thought vacillated between collectivism of Black nationalism and the individualist desire to "get a piece of the pie," Shaft is individually capitalizing on his "dual citizenship" in both the "the ghetto" and the "white world." When white officers need information about what is happening up in Harlem, they send for him. At the same time, Bumpy Jonas sends for Shaft to rescue his daughter captured by the Mafia. "My people are not worth a damn outside of Harlem." Shaft's roots in the ghetto allow him to recruit Black militants as he makes a daring raid on a mafia "safe house."

Shaft's character is a variation on the theme of double consciousness.[22] Shaft not only moves between the ghetto and uptown, between different social strata, he bridges the seemingly unbridgeable gulf between "white norms and Black

Figure 7.2 Richard Roundtree as Shaft.

Source: Photograph, https://www.alamy.com/richard-roundtree-shaft-1971-mgm-file-reference-32557-345tha-image219066056.html?imageid=54156C16-B018-4F55-8515-A9AE301061DF&p=729462&pn=1&searchId=8f 83adaaf5ac252fc4459e82e8de4487&searchtype=0, taken December 31, 1970.

ones." Whiteness, on the one hand, requires that to have the good life one must get a decent job, obey the law, and observe a politics of respectability. But in the 1970s, Blacks saw the law as only the enemy. To be Black required a defiance of the very structures of authority that whiteness demands allegiance too. Shaft goes after bad guys, the mafia. But Shaft is still an outlaw in that while he fights for justice—street justice—he does it "gangster" style. When Shaft swings through the window and shoots down the white men holding an innocent Black girl hostage, a million Black voices across urban America cheered with one voice. Shaft "stuck it to the man," but the police can't touch him.

Super Fly

Oh, Superfly
You're gonna make your fortune by and by
But if you lose, don't ask no questions why
Curtis Mayfield, Superfly[23]

Figure 7.3 Super Fly.

Source: Alamy.

Super Fly[24] opens with two nameless junkies trying to rob Youngblood Priest, a dapper Black and Latino dope dealer, in the vestibule of a Harlem tenement (see Figure 7.3). After a scuffle, Priest disables one of the attackers while the other runs away with his money. As Curtis Mayfield unforgettably sings, "Little child, running wild …," Priest gives chase, taking the audience on a tour of "grimy dilapidated tenements of Harlem." No matter what we think of Priest, or his nameless junkie victim, the social setting of this vignette "forces us into a disturbing awareness of urban poverty, drugs, and the wicked symbiotic power relation between the junkie and the pusher man."[25] Priest chases the junkie into his home and takes back his money. Having established his Black machismo, we learn that Priest has grown a conscience and plans, with his partner Eddie, one last big score to provide his golden parachute out of the drug business.

Super Fly exemplifies another aspect of the dilemma of Black identity. Schools are disaster factories, there are no jobs, poverty and hopelessness sit over the ghetto like permanent cloud. But the same society holds up having one's own place, nice clothes, and a car as the elements of success. How does one survive, much less achieve success, in the ghetto? This creates a feeling of anomie, of being trapped, of having no way out.

What arises out of this tension between structural inequality and perceived needs is a culture—the culture of the street—which holds that one is justified in doing whatever one has to do to survive. Drug selling in this culture of the street is called "the game." In the context of the structural inequality of the ghetto, playing the game is a rational choice, albeit an extremely immoral one. Eddie, Priest's partner, expresses it this way: "It is a rotten game but it's the only one the man has left us to play."

Priest is good at it. He runs a drug organization with at least fifty employees selling cocaine. But the game is a trap. Priest lives in a posh apartment, is sought after by alluring women, and drives an iconic luxury car (a 1971 Eldorado Cadillac). Priest has all that and hundreds of thousands of dollars in ill-gotten gains. But he has no freedom. Being drug boss—working for the bigger (white) boss—is not a way out of the ghetto; it is just another level of control. "Another junkie plan, pushing dope for the man."[26] Once in the game you can never retire, until the bosses retire you through execution. This is moral slavery. Priest's "last big score," from the standpoint of the dominant society, is a crime. But from Priest's perspective it is a victory over "the man." *Super Fly* thematized the moral dilemma of life in the ghetto, the tension between "decency" and survival.

Despite the low budgets, the super-humanization, and the stereotyping from a ghetto-centric perspective, all these early films—*Sweetback*, *Super Fly*, and *Shaft*—were empowering.

What follows these early films by Black directors was true commodification. From 1973 to 1976 there was an explosion of Black-oriented films that lacked a social message but blatantly exploited the studio's desire for Blacks for films which featured familiar stereotypes of violent and hypersexual Black men and women.

There were some genuine efforts, such as *Buck and The Preacher*[27] by Sidney Poitier, about re-enslavement of Blacks after the Civil War and *Across 110th Street*,[28] about the struggle to get out of the ghetto. And I would also exempt the charismatic, fiercely assertive performances of Pam Grier and

Tamara Dobson, who through their portrayals empowered many young Black women.

Tamara Dobson debuts in *Cleopatra Jones*,[29] the Black female James Bond. Even more sensationally, the great Pam Grier electrified the screen with *Coffy* (1973),[30] *Foxy Brown* (1974), and *Sheba Baby* (1975). Pam Grier's signature was her incomparable combination of beauty, charisma, and warrior spirit, a baadasssss woman as resourceful as she was brave. "Grier deliberately uses the sexual stereotype to her advantage, reclaiming and transforming Black female sexuality."[31] She took on pimps, pushers, the mafia, and crooked politicians and always won. K. Jewell writes, "the media have defined African American womanhood into four categories: Mammy, Aunt Jemima, Sapphire and Jezebel/the Black bad girl." Dobson, Grier, and others showed African American women in a new light—tough no-nonsense women who fully embraced their sensuality, but, according to Alan Ebert, "took no shit from The Man."

There were notable exceptions. But overall, the moral ambition to tell an authentic story about the Black experience was gone. Until the 1990s, Hollywood, notable exceptions aside, produced race porn.

From Fred Williamson's *Black Caesar*,[32] a Harlem hit man who murders over thirty mobsters for revenge, to *The Mack*,[33] *Shaft in Africa*,[34] *Boss Nigger*,[35] and *Bucktown*[36] (literally), the genre featured a Black underworld crime boss, a pimp, a killer for hire. There was almost a comic aspect to this, as Blacks were super-humanized and often presented as violent psychopaths or sometimes monsters: *Blacula*,[37] *Blackenstein*.[38]

The Eurocentric Perspective

White audiences, white critics, and many in the Black middle class viewed these films either through the lens of pre-existing notions of Black deviance or criminality, in the case of whites, or through the window of a politics of respectability in the case of the Black middle class. Both perspectives were Eurocentric. For white audiences, the films reinforced the presumption that Blacks were dangerous or criminal, a presumption that never dissipated despite the introduction of equal opportunity laws. For these white audiences, the new Black-era heroes were all race porn, a parade of violent, hypersexed Black "super-dudes" and "super-gals" who titillated their taste for Black stereotypes. The Black middle-class view was expressed by Junius Griffin, the head of the Hollywood Branch of the NAACP. "We must insist that our children are not constantly exposed to a steady diet of so-called Black movies that glorify Black males as pimps, dope pushers, gangsters and super-males."[39]

More bluntly, Roy Innis stated that these movies promoted "Black genocide in the Black community."[40]

The denigration, in my view, was less something that was intrinsic to the films—some were works of art. Just as police cannot distinguish between law-abiding Black citizens and urban criminals, the reductionist, Eurocentric lens of the audience that viewed the films only saw denigrating stereotypes.

The reductionist view of these films became hegemonic. All the films were lumped to together under the heading of "Blaxploitation." The stereotype of the ghetto as a place of violence, drugs and sin, as well as the stereotype of hyperviolent Black "outlaws," was deeply inscribed into our culture through these films.

Intersectionality Arrives

As we have noted, between 1970 and 2000, millions of Blacks escaped the ghetto and moved to the suburbs. Increasingly during this period, inner city and underclass, both spatial metaphors, became code words for race. Race and urban space became signifiers of each other. Race became a spectrum: Black underclass is stigmatized, but the Blacks who make it out of the ghetto, the talented tenth, the John Prentices, have access to a kind of "respectability."

This gives rise to two new cinematic tropes, new vehicles for the old racial stereotypes that Blacks were presumptively dangerous and prone to crime. One image is the trope of the ghetto as war zone, another America, another continent, another world: a hyper-violent lawless space populated by criminals. The other image is that of the urban gangster or thug. Race thus becomes a spectrum, with decent, law abiding, credentialed, affluent Blacks on one side, in the suburbs, and dangerous, criminal, saggy-pants, hoodie-wearing Blacks in the ghetto on the other.

Two elements of the new era of films served as a foundation for this narrative. First, the new era of Black films typically featured pimps, pushers, hit men, or criminals as their central characters. The second was that the action was typically set in the inner city, a place already associated by a generation of blaxploitation films and years of evening news with violence and crime. A new Black criminal emerges in these cultural productions; he is both Black and underclass, defined both by race and place: the urban ghetto. The flip side of this new stereotyping was the narrative that the ghetto is a war zone. At the same time these narratives played out on film, they mirrored the evening news.

In 1988 Dan Rather did a special which typified evening news coverage of the time. The recasting of South Central as a U.S. war zone was brought to us by NBC news on Dan Rather's special report, "48 Hours: On Gang Street." A year later *COPS* premiered as a reality show, which purported to film police doing their jobs, but focused overwhelmingly on the arrest of suspects in Black communities. However, as Richard Benjamin writes,

> To enjoy "Cops" is to relish seeing black, Latinx, and poor men harangued, choked, slammed, shot at, and handcuffed by police officers, with no meaningful context or resolution to any given human being's situation.[41]

In 1990, Robert Entman did a famous study[42] that quantified statistically the way Blacks in the ghetto were caricatured. He looked at three 10-day periods covered by ABC, CBS, and NBC news.

1. About 77 percent of the stories, in which Blacks were accused, concerned a violent or a drug crime. … In other words the overwhelming majority of Black crime stories concerned violence or drugs.
2. Blacks were twice as likely as whites to be shown in the grasp of a police officer.
3. The image of police breaking into a house was shown seven times during the period. In six of the cases, the occupants were Black.
4. Ten stories during the period focused on people selling drugs. In six of those cases, such images were of Blacks.

Stereotypes found in news are harder to resist because the news is real. While the images are entirely stereotypical, they are presented as neutral. Entman notes that "the benign guise" of these stereotypical images encourages the racial coding of "criminal behavior."[43] In effect, viewers are "primed" to consider crime through the lens of their racial stereotype.

By the 1990s, blaxploitation films, with super-Blacks sticking it to the man, gave way to Hood films, which aimed more at authenticity than super-humanization.

Boyz n the Hood[44] is the classic example. The film, which would be nominated for Academy Awards, was a "coming-of-age" drama set in South Central. Directed by John Singleton, it starred Ice Cube, Laurence Fishburne, Cuba Gooding, Jr., Nia Long, Angela Bassett, and Regina King. The film opens with the quote: "One out of 21 Black American males will be murdered in their lifetime. Most will die at the hands of another Black male."

Singleton's film delivers the heart-stopping urgency of this issue through a story of three young Black men, Tre, Doughboy, and Ricky, growing up in South Central L.A. It tells the story from their point of view. South Central is not the ghetto of *Shaft* and *Super Fly*. This is much worse. This is the post-industrial ghetto. Structural inequality of the 1970s inner city has festered into concentrated poverty, joblessness, and despair. Heroin has given way to crack. Drugs and crime—particularly gang violence—have reached epidemic proportions. Social programs were replaced with more police. Los Angeles Police Department (LAPD) helicopters fly constantly overhead, invoking the narrative of the ghetto as a war zone. Ice Cube, who plays Doughboy, calls it "concrete Vietnam." The central character is Tre Styles, played by Cuba Gooding, Jr. Tre is a talented young man on the path to college—if he can stay out of trouble. But in his Watts neighborhood, trouble lurks around every corner.

Tre and Ricky go to the store and on the way home encounter a car full of thugs with whom Ricky has had an altercation. They kill Ricky in a drive-by execution. Tre faces a dilemma of whether to continue his path to college, or to avenge the death of his friend. The film thematizes yet another dilemma of the Black urban experience. Singleton paints the dilemma as a choice between self-destruction and the potential for building a better community. At an individual level, Singleton's catechism rings true. Singleton was nominated for an Academy Award and won the NAACP image award and the MTV Movie award for best new filmmaker. It's a brilliant film.

In the same year as *Boyz n the Hood*, *New Jack City*[45] made its debut. While *Boyz n the Hood* looked at the ghetto from its point of view of the Blacks in the underclass, *New Jack City* looks at the ghetto through the lens of decent society.

Variety's critic called it "a provocative, pulsating update on gangster pics … (the) powerful anti-drug sentiment will pack a punch with urban audiences." The film thematizes the plight of the Black community as the crack epidemic takes hold. Wesley Snipes, Ice T, and Melvin Van Peebles all perform their roles with charisma against the background of Queen Latifa's vocals and a driving beat. The film's rhythm and realism about how the crack epidemic began are engaging. It remains a hip-hop classic. It tells a story about the rise, and fall, of the ruthless Nino Brown, leader of what in the beginning is a small-time gang of hustlers called the Cash Money Brothers. Nino devilishly seizes upon the emergence of what is at the time (1986) a new drug called "crack" to build a criminal empire. His base is an apartment building, famously called the Carter, that he has taken over by force. Nino Brown and his lieutenants use computers, they have sophisticated marketing skills, and they turn their employees into "crack slaves." In turn, the residents in the Carter are both hostages and prisoners of Nino and his gang.

New Jack City sermonizes against drugs, showing "a drug dealer's hollow triumph" and his "tragic end." Nino, who lives by the sword and is virtually untouchable by the police, is brutally gunned down in the end by an elderly vigilante whom Nino had earlier humiliated.

But Van Peebles balances his moralizing with what is tacitly a sophisticated economic analysis of the problem. Jeffrey Miron, in his book *Drug War Crimes: The Consequences of Prohibition*,[46] shows that always criminalizing drugs created an international Black market for drugs driven by supply and demand. Miron goes on to show that taking one drug dealer off the street affects the price of drugs but has no effect on supply or demand. Van Peebles channels Miron through Nino Brown's soliloquy on the witness stand:

> I'm not guilty. You're the one that's guilty. The lawmakers, the politicians, the Columbian drug lords, all you who lobby against making drugs legal. Just like you did with alcohol during the prohibition. You are the one who's guilty. I mean, c'mon let's kick the ballistics here: Ain't no Uzis made in Harlem. Not one of us owns a poppy field. *This thing is bigger than Nino Brown.* This is big business. This is the American way. [emphasis added]

Menace To Society II:[47] Struggling to Achieve Respect

White racism created the ghetto. White racism maintains it and keeps the Black poor trapped there. The crimes of Blacks who live in the ghetto are popularly conceived of as manifestations of broken families, cultural pathology, or simply bad choices. But given the fact that racism has created the social conditions underlying the pathology and keeps the Black underclass trapped in this ethos, there is a political dimension to these so-called bad choices. Therefore, Blacks are not mere hoodlums or criminals. Their crimes, while not political crimes like criticizing a tyrant, are not conventional crimes against persons and property either, or even, as one sociologist put it, "a distorted form of social protest." "Instead, their words and deeds must be seen as part of a struggle to right wrongs as much as to enrich themselves. The underclass are soldiers in a race war, activists in a social movement."[48]

While the violence of the ghetto seems random, it is part of a larger pattern of structural violence. The same white racism that created the ghetto created conditions of joblessness and lack of opportunity, which, working in tandem, create a sense of no future and despair. Compounding these conditions, there is a constant sense, as the police stop and sometimes arrest Blacks for no good reason, that to be Black, especially a Black man, and live in the ghetto is to have a target on one's back. These conditions create a sense of "anomie,"[49] or what Elijah Anderson calls alienation.[50] This can be read equally as anxiety about survival itself. What arises out of these conditions is street culture, or what Elijah Anderson calls the code of the street. The code of the street is about a struggle for survival, as a mature adult character instructs the youths, "Being a Black man in America isn't easy. The hunt is on, and you're the prey. All I'm saying is … all I'm saying is … Survive."[51]

The currency of survival in the ghetto is respect. Tragically, getting respect in the ghetto generally comes at the expense both of law and order and the well-being of the community. Respect comes from being large and in charge, the leader of a gang, a drug kingpin, having money, a hustle, or beating down others, robbing, or intimidating those around you. The violence of living in these ghetto conditions is internalized.

Menace to Society II, filmed in the Jordan Downs Housing Project in Watts, is a great film which explores how the then brutalization of Blacks by social conditions and the violence in the ghetto are at the root of this cruel code of respect. While the violent acts which take place in the ghetto are seen as evil, they are in part the expression of this internalized trauma. There are two main characters: Kaydee "Caine" Lawson played by Tyrin Turner and Kevin "O'Dog" Anderson, played by Lorenz Tate. In the first scene of the film, O'Dog kills a Korean shopkeeper who made the mistake of commenting on his mother, and then (for good measure) kills the shopkeeper's wife, as well. Although he lives by intimidation, O'Dog is so bereft of inner resources that avoiding shame and punishing those who shame him consume his life. The film flashes back to Caine as a child in onesies watching his father, a drug dealer, commit a senseless murder. Played by Samuel L. Jackson, Caine's father Tat Lawson shoots down his own friend because he disrespects him while playing cards. The film laments the cycle of violence—Caine becomes a drug dealer and a violent thug robbing and killing with O'Dog in the streets of South-Central L.A.

While *New Jack City* moralized, *Menace to Society II* makes no judgments. Imagine you are exiled to a place, a "God-forsaken" place where there is no law except the law of survival. There is no way out except by taking what others on the island have. Brother robs brother. Everyone on the island feels trapped in a cycle of violence that constantly repeats from one generation to the next. The film invokes this "God-forsaken place" metaphor explicitly. Caine's grandfather, trying to turn Caine and O'Dog away from their lives of crime, invokes God's commandments in the Bible: "Thou Shalt Not Kill," he says. O'Dog replies, "I don't think God cares too much about us or he wouldn't have put us *here*."

From a realist point of view, from the point of view of someone who grew up in the inner city, I identify with the characters and the urban dilemmas that are thematized. I embrace the truth of both *Boyz* and *New Jack* as art and as testimony.

But the received message of the films was very different.

As Linus Abraham writes, "even in situations where the director's ideological leaning is toward anti-violence … [the film] draws its dramatic visual force from the film's insider depiction of gangster culture," and "the [film's] visual violence critical to the film's appeal contradicts and defeats the director's antiviolence message."[52]

The films merge and reinforce the racial coding of the inner city and the inner city's underclass that was daily occurring on the evening news. Jacquie Jones writes,

> The stories that predestined 1991's summer ghetto blockbusters *New Jack City* and *Boyz n the Hood*, ... first came to the American public in the form of television news. From the advent of drive-by shootings in L.A. and leather-jackets-for-lives in Detroit, gangs, drugs, and the accompanying violence became an expected fixture from six to seven, and then again at eleven, in American homes. The news became the factory for black mass media imagery.[53]

Thus, it appears "distinctions no longer exist between movies, news, television in their depictions of African Americans. They all supply a steady diet of negative images that tap into long standing stereotypic character traits of sambo and the savage."[54] What emergences from the films like this—as a result of the reductionist gaze of the dominant society—is that the Black inner-city underclass is criminalized and racialized. In turn, the ghetto is another country, deadly dangerous, a no-man's-land populated by junkies, criminals, and psychopaths.

These 1990s themes continue through a genre of hood films which double as horror films like *Judgement Night*, *Trespass*, and *Training Day*. These later projects seem to accept the tropes of the underclass as a community of criminals and the ghetto as war zone—not as metaphor or hyperbole but as fact. The ghetto is exoticized as the nightmare world next door.

Judgment Night[55] is typical of the genre. Premised on a crudely drawn binary opposition between the comforts of suburbia and the mortal dangers of the inner city, it tells the story of a group of suburban men driving to a boxing match who take a wrong turn into a bad neighborhood on Chicago's South Side, witness a murder, and spend the rest of the night running from the drug dealers who are responsible for the killing.

"In *Trespass*, white middle-class main characters are trapped in an abandoned East St. Louis factory where they are forced to fight for their lives against an Uzi-wielding Black gang."[56] These scenes of crossing over into the netherworld of urban decay "exude the Manichean, middle class paranoia that once you leave the bourgeois life you are immediately prey to crime, madness, squalor and poverty."[57] The horror story genre is only the most obvious mainstream effort to exploit the stereotypes whites have about the ghetto. There is a whole genre of films that, while not explicitly focusing on race, use the ghetto as a backdrop and have major Black characters. Whenever Hollywood situates itself in the ghetto, the film is populated with demeaning images.

In *Training Day*,[58] Denzel Washington stars in a police drama which explores the issue of police corruption. The film clearly individualizes the problem as a function of character rather than something rooted in the system itself. Alonzo Harris, senior narcotics detective, played by Denzel Washington, is a criminal with a badge. Jake Hoyt, played by Ethan Hawke, the ramrod-straight rookie, is the good cop. Jake is white. Alonzo is Black.

When we meet Jake, he is with his wife and family. It is a place of warmth and of dreams. He speaks of the house he wants to buy and his goals for his career. Jake moves up from patrolman to work with Alonzo as trainee detective in the drug war. The war is being fought in the Los Angeles ghetto. The ghetto in the film is called "The Jungle." It is so dangerous that Alonzo will not let Jake, a policeman, go there by himself. In this jungle, the image of the black criminal and the animal are knotted together. Concomitantly, the ghetto really is a jungle. "The stereotypes are true." Harris, though he wears a badge, is an animal as well, a brute, a savage. The notion is, however, that Hoyt, the white cop, is the polar opposite of Harris, and that the suburbs are a polar opposite to the ghetto. Listen to an exchange between Alonzo and Hoyt. It captures this symbolism quite well. Alonzo, corrupting the law, has just released two would-be rapists.

> Harris: You know they would have killed you without hesitating.
> Hoyt: That's why they belong in prison.
> Harris: For what they did they got beat down. They lost their rock; they lost their money. Those eses from the Eastside are probably gonna smoke 'em. What else do you want?
> Hoyt: I want justice.
> Harris: Is that not justice?
> Hoyt: That's Street justice. Oh, just let the animals wipe themselves out.
> Harris: God willing. Fuck 'em and everybody who looks likes them …. To protect the sheep, you gotta catch the wolf. It takes a wolf to catch a wolf.

What drives this stereotyping home is that throughout the film in the ghetto that Hoyt and Harris patrol we meet crews, posses, crack addicts, and thugs, but no decent families. In the real world, the criminals in the ghetto are a small minority. The media and Hollywood films treat them as the norm, however. The part stands for the whole. Hoyt's worldview of the underclass in the neighborhood he patrols is precisely the worldview of the film, which also echoes, as it is the worldview of the evening news.

The Visible and the Invisible:
The Legacy of a Culture of Fear in Film

> Race has become metaphorical—a way of referring to and disguising forces, events, classes, and expressions of social decay ... far more threatening to the body politic than biological race ever was.[59]

In Lewis Payton Jr's film *The Slowest Car in Town*, a Black man dressed in a business suit enters an elevator on the eighteenth floor of an office building. The elevator makes four stops. At each stop the Black man is stereotyped a different way by the white[s] he encounters. First a white woman gets on and, seeing it is a Black man, exits at the next stop. Then two whites enter the elevator and they "see" not a businessman but an African bushman holding a spear and "hear" roaring drumbeats. The next whites to enter the elevator see him as a shackled convict, dressed in prison stripes. Other passengers see him as a drooling crack addict.

Payton's film captures the idea that the stereotypical image of the Black person in the white mind has many faces. These images are in large part a function of media portrayals, from the evening news to Hollywood films over the last forty years. How does this happen? The images of Blacks we see on our screens function as metaphors. All metaphors function by borrowing an image of something we can see, like color or blood, and linking that to something abstract such as race. In this case it is not merely linkage but substitution. In Ellison's *Invisible Man*, he thematizes this problem arguing that racism made him invisible as an individual.

> I am an invisible man. No, I am not a spook like those who haunted Edgar Allen Poe; nor am I one of your Hollywood movie ectoplasms. I am a man of flesh and bone, fiber and liquids—and I might even be said to possess a mind. I am invisible, understand simply because people refuse to see

me. Like the bodiless heads you see sometimes in circus sideshows, it is as though I have been surrounded by mirrors of hard, distorting glass. When they approach me, they see only my surroundings, themselves, or figments of their imagination—indeed everything and anything except me.[60]

Franz Fanon makes a similar argument. He describes how the whites not only refuse recognition of the Black but reduce him through their colonialist gaze to a "savage". "I was battered down by tom-toms, cannibalism, intellectual deficiency, fetichism, racial defects, slave-ships, and above all else, above all: 'Sho good eatin.'"[61] Ellison and Fanon speak of the same phenomenon.

Whether we speak of Fanon's colonialist gaze or Ellison's concept of invisibility, we speak of the power of denigrating racial images. These images of Blacks in Hollywood films and on the evening news—as criminals spread-eagled over the police car or thugs chillin' and killin' in the hood—anchor the presumptions we have been talking about in this book. They go before Blacks when they enter an elevator, a taxi, a courtroom. They distort not only the perception of police, but also judges, mayors, legislators, and governors when they craft criminal justice policies.

On June 6, 1986, Massachusetts Governor Michael Dukakis released Willie Horton from prison as part of a weekend furlough program. Horton had been sentenced to life imprisonment without the possibility of parole.[62] But Horton did not return to the prison as planned. On April 3, 1987, in Oxon Hill, Maryland, Horton twice raped a woman after pistol-whipping, knifing, binding, and gagging her fiancé. He then stole the car belonging to the man he had assaulted.

Consider the case of Willie Horton. By 1988 Governor Dukakis was a candidate for president, running against George H. W. Bush. A political action committee that supported Bush seized on the Horton incident to run a series of political attack ads accusing Dukakis of being soft on crime. The attack ad series was called "Weekend Pass."[63] It flashed Horton's picture and portrayed Horton's vicious criminal acts as the proximate result of Dukakis's "liberal" crime policies. Later ads showed a series of prisoners walking through a revolving door. Dukakis would lose the election. But what was interesting here was that while most rapes and murders are committed by whites, Horton, a Black man, became the poster child for violent crime. This demonization is possible in large part because of a presumption not merely that Blacks are prone to crime but that they are beasts and savages. "Willie Horton symbolized the threat that Black males aided by liberal politicians, pose to innocent whites."[64] But how is it possible that the mere image of a Willie Horton, associated with a story about what this particular Black man did, could result in moral panic against Black men as a class of people? This is the mischief of decades of Hollywood images. The image of Black men as murderers and rapists was already "there."

These images have a lot to do with the scapegoating—Willie Hortonizing— of Black men as the cause of crime in the streets, from the drug war to the war against guns; with the Reagan-era scapegoating of Black women as welfare queens; the super-predator hysteria of the 1990s; the demonizing and conviction of five young Black men in the Central Park Jogger case;[65] the constitutional apartheid we see in the programs of stop and frisk; the public humiliation and shaming by arrest of Black people in public spaces for sitting in Starbucks without buying coffee or for falling asleep while reading a book in a Yale College dorm; and with the epidemic of Black men, women, and children gunned down unarmed by police who do so with impunity.

This is what happens when real people become invisible. The presumption of guilt/dangerousness and invisibility are two sides of a single coin of social identity.

Ava DuVernay, writing about the Central Park Five, titles her film, "*When They See Us.*" I ask, "Do they see us?" Do they see us or do stereotypes drawn from film or the evening news block out our individuality like Ralph Ellison's hard opaque glass?

Notes

1   See Harriett Beecher Stowe, *Uncle Tom's Cabin: Authoritative Text, Backgrounds, Contexts, Criticism* (New York: W.W. Norton, 2018). Sambo was the overseer to Simon Legree. In *Uncle Tom's Cabin* he was essentially a cruel person. Ironically, the term Sambo seems to have entered the lexicon following the publication of Stowe's book (1852) as a stereotype of a child-like Black person. See also Joseph Boskin, *Sambo: the Rise and Demise of an American Jester* (New York: Oxford University Press, 1986).

2   John W. Blassingame, *The Slave Community: Plantation Life in the Antebellum South*, revised edition (New York: Oxford University Press, 1979), 230; See also D. Marvin Jones, *Race, Sex and Suspicion: The Myth of the Black Male* (London: Bloomsbury Academic, 2005), 18.

3   Richard Wright, *Native Son* (New York: Harper Collins, 2005).

4   Tupac Shakur, "Words of Wisdom", track no. 6, on *2Pacalypse Now*, Interscope Records, 1991, Audio CD.

5   David Pilgrim, *Understanding Jim Crow: Using Racist Memorabilia to Teach Tolerance, and Promote Social Justice* (New York: PM Press, 2015).

6   Lori Latrice Martin, *White Sports/Black Sports* (Santa Barbara, CA: Praeger, 2015) quoting Pilgrim, *Understanding Jim Crow*. See also Donald Bogle, *Toms, Coons, Mulattoes, Mammies, and Bucks: An Interpretive History of Blacks in American Films* (New York: Bloomsbury Academic Press, 2016).

7   Bogle, *Toms, Coons, Mulattoes, Mammies, and Bucks*.

8   Paul Oliver, *Songsters and Saints: Vocal Traditions on Race Records* (New York: University of Cambridge Press, 1984). All the facts concerning the song Stagolee are taken from this source. Excellent book.

9   Cecil Brown, *Stagolee Shot Billy* (Cambridge, MA: Cambridge University Press 2003).

10   Vincent E. Kappeler, *The Mythology of Crime and criminal Justice, Fifth Edition* (Long Grove, IL: Waveland Press, 2018); James C. Howell, *Preventing and Reducing Juvenile Delinquency* (Thousand Oaks, CA: Sage, 2003), 17. The super-predator myth originated when James Q. Wilson predicted a massive increase in juvenile violence in the 1990s. John Dilulio in 1995 coined the term super-predator to refer to "a new breed" of offenders, "kids that have absolutely no respect for human life and no sense of the future … these are stone cold predators!" Dilulio warned that by the year 2000 an additional 30,000 young "murderers, rapists, and muggers" would be roaming America's streets, sowing mayhem. See John Dilulio, "The Coming of the Super-Predators," *The Weekly Standard* (November 27, 1995). See also Bennett, Dilulio and Waters, *Body Count: Moral Poverty: How to Win America's War against Crime and Drugs* (New York: Simon & Schuster, 1996). The super-predator myth was a driving force behind a wave of moral panic which crystallized in the form of laws like the 1994 Crime Bill, championed by then Senator Biden and President Bill Clinton. The bill included 9.7 billion dollars for new prisons and putting 100,000 police on city streets. Over forty States passed laws pushing juveniles into adult courts and authorizing life without parole.

11   See D. Marvin Jones, *Fear of a Hip-Hop Planet: America's New Dilemma* (New York: Praeger, 2013).

12   Loïc Wacquant, "Deadly Symbiosis: When Ghetto and Prison Meet and Mesh," *Punishment and Society* 3, no. 1 (2001) 95–133.

13   The decolonization of Africa took place from the late 1950s to 1975. For example, Ghana received its independence in 1957. Scott Thompson, Ghana's *Foreign Policy, 1957-1966: Diplomacy, Ideology, and the New State* (Princeton, NJ: Princeton University Press, 1969). Angola received its independence under the Alvor agreement from Portugal in 1975, W. James Martin, *A Political History of the Civil War in Angola, 1974–1990* (New Brunswick, NJ: Transaction Publishers, 1992).

14   Michael J. Koven, *Blaxploitation Films* (Harpenden: Oldcastle Books, 2010).

15   Kenneth Clark and William Junius Wilson, *Dark Ghetto: The Dilemmas of Social Power* (Middletown, CT: Wesleyan University Press, 1989).

16   *Sweet Sweetback's Baadasssss Song*, dir. by Melvin Van Peebles, (Original release 1971, Yeah, Inc.).

17   Mark A. Reid, Redefining Black Film (Berkeley, CA: University of California Press, 1993).

18   William R. Grant, *Post-Soul Black Cinema: Discontinuities, Innovations, and Breakpoints* (New York: Routledge, 2004). The quote appears in Appendix B, Brief Plot Summary of Sweet Sweetback's Baadasssss Song (no page number available).

19   Novotny Lawrence and Gerald R. Butters, *Beyond Blaxploitation* (Detroit, MI: Wayne State University Press, 2016).

20   Xavier Mendik and Steven Jay Schneider, *U. S. A.: Filmmaking Beyond the Hollywood Cannon* (New York: Columbia University Press, 2003).

21   *Shaft*, directed by Gordon Parks (1971, Los Angeles, CA: Metro-Goldwyn Meyer).

22   Also, in 1972 the studio presented *Trouble Man* starring Robert Hooks. The film has a character who is similarly split, again reflecting the doubleness of Black life in America. The soundtrack retains cult status. "I grew up hard babe, but now I'm cool, I didn't make it sugar playin' by the rules" (Marvin Gaye, theme from *Trouble Man*).

23   Curtis Mayfield, "Super Fly", July 11, 1971, R.C.A. Studios, track no. 9, on *Super Fly*, R.C.A.

24   *Super Fly*, directed by Gordon Parks (1972, Burbank, CA: Warner Brothers).

25   John David Slocum, *Violence and American Cinema*, New York: Routledge, 2001), 191.

26 Curtis Mayfield, "Freddie's Dead", July 11, 1972, track no. 3 on *Super Fly*, R.C.A. Studios.

27 *Buck and The Preacher*, directed by Sidney Poitier (1972, Culver City, CA: Columbia Pictures).

28 *Across 110th Street*, directed by Barry Shear (1972, Beverly Hills, CA: United Artists).

29 *Cleopatra Jones*, directed by Jack Starrett (Burbank, CA: Warner Brothers, 1973).

30 *Coffy*, directed by Jack Hill (1973, Los Angeles, CA: American International Pictures).

31 Y. D. Sims, *Women of Blaxploitation: How the Black Action Film Heroine Changed American Popular Culture* (Jefferson, NC: McFarland, 2006), 80

32 *Black Caesar*, directed by Larry Cohen (1973, Los Angeles, CA: American International Pictures).

33 *The Mack*, directed by Michael Campus (1973, New York: Harbor Productions).

34 *Shaft in Africa*, directed by John Guillermin (1973, Beverly Hills, CA: Metro Goldwyn Meyer).

35 *Boss Nigger*, directed by Jack Arnold (1975, Dimension Pictures).

36 *Bucktown*, directed by Artur Marks (1975, Los Angeles, CA: American International Pictures).

37 *Blacula*, directed by William Crain (1972, Los Angeles, CA: American International Pictures).

38 *Blackenstein*, directed by William A. Levey (1973, Prestige Pictures U.S.).

39 Junius Griffin, "Hollywood and the Black Community" in *The Crisis*, (Baltimore, MD: The Crisis Publishing Company, volume 80, May 1973).

40 Aram Gouzidian, *Sidney Poitier: Man, Actor, Icon* (Durham, NC: University of North Carolina Press, 2004), 344.

41 Richard Benjamin, "Not Just 'COPS': It's Time to End the Entertainment Industry's Anti-Black, Pro-Police Programming," *The Intercept*, June 20, 2020. "Not Just 'Cops': Culture Industry Must End Anti-Black Content" (theintercept. com).

42 Robert Entman, "Representation and Reality in the Portrayal of Blacks on Network and Television News," *Journalism Quarterly* 71, no. 3 (1994): 511–12.

43 Jones, *Fear of a Hip-Hop Planet*.

44 *Boyz n the Hood*, directed by John Singleton (1991, Culver City, CA: Columbia Pictures).

45 *New Jack City*, directed by Mario Van Peebles (1991, Burbank, CA: Warner Brothers Pictures).

46 Jeffrey Miron, *Drug War Crimes: The Consequences of Prohibition* (Oakland, CA: The Independent Institute, 2004).

47 *Menace To Society II*, directed by The Hughes Brothers (1993, Burbank, CA: New Line Cinema).

48 Thomas Halper and Douglas Muzzio, "Menace II Society? Urban Poverty and Underclass Narratives in American Movies," *European Journal of American Studies* 8, no. 1 (Spring, 2013) 1–31.

49 The concept of anomie goes back to Durkheim. See Emile Durkheim, *Selected Writings* (New York: Cambridge University Press, 1968); see also Robert King Merton, *Social Structure and Anomie* (New York: The Free Press, 1968). Generally, it refers to "normlessness." This is often associated with "strain theory."

50 Elijah Anderson, *Code of the Street: Decency, Violence and the Moral Life of the Inner City* (New York: W.W. Norton, 1999).

51 Mr. Butler, a high school teacher to Caine in *Boyz in the Hood*.

52 See Linus Abraham "Media Stereotypes of African Americans" in Paul Martin Lester, Susan Dente Ross, eds., *Images that Injure* (Westport, C T: Greenwood Press 2003), 89.

53 Abraham, *Images that Injure*.

54 Ibid., 90.

55 *Judgment Night*, directed by Stephen Hopkins (Universal City, CA: Universal Pictures, 1993).

56 *Trespass*, directed by Walter Hill (Universal City, CA: Universal Pictures, 1992).

57 Jones, *Fear of a Hip-Hop Planet*.

58 *Training Day*, directed by Antoine Fuqua (Burbank, CA: Warner Brothers, 2001).

59 Toni Morrison, *Playing in the Dark: Whiteness and the Literary Imagination* (Cambridge, MA: Harvard University Press, 1992), 63.

60 Ralph Ellison, *Invisible Man* (New York: Random House, 1995).

61 Franz Fanon, *Black Skin White Masks* (New York: Grove Press, 2008).

62 Kenneth F. Warren, *Encyclopedia of U.S. Campaigns, Elections, and Electoral Behavior* (London: Sage, Volume 1, 2008), 153.

63 Antoine J. Banks, *Anger and Racial Politics: The Emotional Foundation of Racial Attitudes in America* (New York: Cambridge University Press, 2014).

64 Jones, *Race, Sex, and Suspicion*, 168.

65 For a detailed account of this case see Jones, *Race, Sex and Suspicion*; See also Natalie Bayfield, *Savage Portrayals: Race Media and the Central Park Jogger Story* (Philadelphia, PA: Temple University Press, 2014); see also Yusef Salem, *Words of a Man: My Right to Be* (New York, Omo Misha, 2017), a selection of poems; Iboi Zoboi and Yusef Salaam, *Punching the Air* (New York: Harper Collins, 2020).

8

Conclusion

The presumption was born on the plantation. Slaves were regarded as property and subject to absolute domination by the master. By 1660, throughout the United States, slavery was reserved for "Blacks only."[1] They were deprived of all freedom, all honor, and all rights. In a society which professed the belief that all men are created equal, these deprivations required a rationale. The deprivation of freedom can of course be justified if the individual has committed a crime. But what crime had Blacks committed that they should be slaves from birth? Listen to Justice Taney, who, in 1857, precisely captured the worldview of the master class as he infamously upheld the constitutionality of slavery.

> They had for more than a century before been regarded as beings of an inferior order, altogether unfit to associate with the white race … and so far inferior that they had no rights that the white man was bound to respect and that the negro might justly and lawfully be reduced to slavery for his benefit. He was bought and sold, and treated as an ordinary article of merchandise and traffic whenever a profit could be made by it. This opinion was at that time fixed and universal in the civilized portion of the white race. It was regarded as an axiom in morals as well as in politics, which no one thought of disputing or supposed to be open to dispute, and men in every grade and position in society daily and habitually acted upon it … without doubting for a moment the correctness of this opinion.[2]

Taney refers to this notion of Black inferiority as an axiom. An axiom is something we assume—or "presume"—to be true.

Arthur De Gobineau and other "phrenologists" tried to anchor this "axiom" or "presumption" of inferiority in science. The phrenologists argued that, based on the study of human skulls, there was scientific proof that Blacks were biologically inferior. Theologians, on the other hand, could rely upon the writings of Thomas Aquinas, who held that Blacks were on the lower rung of "the great chain of being," above an ape but lower than a man. But the popular rationalization of this claim of Black inferiority was based on the Bible. The master class viewed Blacks as descendants of Ham, who were cursed by Noah to be slaves. Some call it the curse of Noah,[3] others "the curse of Ham."

Like a curse, Taney's axiom, which I refer to as a "presumption," has followed Blacks down the corridors of history from generation to generation.

Dr. Ossian Sweet encountered the presumption when he bought a house in a white neighborhood in Detroit in 1933. The presumption that he encountered was that because he was Black, he and his family had low morals, or that they were dirty, or prone to crime. It was as if Blackness was associated with a virus that had to be kept out of the neighborhood. Our neighborhood. This was largely a presumption of biological inferiority. The same presumption motivated a mob of whites to riot and attack his home. When someone shot a white member of the attacking mob, Leo Briner, the presumption anchored the decision to prosecute Dr. Sweet in his death. This was true in spite of the obvious claim of self-defense and in spite of the fact that there was no evidence that Sweet had fired a shot or directed anyone to do so.

The same presumption that Ossian Sweet faced in the 1930s shaped the making of what Arnold Hirsch called "the second ghetto" in the 1940s and 1950s. Millions of Blacks migrated to the North during and after World War II in the hope of a promised land of better jobs and equal opportunity. They found neither. They were relegated to urban ghettos. The presumption of Blacks as ignorant, lazy, frightening in their "volatility, carnality, and their utter incapacity to learn the lessons of civilized society" drove the concentration of Blacks on the ragged edge of industry in the inner city. This presumption was the impetus for a policy of redlining by both the federal government and its partners in the banking industry. It was the impetus for the phenomenon of massive white flight.

The presumption was at the root of the backlash against civil rights that occurred at the end of the 1960s. Formal equality did little to change the massive inequality of the masses of Blacks penned up in urban ghettos. Both violently and non-violently, Blacks demanded structural change. In the aftermath of this violence, during the long hot summers of the 1960s, the presumption shifted from a notion of Blacks as childlike—Sambos—to that of Blacks as savages—Nat.

This shift reflected the racialization of Black protest. A literary analogy may be helpful here. Many Black rebels like Toussaint L'Ouverture were inspired to cast off their chains by the writings of Jefferson and other American revolutionaries. In Herman Melville's *Benito Cereno*, he describes Black slaves who revolted aboard a ship as "wolves, red tongues lolling" as they made war on their white captors. Melville was describing the image of rebellious slaves in the white mind. Like light refracted in water, the racial fears of whites refracted, i.e. distorted, the image of Blacks fighting for freedom. They appeared as simply beasts.

When Black communities erupted in anger in the 1960s at continuing conditions of poverty and powerlessness, whites saw this similarly though the lens of their own racial fear. Through this lens, the outpouring of Black anger and violence gave rise to a presumption in the late twentieth century that Blacks were prone to violence, crime, and disorder. Blacks were a threat to law and order.

In the post-civil rights era, from the late twentieth century to today, the beast becomes the urban criminal or urban thug. Because the riots were collective violence this lent itself as well to a notion of the ghetto as a community of savages—or thugs.

The same presumption of dangerousness and criminality drove the scapegoating narratives that Nixon used to justify a "war on drugs." Similarly, the presumption anchored the super-predator myth and the crime control legislation of the 1990s. It is through the presumption of guilt functioning as a lens that white America enacted what was once a 25-to-one differential between crack cocaine and powdered cocaine and thought it "made sense." Through the window of the presumption, it seems to make sense also that Blacks are in massive disproportion arrested, jailed, and incarcerated.

The presumption evolved further in the late twentieth century as race evolved. Race became a spectrum with affluent, educated Blacks on one side and poor, under-educated Blacks on the other. This adds another layer of complexity and obfuscation. As we erased the color line in the post-civil rights era, we have formally erased the presumption that Blacks are universally prone to violence or crime. But we have replaced the color line with the line between the suburbs and the inner city. Race has been spatialized: inner city and underclass have replaced metaphors of color. This becomes the new color line. It is no longer a matter simply of Black and white, but one's zip code. The presumption has followed the new fault lines. To live in the ghetto in the twenty-first century is to be one of "them." To live outside the ghetto is to be one of "us." Black mayors, Black prosecutors, and Black police who are middle class are invited to the predominantly white side of the line, "us," and on the overwhelmingly Black side of the line, "them," the Blacks who live in the city, become the new racial other.

This reconfigured presumption, attaching to whole communities ("the ghetto is a community of criminals"), drives a policy of targeting violence against inner-city neighborhoods relabeled as high-crime areas. The notion of a high-crime area is a code, a reference to the post-industrial ghetto areas that are predominantly or heavily disproportionately populated by the inner-city poor. Here in the ghetto, in this other America, on the other side of the line between us and them, reasonable suspicion is thrown away.

Kalief Browder confronted this insidious duality walking home from a party in the South Bronx. The South Bronx is the quintessential inner-city "hood." Authorities held him in Riker's Island without any evidentiary hearing for three years, two of which he spent in solitary confinement—before the miracle of national publicity allowed him as an individual to be freed. But his treatment was part of a larger pattern in the South Bronx, in which for Blacks, the average time from arrest to trial is twenty months. This is despite the fact that a speedy trial is generally required within six months.

This latest version of the presumption—drawing a line between the suburbs and the inner city—has led to a notion that there are white spaces and Black spaces. Blacks have been arrested for sleeping in a college dormitory, sitting in a Starbucks, wearing socks in an area near an apartment complex pool where socks are not allowed, and for picking up kids (white kids) at a daycare center in an affluent area.

Invisibilization

The presumption functions like the opaque glass that Ellison refers to in his book, *The Invisible Man*. Whites, especially police, don't see the Black person.

They see a reflection of the fear in their mind *but not what is actually there.* Blacks have been shot when spotted holding a cell phone, playing with a toy gun, knocking on a door seeking help after their car has broken down, standing in a doorway, reaching into a pocket for a license when asked by the police for identification, and walking down the street with a bag of Skittles.

In addition to seeing things that are not there, the presumption often magnifies things that are. A small child may appear to be a grown man, a toy gun an automatic weapon. Super-humanization takes place. It causes policeman and juries to imbue ordinary Black people with Herculean strength. Rodney King was said to be the aggressor while prone on the ground being beaten by eleven officers wielding their batons. Michael Brown was considered armed even though he had no gun, no knife, or other weapon. Ben Stein explicitly relies upon this racist, "super-humanized" image in an article he wrote for *Salon Magazine*:

> The idea of calling this poor young man unarmed when he was 6'4", 300 pounds, full of muscles, apparently, according to what I read in *The New York Times*, on marijuana. To call him unarmed is like calling Sonny Liston unarmed or Cassius Clay [sic] unarmed. He wasn't unarmed. He was armed with his incredibly strong, scary self.[4]

But as race has become a spectrum, the meaning also changes between different cultural motifs. We have witnessed the social construction of a criminal who wears a hoodie, saggy pants, twisty braids, and tattoos. We say as a society that we have erased race, but we have racialized culture. What emerges from this is a presumption in which cultural alterity merges with race. Each intersection represents an additional point of intensification of paranoia and fear.

The conventional explanation for all this is filed under the umbrella of white supremacy—whites hate Blacks. From the despicable murders committed by Dylan Roof to the brutal, unbelievable spectacle of a policeman kneeling on the neck of George Floyd, who gasped he could not breathe twenty times while officers continued to press him face down into the ground, the specter of white supremacy driven by hate is very real.

The presumption manifests as hate. But its source is in the realm of cognition, or perception where it operates as a distorting prism. The legacy of decades of reports about crack users, gang bangers, and drug dealers in the ghetto, and decades of hood films, has reshaped the prism—or lens—such that Blacks in the inner city are criminalized even in the eyes of other Blacks. Similarly, affluent America does not see the systemic racism inner-city Blacks experience, the massive stop and frisks, massive arrests, and military-style campaigns for what they are—an "occupation." It appears to this America of the white middle class as crime control. Historically, this was rationalized as, if racism at all, reasonable racism. This is the notion that the stereotypes are true. This "reasonable racism" is rooted not in fact but assumption and received as common sense.

Of course whenever one can say something is common sense one can say this is "ideology." And whenever a person or a society is under sway of an ideology, as anthropologist Clifford Geertz has taught us—they are often unaware that they are. The more the presumption—the notion that Blacks are prone to crime and violence—is received as "common sense" the more it is able to hide in plain sight.

When the New York police commissioner talks about arresting "the right people," when Bernard Goetz was confronted on a subway by five youths who smiled at him with shiny eyes, and therefore "knew they wanted to kill him," when city of Chicago attorneys spoke of the "visible lawlessness" of kids who met a certain profile, this reflects the pervasiveness of this so-called common sense. But when policies and programs that target Blacks under the cloak of high crime areas (the New York Stop and Frisk program) or target kids who wear "gang attire" (the Chicago Loitering Ordinance in *Chicago v. Morales*), many cheered on these programs. Even when Bernard Goetz justified his shooting of kids who had done no more than ask him for five dollars by the fact that "they smiled at him with shiny eyes," many in New York cheered him. They either didn't see or claimed not to see the tacit racism.

In the 2009 film *Sherlock Holmes*, Holmes intervenes to save the life of a girl Lord Blackwood was about to murder.[5] Blackwood is a Satanic cult leader and a serial killer. Before he is hanged, he says, "three more will die and there is nothing you can do to save them." A series of mysterious murders do in fact take place and appear to fulfill Blackwood's curse. Blackwood is actually committing the murders but somehow remains "invisible." Racism, in the form of a tacit presumption of dangerousness or guilt, like Holmes's Lord Blackwood, is invisible as well. We must be like detectives in looking for it within our polices, practices, and attitudes.

Students of implicit bias would say that the "presumption" is unconscious bias. On the surface this is appealing. But implicit bias is Freudian. As such, the unit of inquiry is the individual.

The racism of explicitly targeting inner-city communities, of explicitly legitimating double standards for high-crime areas, which in practice are almost always inner-city areas, is not usefully thought of as a problem of individual bias. This individualizes a worldview that is received as common knowledge, one that whole communities consciously share and operate on routinely. *It is in the first instance a problem of identity construction—more specifically the essentializing of an entire community to a stereotype through the lens of a shared narrative.* I'm reminded of Kima Griggs in a scene from *The Wire*. Kima sings to her adopted son, Elijah, a kind of sing-along lullaby while sitting in a windowsill in an apartment in the inner city.

> *Kima: Let's say goodnight to everybody. Goodnight moon …*
> *Elijah: Goodnight moon …*
>
> *Kima: Goodnight stars …*
> *Elijah: Goodnight stars …*
>
> *Kima: Goodnight po-pos …*
> *Elijah: Goodnight po-pos …*
>
> *Kima: Goodnight fiends …*
> *Elijah: Goodnight fiends …*
>
> *Kima: Goodnight hoppers …*
> *Elijah: Goodnight hoppers …*
>
> *Kima: Goodnight hustlers …*
> *Elijah: Goodnight hustlers …*
>
> *Kima: Goodnight scammers …*
> *Elijah: Goodnight scammers …*
>
> *Kima: Goodnight to everybody …*
> *Elijah: Goodnight to everybody …*
>
> *Kima: Goodnight to one and all …*
> *Elijah: Goodnight to one and all.*[6]

In a few lines she reduces a whole diverse community to a set of stereotypes. But Kima sings the song about the denizens of the inner city with affection, not hostility. The song captures the fact that for Kima, for the media, for the Black middle class the notion that the Black community is a community of criminals, "fiends" (as in dope fiends), "hustlers", and "scammers" is just a "fact of life."

This essentializing does not originate within any individual but rather an ideology which manifests as a *culture* of fear. Let's think of this culture as a lake: a toxic lake in which historical experiences—slavery, segregation—as well as literature, film, and television have all deposited their streams.

Notes

1 Robert S. Smith, *Three Centuries of Slavery*, https://www.abhmuseum.org/how-slavery-became-legal-for-blacks-only/.

2 See *Dred Scott v. Sanford*, 60 U.S. (19 How.) 393 (1857).

3 Stephen R. Haynes, *Noah's Curse: The Biblical Justification of American Slavery* (New York: Oxford University Press, 2002); see also D. Marvin Jones, "The Curse of Ham," in Richard Delgado, Jean Stefancic, eds., *Critical White Studies: Looking Behind the Mirror* (Philadelphia, PA: Temple University Press, 1997), 255–7.

4 Joanna Rothkopf, "Ben Stein: Michael Brown was armed with his 'strong scary self,'" *Salon*, August 27, 2014.

5 Guy Ritchie, *Sherlock Holmes*, Warner Brothers, 2009.

6 David Simon, *The WIRE*, Season 5, Episode 7 "Took", February 17, 2008.

Afterword

We have to drain the lake. This is a difficult feat of social engineering. It requires more than empathy on the part of individuals. It requires a massive national effort. We need nothing less than a Third Reconstruction.

What Congress Should Do: Repealing the New Black Codes

In the aftermath of the Civil War, Southern states required former slaves to make an employment contract with local landowners, who were designated as "the master." If the former slaves failed to secure an employment contract, they were incarcerated and later rented out to their former masters under the infamous convict lease system. Blacks were re-enslaved.

The conditions of the ghetto are at the core of the caste-like status of Blacks in the twenty-first century.[1] Our criminal justice system plays a huge role in perpetuating racial caste. Our drug laws, more specifically, perpetuate this caste system in a manner reminiscent of the Black codes.

Like the Black codes, drug laws are used to systematically criminalize and incarcerate Blacks. One in four people arrested for drugs in the United States is Black—though Blacks use drugs at rates statistically identical to those of whites. In seven states, Blacks make up 80 to 90 percent of all drug offenders sent to prison. This reflects in part the stunning disparity between the way Blacks are arrested, sentenced, and imprisoned for marijuana and crack cocaine in comparison to whites on opioids or cocaine powder. And if one in three Black men are likely to spend several years in prison before they are 35, the drug war (which put the inner city populations in the crosshairs) is largely responsible.

Like the Black codes, drug laws recreate conditions in the urban ghetto analogous to those that existed on the slave plantation. Both hip-hop artists and historians find a strong analogy between the modern ghetto and the old plantation. The plantation was a prison. The ghetto is increasingly becoming like the prison and prisons increasingly like the ghetto. The drug war plays a huge role in creating this carceral regime.

The Black codes kept Blacks in a constant state of peonage. The drug war has a similar effect. The racism of the drug war begins with the targeting of Black communities for military-style campaigns. It results as well in massive economic harm.

Each Black or brown person arrested or imprisoned is someone who too often loses their ability to find employment, their ability to get an education, their ability to obtain housing. Families lose breadwinners: fathers, brothers, sisters, cousins, uncles, aunts, each of whom could otherwise contribute to the community. Beyond the educational, economic, carceral consequences there is a vast stigma that hangs over the community like a cloud.

What Courts Should Do

A criminal justice system punishes individuals. A police regime does not; its goal is not punishment but control, control of a dangerous population. Thus, individual rights are routinely ignored. Plantation society was a police regime; the Bantustans in South Africa were a police regime. And in inner-city America, what is called the criminal justice system bears disturbing earmarks of a tacitly sanctioned police regime as well. In many urban areas, reasonable suspicion and probable cause are routinely ignored.

When New York Judge Sheindlin found that police routinely violated the rights of Blacks and Latinos in their massive stop-and-frisk campaign, and that police targeted neighborhoods, she opened America's eyes to the systemic nature of the problem in New York City. But New York is not an isolated case. In Ferguson, the Justice department documented a pattern and practice of police making arbitrary arrests, in part due to a desire on the part of the municipal government to raise funds through fines, utilizing the Black community "as an ATM." Evan Howard's arrest, for merely walking down the street in his West Baltimore neighborhood is yet another a case in point. The Black students at Miami Edison High who were arrested *en masse* following a disturbance at the school—despite the fact that police had neither witnessed the Black students engaged in fighting nor had eyewitnesses to that effect—are yet another. Beyond this anecdotal information, stunning statistical disparities expose a national pattern. Blacks are disproportionately arrested for marijuana and crack cocaine at a level which is startling enough that many of my students, many judges, and many scholars argue the single explanation is race.

But arrest is only the first level of the police regime. The court system is not distinct, but represents another level of subordination and control. I remember the poem in which a Black man says when he went to court there were two doors: one marked white and another door marked Black. He went through the Black door and fell nine stories to the street. There is a deep sense in which this is still true. It is not so much that they fall to the street but into a racialized version of the justice system, which formally is the same as that of white affluent defendants but which operates in practice as if the defendants who come in are already guilty.

The hallmark of our system of criminal procedure is the presumption of innocence, a fair trial, and control by an independent judge or magistrate. But the bureaucracy the Black poor defendant confronts is the exact opposite. Few can afford counsel. Public defender systems are overburdened. Most criminal cases, especially those in urban areas, are disposed of by plea. The plea-bargaining system explicitly assumes guilt; the prosecutor controls the system, and there is no trial.

Of course, all defendants have a right to a speedy trial. Black poor defendants have these rights as well. But they are often waived by their attorneys. Disturbingly, there is often never any record as to what specific factual grounds—if there are any— that allegedly justify sometimes weeks or months of incarceration.

This is true because too often police rely not on specific facts but guilt by association,[2] walking in a particular so-called high-crime area,[3] driving in a high-crime area, running in a high-crime area,[4] or mere appearance. In many jurisdictions police are not even required to provide specific facts on the arrest form as to why the individual was detained. The individual has notice of the elements of the statute on which he or she is charged. But the narrative may be conclusory or vague. This is not necessarily a problem. If criminal complaints were routinely tested by preliminary hearings, discovery, and trial, if defendants could afford this, or afford bail, or if public defender services could provide this level of representation routinely, it would be a different world. But in the real world, many of these defendants stay in jail for weeks or months without evidentiary hearings of any kind unless they plead guilty.

There is overwhelming evidence that systemic discrimination in stops and arrests is a national pattern. Underlying this, I posit Blacks—and it cannot be reduced to class[5]—face pervasively a presumption of guilt in confronting police and courts. The legislature and courts should work together to develop policies and practices that affirmatively guarantee the presumption of innocence.

Again, we need to abolish incarceration for simple possession of marijuana and similar drugs. Similarly, we should abolish laws that give police the power to arrest for quality-of-life crimes such as sleeping on a subway or riding a bicycle without registration.

But until then, we need a due process revolution.

In every urban area, courts should have a magistrate's panel of lawyers or *law students* who review *each charging document* promptly after any arrest for simple possession of drugs, loitering, or so-called quality-of-life crimes. In all these cases, the burden should be on the state: Has the city or state provided specific articulable facts to show probable cause? If there is not probable cause *based on the affidavit of the arresting officer*, the case should be subject to dismissal.[6] If the state cannot give defendants a trial in six months, the case should be dismissed. If the speedy trial rule is defendants should be brought to trial in six months, the rule should be strictly construed. Also, if defendants are arrested for crimes like riding a bicycle without a registration, "loitering," or jaywalking, the court should simply dismiss these cases. While the Supreme Court has placed its imprimatur on jailing individuals for these quality-of-life crimes, local courts should not.[7]

Theorizing the End of Police Violence: Community Control of Police

Now when this begins to move, the pig power structure is gonna say, "OK, you can have civilian review boards." But all that does is allow the same old fascist power structure to keep control of the police … What we're talking about is righteous community control, where the people who control the police are elected by the people of the community.—Bobby Seale[8]

In the aftermath of the unwatchable murder of George Floyd by Derek Chauvin, we as a nation began a wrenching process. We searched through dialogue, demonstrations, debate, and struggle in the streets for a way to move forward against the scourge of police violence. That violence continues apace: in 2022 two hundred and twenty-five Blacks were shot by police. Among Black Americans 5.8 Blacks per million are shot in an average year, more than twice the rate of whites.

Two schools of thought have emerged as to how we end police violence. One school of thought is captured by the iconic "defund the police" slogan seen during many Black Lives Matter demonstrations. Others, less radically, argued for more training, more prosecutions of police. In essence, we vacillated between abolition of police or reform. These slogans and rhetoric inspire and galvanize, but conceptually they miss the mark. Neither reform nor abolition is a viable path to real change.

Why Reform Approaches Will Not Work

Civilian review boards, citizen police academies, community policing, predictive policing, body cameras, implicit bias training … and focused deterrence are some of the more common themes that immediately come to mind. None of these approaches are designed to shift policing power and control to the Black community. They are designed to shift the power of policing to white liberals.[9]

As Baldwin wrote, "the police cannot be reformed." First, we cannot train our way out of the problem. Studies that have been done on training show that while police are often engaged in the training, and it makes them aware of new concepts and ideas, it has little effect on behavior. Similarly, we cannot prosecute our way out of the problem.[10] Prosecutors are inherently conflicted when it comes to prosecuting the same group of people—police—they rely on for their investigations. The dismal historical record bears this out. Ultimately both the public and prosecutors rely on the police for security.

We, of course, should hold police accountable. But this is not enough. The media seems to promote a narrative that the police who kill Blacks are "the bad apples." The problem of police violence is less a problem of bad apples than of a rotten barrel. Police violence is structural and rooted in a culture of stereotyping and disrespect. We must change the culture.

Why Defunding the Police Will Not Work Either

Wealthy liberals and the very poor—the tops and bottoms of the economy often do support defunding the police. In a perverse way it will benefit the wealthy upper-east-side liberals: they already have their own private security. It will mobilize the whites in low-income communities, who are already well armed, like the whites who murdered Ahmaud Arbery, to double down on neighborhood watch, looking for Blacks who "do not belong" in the neighborhood. We have a glimpse of what the Black community would be like when we consider communities like Haiti, or Kingston, where the police serve only the rich. These poor neighborhoods become garrison communities lorded over by local warlords. We already have the beginning of this feudal infrastructure in the form of drug gangs who populate many urban areas.

What Will Work

We are going to start out with community control of that particular community institution that's affecting our lives, and this is the police department. We're going to try to implement what we call community control of police.[11]

The only way the police can represent and enforce the interests of the Black Community—rather than the interests of outside colonial powers—is to shift power so that the Black Communities have power over their own police departments. This historic moment calls for something more significant than additional training or even civilian oversight boards. We must fight for Community Control over Police.[12]

The most important direct change needed is community control of police. This model was proposed by the Black Panther Party for self-defense in the 1970s. The underlying premise of this proposal was, as noted earlier, that the Black community was to the dominant society what the colony is to the mother country. Colonial rule was defined by police who answered to a central command composed of members of the colonizer group. This new model replaces "the imperial model" with one that allows the community to participate democratically at the neighborhood level.

The Panthers called these neighborhood-level control mechanisms "Community Commissions." They could decide whether police must live in the neighborhoods they police, whether police carry guns, whether they ride in cars or walk the beat, how much training they need, what kind, and what budget priorities to implement. The community control notion still resonates as innovative and new today, and it is on the agenda of a new generation of activists, as Max Rameau's position paper exemplifies.[13] This is a paradigm shift away from civilian complaint review boards. The civilian review board is part of the "imperial model"—that power resides in a centralized authority. Under the community control approach, the power would reside in the community.

Police are not inherently bad. Police are necessary for democracy. But in the inner city, police have functioned, in the eyes of many community leaders and scholars, as more of "an occupying force"[14] than a force which protects and serves. They are part of a system which operates based on policies that deeply assume—presume—Blacks are prone to crime. The issue is in large part one of power; who controls the police? Community control will give the community the power to reverse this presumption. In the inner city, this represents a paradigm shift from centralized control, from the white power structure, back to the precincts of the Black and brown people who live there.

What the American People Must Do

Slavery was America's original sin. The first reconstruction led to the re-institution of slavery by another name. This left a legacy in the form of urban ghettos, systemic disparities in education, jobs, wealth, health, and political power. The Second Reconstruction from 1945 to 1977 did not confront this legacy.

The legacy of slavery is a criminal justice system that functions as a system of racial caste. The legacy is also the social isolation of Black children in inner city schools. The legacy of slavery is the landscape of despair one sees when entering or living in an inner-city Black neighborhood. The legacy of slavery is the pervasive joblessness, squalor, violence, and despair which define the bleakness of life in the post-industrial ghetto. Blacks experience this as powerlessness.

Blacks confront that powerlessness when they cannot find a job, or housing, or cannot get a decent education. This powerlessness becomes alienation and despair. In turn, this feeds the narrative that the only way out is through crime: selling drugs and pills—"It's the only game the man has left us to play." In turn, such alienation turns to lack of self-esteem.

What has emerged is a street ghetto culture in which individuals and gangs engage in violence, often for what Elijah Anderson calls "respect." We cannot defeat crime with police, or a drug war, or a war crime. We can defeat it if we remove the root causes. But we are up against not merely social conditions, but narrative—a mentality. The veil that Dubois talked about is no longer a problem of formal laws. The veil is anchored by the social conditions that Blacks experience that produce powerlessness and alienation. And as these conditions are internalized they become understood as part of the condition of being Black. I posit that this veil, and even social identity itself, is a function of power. *We must empower those who have been powerless.* When we do so we remove the root source of stigma.

Of course the operative phrase in talking about how to address the legacy of slavery is reparations. Of course Blacks richly deserve reparations for slavery! But reparations has been thinly conceived. As it is now being discussed, reparations is framed in terms of payments to individuals. But will these payments to individuals—which I think of as comparable to a stimulus check—address, in itself, the legacy of slavery?

What we need is a Third Reconstruction.

We need massive investment to rebuild the infrastructure of the inner city, to rebuild the educational system, to build back jobs, businesses, and churches lost in the era of de-industrialization. It is by changing educational, and economic conditions of the masses of Black people—in addition to democratizing policing—that we change power relationships. This begins to address the legacy of slavery. I posit the legacy of slavery is the root of both racial caste as it continues to exist in our society and " the presumption" itself.

Blacks must lead the reconstruction process. Black mayors, Black political leaders, Black businessmen, Black artists, and Black thought leaders should all lead on the various stages in which the reconstruction takes place.

Of course we will never be a post-racial society. DuBois warned us the veil could not be lifted. In this true democracy, we will of course see race. But because power relationships will have changed, it will no longer matter.

Notes

1   Historians August Meir and Elliot Rudwick, *An Interpretive History of American*, 3rd edn (New York: Hill & Wang Publishers, 1967), for decades have suggested both a continuum and an analogy between plantation and ghetto. See also Glenn C. Loury, *An American Tragedy: The Legacy of Slavery Lives on in our Cities*, Brookings.edu.

2   The classic case is *Sibron v. New York*, 392 U.S. 40 (1968). According to Rod Vareen, a prominent high profile lawyer in Miami, a typical arrest in the inner city occurs where two kids are sitting outside of a laundromat and a policeman recognizes one of them as someone he has arrested for possessing or selling marijuana. The policeman walks up to the kid who he has arrested, immediately puts his hand in his pocket, finds marijuana, arrests him for possession with intent to sell, and arrests his friend for trying to purchase marijuana from him.

3   See "Strolling while Poor: How Broken Windows Policing Created a New Crime in Baltimore," *Georgetown Journal of Poverty Law and Policy* 14, no. 419 (2007), documenting the case of Evan Howard arrested, ostensibly, for "loitering." The Police department settled Howard's case and many others. The claim was that in Baltimore police systemically violated the 4th Amendment rights of inner-city residents. The city did not context this. See also "Investigation of the Ferguson Police Department" (Washington, D.C.: United States Department of Justice, Civil Rights Division, March 4, 2015).

4   Freddie Gray was stopped for "running" in a high crime area. He was then arrested when police found a pocket knife in his pocket, which was not necessarily illegal. Subsequent to Gray's arrest, and while he was in police custody, Gray's spine was partially severed. Gray was taken to a nearby hospital where he underwent spinal surgery, lapsed into a coma, and died a week later. Comment: J. T. Vanderford, "Wardlow Revisited: How Media Coverage of

Police Brutality Makes Empirical Data More Relevant Than Ever," *University of Pennsylvania Journal of Constitutional Law* 22 (2020), 1523–4. Prosecutor Marilyn Mosby stated, "no crime had been committed." Alan Blinder and Richard Perez Pena, "6 Baltimore Police Officers Charged in Freddie Gray's Death," *The New York Times* (May 1, 2015).

5   In New York, for example, Judge Sheindlin found that police targeted neighborhoods which were predominantly Black or Latino. Moreover, the drug war and the war on crime are clearly aimed at communities of color.

6   There will be many who will say, "but due process does not require this." As a general rule due process may not require this. This is not my argument. However, where there is compelling evidence that Blacks systemically face a presumption of guilt, the state has the power to provide enhanced due process protections. At the local level courts and legislatures must confront the question of "how bad is it out there." They should hold hearing, do the studies, do whatever is necessary to apprise themselves of the true nature of the crisis. But something must be done.

7   See *Atwater v. City of Lago Vista*, 532 U.S. 318 (2001).

8   Bobby Seale, *Seize the Time: The Story of the Black Panther Party and Huey P. Newton* (Baltimore, MD: Black Classic Press, 1991).

9   Tony Gaskew, *Stop Trying to Fix Policing: Lessons Learned from the Front* (Lanham, MD: Rowman & Littlefield, 2021), 63 (quoting a 1970 Black Panther Party Newsletter entitled "Community Control of Police").

10 The U.S. Civil Rights Commission has found that state District Attorneys are inherently conflicted when they prosecute police. In most cases the person charging the police is himself or herself a defendant. The District Attorney has to investigate two cases simultaneously. Moreover Professor Louis Swartz in his study of police violence found that DAs are hopelessly conflicted also because they rely on police to investigate their cases. Similarly, the notion of appointing a Special Prosecutor will work no better. In his study of police brutality in Philadelphia, Swartz found that, "the District Attorney's office has not been, and, in the nature of things, could not be, an effective instrument for controlling police violence."

    The whole idea that we can prosecute our way out of this is deeply linked to a narrative that police violence is deviant. It is not. The problem is not the rotten apple, it is the rotten barrel. Police operationally, in the drug war and in the war on crime do function in a manner more like an occupying force than an institution that provides security and order. Police themselves often see the members of the inner city collectively as "them." The problem stems from who controls the police, from the fact that the residents live in concentrated poverty, because police operate within a culture of stereotyping and fear. A case by case approach will not address these structural factors. We need to change the social conditions in the inner city as well as power relationships—the community should control the police, not some centralized bureaucracy as we discuss below.

11   Stephen Shames and Bobby Seale, *Power to the People: The World of the Black Panthers* (New York City: Abrahams, 2016).

12   Max Rameau, "Community Control of Police: A Proposition" (The Next System Project: November 10, 2017—thenextsystem.org).

13   Rameau, "Community Control of Police."

14   Huey Newton uses this frame in a publication entitled "A Functional Definition of Politics: Because Black People Desire to Determine Their Own Destiny They Are Constantly Inflicted with Brutality by the Occupying Army." Originally published in *The Black Panther* newspaper (January 17, 1969) and republished online as part of The Marxist Internet Archive 2021, https://www.marxists.org/archive/newton/1969/01/17.htm; see Joshua Bloom and Waldo E. Martin, *Black Against Empire: The History and Politics of the Black Panther Party* (Berkeley, CA: University of California Press, 2016). See also David Hilliard, *Huey: The Spirit of the Panther* (New York: Thunder's Mouth Press, 2006), p. 36. But this frame has been adopted by many progressive leaders in the Black community. See e.g., Keith Koffler, "Police Can Be An Occupying Force," White House Dossier, December 2, 2014, quoting then Attorney General Eric Holder, "Holder Suggests Police Can Be an 'Occupying Force'"—White House Dossier.

Index

Author Bio

D. Marvin Jones is Professor of Law at the University of Miami, where he has taught constitutional law and criminal procedure for more than thirty years. He has published numerous articles in leading law journals, including those of Georgetown, the University of Michigan, and Vanderbilt University. His published work includes *Praeger's Dangerous Spaces: Beyond the Racial Profile*; *Fear of a Hip-Hop Planet: America's New Dilemma*; and *Race, Sex, and Suspicion: The Myth of the Black Male*. He received the James Thomas prize from Yale University, recognizing him as one the nation's foremost scholars on civil rights issues.